HOT GRAPHICS USA

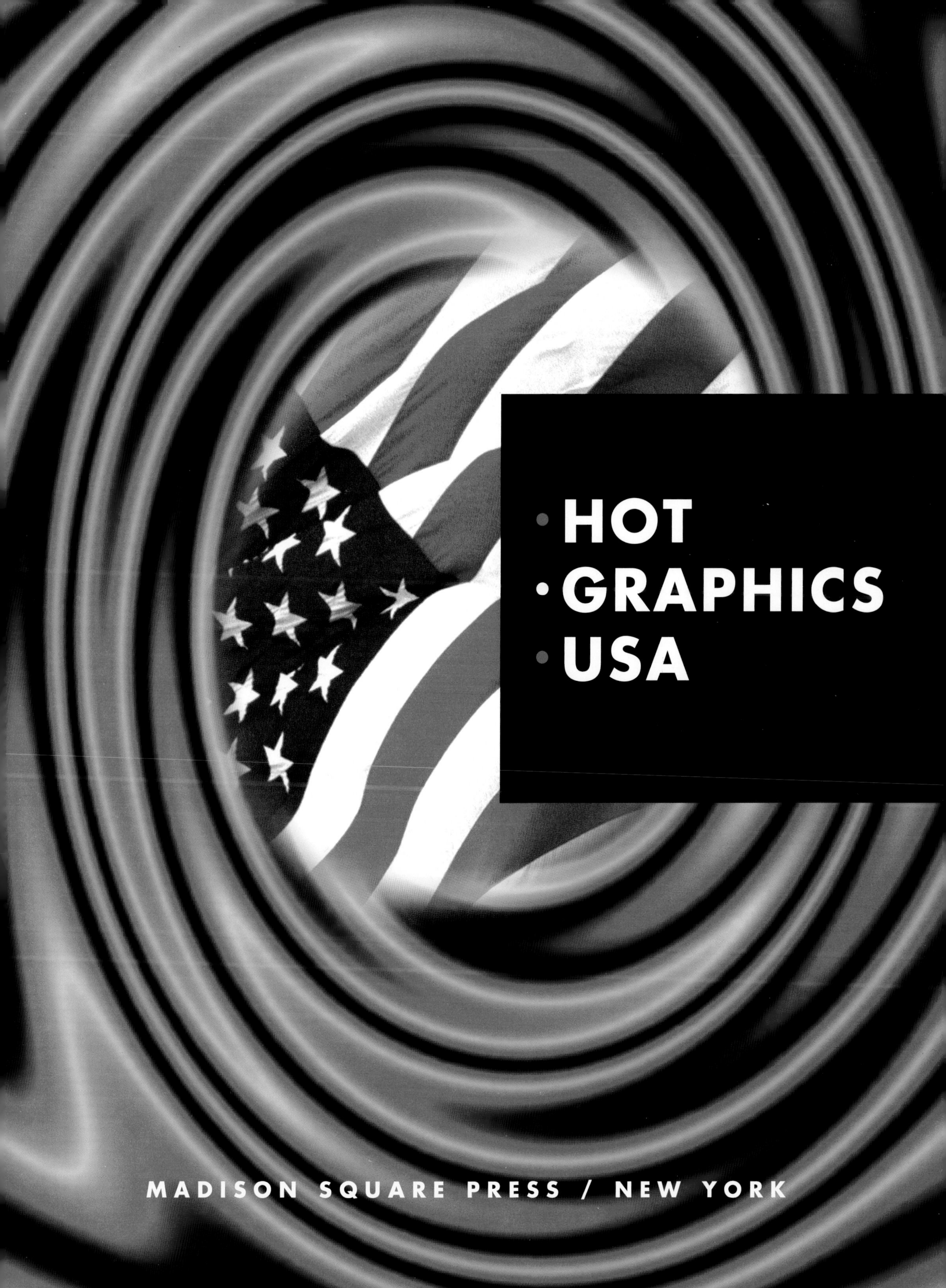

• HOT • GRAPHICS • USA

MADISON SQUARE PRESS / NEW YORK

Madison Square Press
10 East 23rd Street
New York, NY 10010

Distributors to the trade in the United States and Canada
Watson-Guptill Publications
770 Broadway
New York, NY 10003

Distributors outside the United States and Canada
HarperCollins International
10 East 53rd Street
New York, NY 10022

Library of Congress Cataloging in Publication Data:
Hot Graphics USA

Printed in Hong Kong
ISBN 0-06-621361-4

CONTENTS

INTRODUCTION

Do you speak Coca Cola? Walt Disney? Or how about IBM? Though music has often been described as the universal language, one glance at the pages of Hot Graphics USA will make you suspect graphic design has attained the same status. The brands, products and other visual representations of leading businesses and institutions are becoming increasingly recognizable around the world, and much of the credit goes to graphic design.

Providers of goods and services are increasingly turning to graphic design to create powerful visual tools for establishing and building unique identities that can attract and retain customers. What they have discovered is that the ability to escape anonymity and embrace a desirable corporate persona has become virtually mandatory in an ever more crowded marketplace. Far from being an abstract idea, graphic design helps them market and sell products in very specific ways. Organizations that wish to position or reposition themselves in the market, define differences between themselves and competitors, signal internal changes to the outside world, attract attention for whatever reason, or trigger specific intellectual and emotional responses can turn to graphic design for help.

One of the reasons graphic design can do this, of course, is that it is being applied more intensively than ever before. Just as any language has unlimited use when it is spoken by a growing number of speakers, graphic design is a visual language that attains astonishing utility when consumers can see it on as many visible aspects of life as possible. Just look at how effectively a business selling an express delivery service, such as Federal Express, has harnessed the power of graphic design to give its business forms, Web site, retail stores, aircraft, packaging, trucks, signs, delivery workers' uniforms and advertising an unmistakable character that people recognize instantly from Market Street in San Francisco to Park Avenue in New York—and countless places overseas.

Another reason for the ascendance of graphic design is the spread of international commerce, which depends on visible symbols that are easy to comprehend no matter what spoken language or cultural norms prevail wherever multinational corporations collide in their quest for market share. Graphic design has evolved into a highly condensed form of communication that can deliver its message at the speed of light when that's all the time it has. Where once the developed world tried to judge a book by more than its cover, we now appreciate the packaging and presentation of a product as much as the product itself. This isn't just an Internet phenomenon. As anyone who receives a gift from Tiffany knows, the cherished "blue box" from the fabled jeweler is as much a part of the experience as its content.

Still another reason for graphic design's unusual power is the growing reliance of the modern world on visual communications to express its messages. Much of the dominant media of our time, including books, magazines, newspapers, television, movies and the World Wide Web, deliver a high percentage of their information in visual rather than verbal form. For better or worse, this reliance on visual language makes consumers acutely aware of even the tiniest incremental nuances in the images they see, giving graphic designers an unprecedented opportunity to manipulate the man-made environment through their work. For example, graphic design is one of the most significant ways that online retailer Amazon.com defines itself to its millions of customers, who may never have the chance to set foot inside a non-existent Amazon.com retail store.

So join us on the following tour of new work from some of the most talented graphic design studios in the United States. The variety and range of activity documented in Hot Graphics USA will surprise you. The projects on display can be as small as a calling card or hang tag, or as big as a building facade or highway intersection. Hot Graphics USA is an invitation to shape the world using every conceivable medium that can speak in the universal language of graphic design.

Roger Yee

AMPdzine Studio
8236 Needles Drive
Palm Beach Gardens
Florida 33418
ph. 561.627.2600
em. ampdzine@aol.com
Founder / Creative Director
Annette M. Piskel

AMPDZINE STUDIO

Creativity is the craft, the passion, and the center for more than its 20 years in the business of design.

AMPdzine finds its own point of view, its own vision and style. It's a hands-on studio with an energetic approach,
a visual communicator with an eye for unique perspectives.

Its measure of success is the performance of hard work, perseverance, adaptability with creative forward-thinking solutions. The studio style is varied, as are its projects, but its way of thinking is logical. Its creative solutions attain tangible results through taking calculated risks to create something new.

With this conceptual framework AMPdzine resolves problems that are present in the images of individuals, companies, institutions and products from regional, national and international markets.

The area of effectiveness is across all print media. The fresh sensibility and marketing sense is reflected in identity systems, collateral, advertising, packaging, new product, merchandising & new media format.
Over the past 2 decades its clients' diversity include leaders in professional sports, consumer goods (healthcare.fashion.food), technology and telecommunications, toys, medical, travel and tourism, finance, non-profit and the entertainment industry.

Ability Motivation Process

AMPdzine Studio

Artful Messenger Perspective

AMPdzine Studio

Ambition Mastery Perseverance

AMPdzine Studio

Portfolio Showcased

1st Spread L>R

1. Ocean Sanctuary Novelty Merchandise
2. PGA National Sports & Racquetball Brochure
3. NHL Florida Panthers Mascot Packaging

2nd Spread L>R

1. NHL Florida Panthers Playoff Promo
2. Medtronic AVE Product Print Collateral
3. AIGA Miami Annual "Hunger" Newsletter
4. PGA Executive Wedding Invitation
5. Intersource Product Design Trade Literature

3rd Spread L>R

1. Pottery Barn In-store Banner Concept
2. Origins Face & Body Product Line Layout
3. Optometrist Eyewear Advertisement
4. Mamiya Digital Camera Fashion Test Promo
5. Sanchez Cocktail Rings Jewelry Art

Credit > Art & Photography Imagery

- Woodbury & Associates Photography
- Photographer: Fernando Arias
- Stylist: Sonya Sanchez-Arias
- Design & Layout: Annette M. Piskel

Icons-I-Like™

▾ Created for PennyCandy Studio

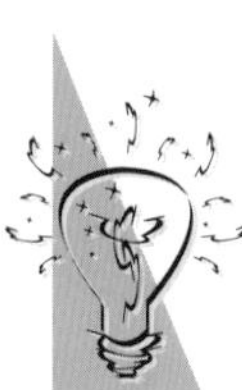

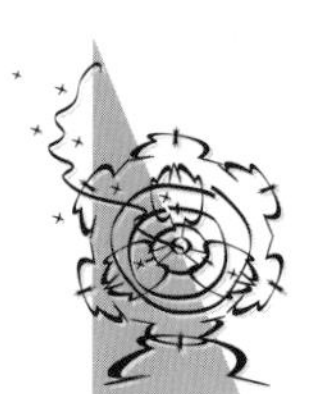

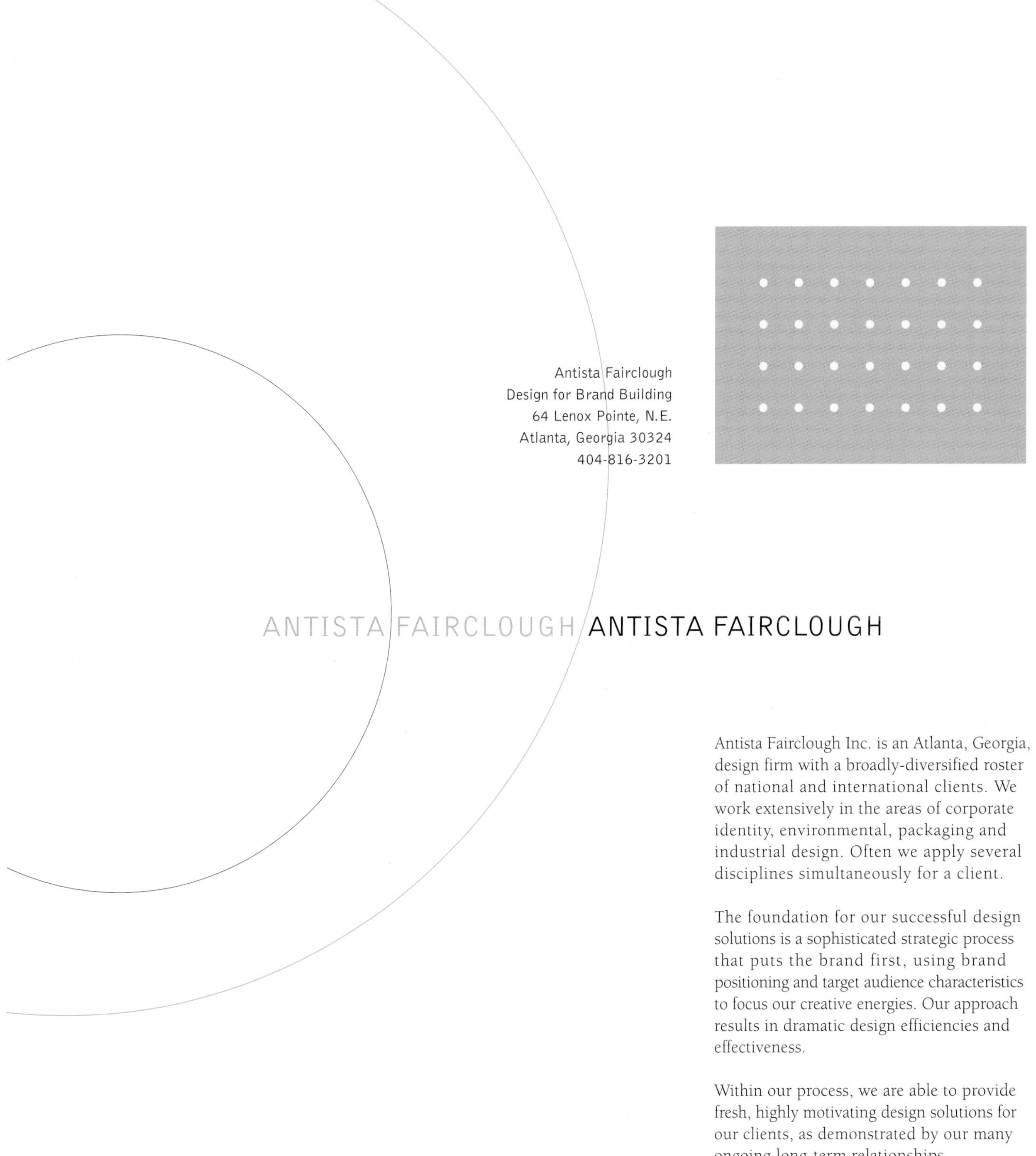

Antista Fairclough
Design for Brand Building
64 Lenox Pointe, N.E.
Atlanta, Georgia 30324
404-816-3201

Antista Fairclough Inc. is an Atlanta, Georgia, design firm with a broadly-diversified roster of national and international clients. We work extensively in the areas of corporate identity, environmental, packaging and industrial design. Often we apply several disciplines simultaneously for a client.

The foundation for our successful design solutions is a sophisticated strategic process that puts the brand first, using brand positioning and target audience characteristics to focus our creative energies. Our approach results in dramatic design efficiencies and effectiveness.

Within our process, we are able to provide fresh, highly motivating design solutions for our clients, as demonstrated by our many ongoing long-term relationships.

The firm has been recognized in many design shows and publications and has been selected for permanent collection in the Library of Congress.

1

BLUE POINTE

2

3

4

5

6

1-2 Atlanta area restaurants identity development.

3- Smoke House retail brand identity for fine tobacco products, liquors and gourmet foods.

4- Phoenix Communications corporate identity - Atlanta area printer.

5- Cloud Nine Chocolates brand identity and packaging system.

6- Budweiser secondary packaging system - Anheuser-Busch, Inc.

7- Zerex brand revitalization and packaging system - The Valvoline Company.

8- Formula Nine product naming, brand identity and packaging system - Califrance Food Company.

9- Valvoline brand packaging, new product launch - The Valvoline Company.

10- Mont Source brand identity and packaging system for a line of men's skin care products.

11- Turner Home Entertainment video box set for Gettysburg, a special movie series.

ZEREX
Valvoline
RADIATOR
Super
Flush
10 Minute Flush
CAUTION:

7

Valvoline
RACING
SAE 10W-30
MOTOR OIL
Valvoline
max LIFE
SAE 10W-30
MOTOR OIL

9

MONT SOURCE
FOR MEN

10

FORMULA 9
GINGER
KETCHUP
1
12 FL. OZ. (360mL)
UNIQUE BLEND
FORMULA 9
CRANBERRY
KETCHUP
2
GOURMET
12 FL. OZ. (360mL)
UNIQUE BLEND
FORMULA 9
ROASTED
RED PEPPER
KETCHUP
3
GOURMET
12 FL. OZ. (360mL)
UNIQUE
ROASTED
GARLIC
4
12 FL. OZ.

8

GETTYSBURG
GETTYSBURG
GETTYSBURG

11

1

2

3

4

5

6

7

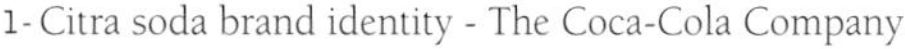

1- Citra soda brand identity - The Coca-Cola Company.

2- Culinary Concerts brand identity - for music and culinary products .

3- Arby's - ArbyQ national sales promotion logo.

4- Roscoe's Red brand identity (UK) a red beer - Anheuser-Busch, Inc.

5- Fetzer Reserve brand packaging and labeling.

6- Tequiza brand identity and packaging - Anheuser-Busch, Inc.

7- Alaska Natural brand identity and packaging - Superette grocer (Mexico).

8- Bud Light brand revitalization and packaging system - Anheuser-Busch, Inc.

9- Mello Yello brand identity and packaging system - The Coca-Cola Company.

10- Surge brand identity and packaging system - The Coca-Cola Company.

11- MoJava brand identity, bottle design and packaging - Royal Crown Company.

12- Bel Arbor brand packaging and labeling - Bel Arbor Vineyards

BUD LIGHT
BEER
BREWED WITH THE FINEST INGREDIENTS FOR A SMOOTH REFRESHING LIGHT TASTE
ONE PINT
PREMIUM QUALITY

8

CLEAR LABEL
LONGNECKS
BUD LIGHT
BEER

Tastes like java
MOCHA
Mo Java
Artificially Flavored
Coffee Soda

11

BEL ARBOR
VINEYARDS
1997
MERLOT
BEL ARBOR
VINEYARDS
1997
CHARDONNAY
CALIFORNIA

12

mello yello
CITRUS FLAVORED

9

SURGE

10

1

2

3

4

5

6

7

8

1- Sunoco brand identity - Sun Oil Company.

2- A Plus convenience store brand identity - Sun Oil Company.

3- Corner Store brand identity - convenience store Ultramar Diamond Shamrock.

4- Star Mart convenience store brand identity - Texaco Petroleum.

5,6- BP Connect retail brand identity and store design - BP Amoco.

7- Roswell Market Place street signage - McCurry Properties.

8- Nava identity - southwestern cuisine Atlanta area - restaurant - The Buckhead Life Restaurant Group.

9- Texaco Petroleum global facility design - Texaco Petroleum.

10- LensCrafters retail identity and store design - U.S. Shoe.

11- Express Care retail identity, signage and facility design - The Valvoline Company.

12- Light House retail identity and store design - Clark Refining & Marketing.

13- Inland Oil retail identity and facility design - Southwest Georgia Oil Company.

9

TEXACO
Take it to the Star
12 345 67890 12345
JOHN Q CUSTOMER
1975
Member Since
0999
Valid Thru

LENSCRAFTERS

10

1
Inland

13

Express
CARE
Valvoline
QUICK LUBE

11

SMOKING LOUNGE
CIGARETTES
CAMEL

12

CAMEL
FILTERS

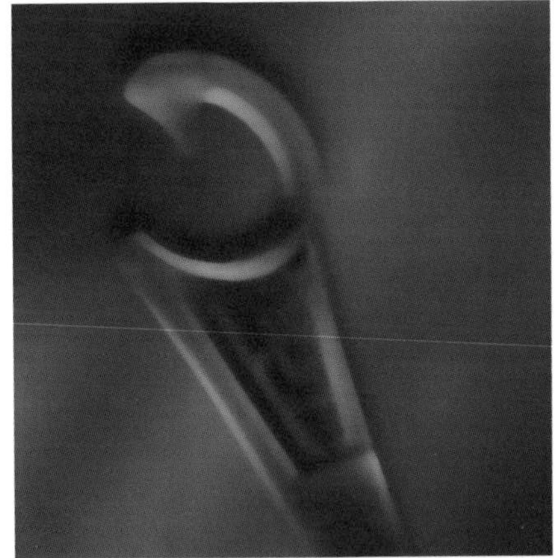

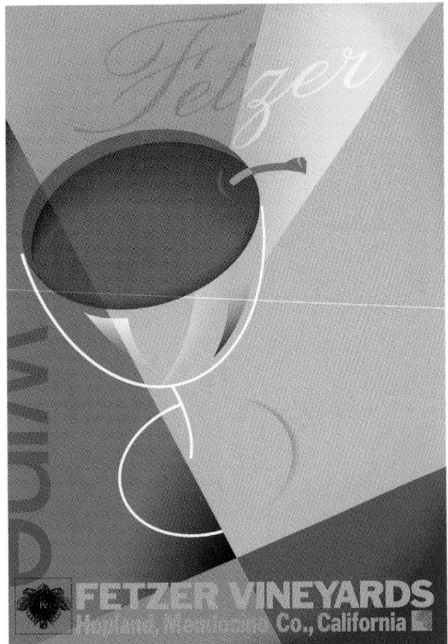

Fetzer
wine
FETZER VINEYARDS
Hopland, Mendocino Co., California

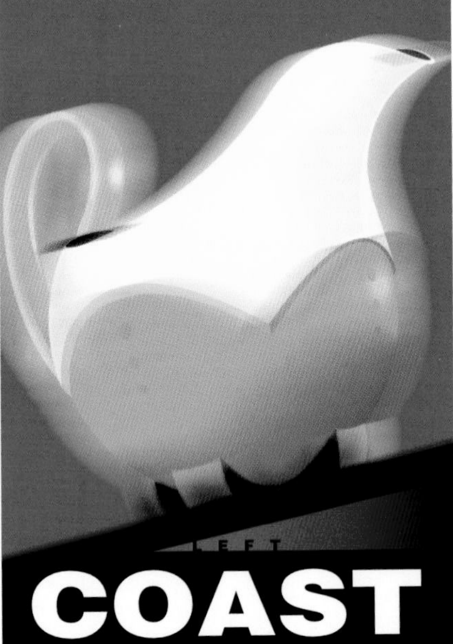

LEFT
COAST

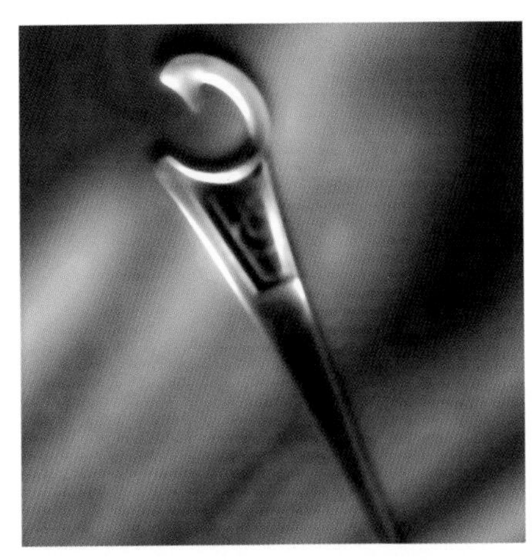

THE BIG
SHOW

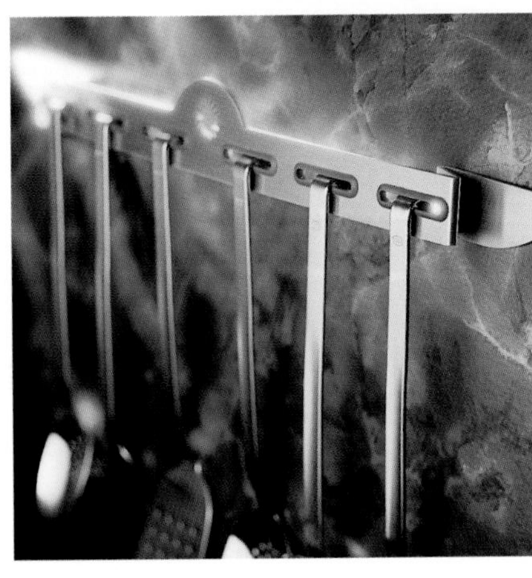

1250 Tower Building
1809 Seventh Avenue
Seattle, Washington 98101
p 206.682.4895
f 206.623.8912
www.belyea.com

BELYEA

Among Seattle's hot bed of graphic design, Belyea is a pleasant surprise. We are not too big, yet we think big. We are not too small, yet we treat each client with singular service. Best of all, every member of our well-seasoned team is brilliant, professional and downright nice.

Intelligent Creativity

These are our watchwords. Belyea offers a lively combination of smarts and artistic originality that produces results. Our work is based on the needs of our clients—solving their marketing challenges. Our solutions are innovative and hard-working, often earning us awards along the way.

Our work is also a reflection of who our clients are—exceptional companies striving to be leaders in their industries. Weyerhaeuser, Holland America and Hogue Cellars to name a few. Some of these clients have been with Belyea for over ten years. We don't think this is just luck.

Strategic Design

At Belyea, we look to the Big Picture. Be it branding, premium print collateral, web development or environmental design, we focus on how everything works together to enhance resources and results.

Some projects require completely novel design approaches, while others need to be consistent with existing collateral. Recognizing the true needs of a company and its brand are key to our work. We have the enthusiasm to be inventive, yet we have the control to create within defined constraints.

We are interested in everything about our clients. We ask questions, make surveys, read everything we can, take field trips, attend training seminars, or do whatever it takes to understand our clients and their businesses. The more we know, the more we have to offer.

A Flexible Partner

Many of our clients have strong marketing departments with well-laid plans. For these companies, Belyea is the creative partner. Original concepts, distinctive design capabilities, and project management skills turn complex plans into reality.

Some of our clients utilize Belyea as their marketing department. Our first step for these groups is to research and develop a marketing plan. Then we build high-level communications to make their enterprises soar.

Belyea serves a select group of motivated companies. We appreciate their determination, sense of adventure, respect and trust. Their success is our success.

Welcome to Belyea.

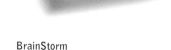

BrainStorm
Self-promotional journal by Belyea

1

2

3

K/P Corporation

Printing, mailing, and fulfillment company

1 Capabilities Brochure

2 Print Ordering Web Site

3 Service Brochure

4

5

6

Hogue Cellars
Washington State winery
4 Bottle Necker
5 Folder and Menu Card
6 In-Store Display

1

2

3

VeenendaalCave

Atlanta space planning firm

1 Marketing Collateral System

2 Web Site

3 Business Paper Suite

5

4

6

Genie Industries
International construction
equipment manufacturer

4 Save The Date Postcard

5 Promotional Button

6 Invitation System

1

2

3

Les Piafs

Vintage living boutique

1 Store Identity

2 Business Cards

3 Direct Mail Postcards

4

5

Weyerhaeuser
International forest products company

4 Bilingual Product Brochure

5 Folder System

1

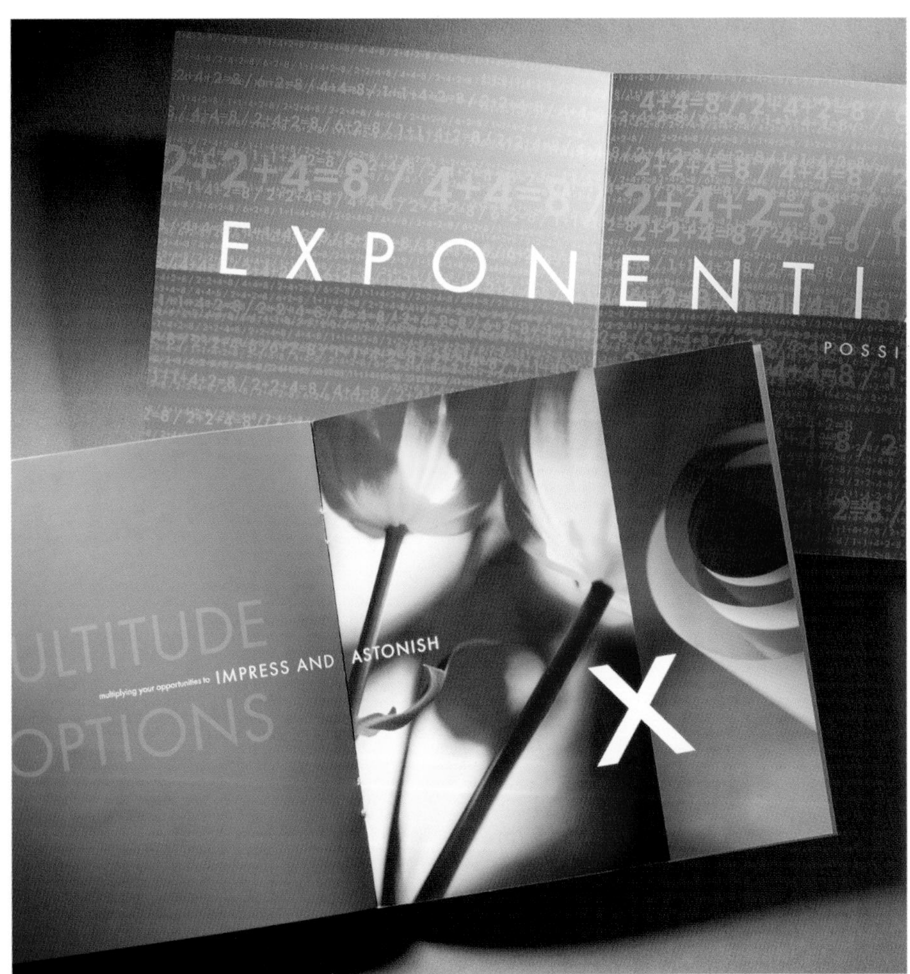

2

ColorGraphics
West Coast printing company
1 Invitation
2 New Service Brochure

Arizona
345 E. University Blvd.
Tucson, AZ 85705
520.792.1026

Colorado
4430 Hanover Ave.
Boulder, CO 80305
303.543.7521

bba@boelts-bros.com
www.boelts-bros.com

Balfour Walker

BOELTS BROS. ASSOCIATES

If setting is the wellspring of inspiration, it is no surprise that Boelts Bros. Associates has become one of the most heralded design and advertising firms in the U.S. today. With offices in the verdant foothills of the Colorado Rockies and the majestic heart of the Arizona Sonoran, Boelts Bros. specializes in the creative development of identity design, collateral materials such as posters, brochures and annual reports, advertising and promotions, internet and multimedia applications, and environmental and wayfinding projects.

While linked geographically to the American West, the work of Boelts Bros. has been critically acclaimed throughout the world. Over 400 national and international awards testify to the broad reach and transcendent appeal of their work. Members of the firm are regularly invited to speak nationally on issues of design and visual communication. Boelts Bros. work has been featured in exhibits in Russia, the Czech Republic, Poland, Mexico, and throughout the U.S.

As the following pages illustrate, Boelts Bros. has earned a well-founded reputation for producing work as visually rich as it is intellectually compelling.

2 

3 

1 

Tim Fuller

1 Collateral system for Tucson FOX Theatre renovation

2 Logo for Peccary King productions

3 Logo for Epic Cafe

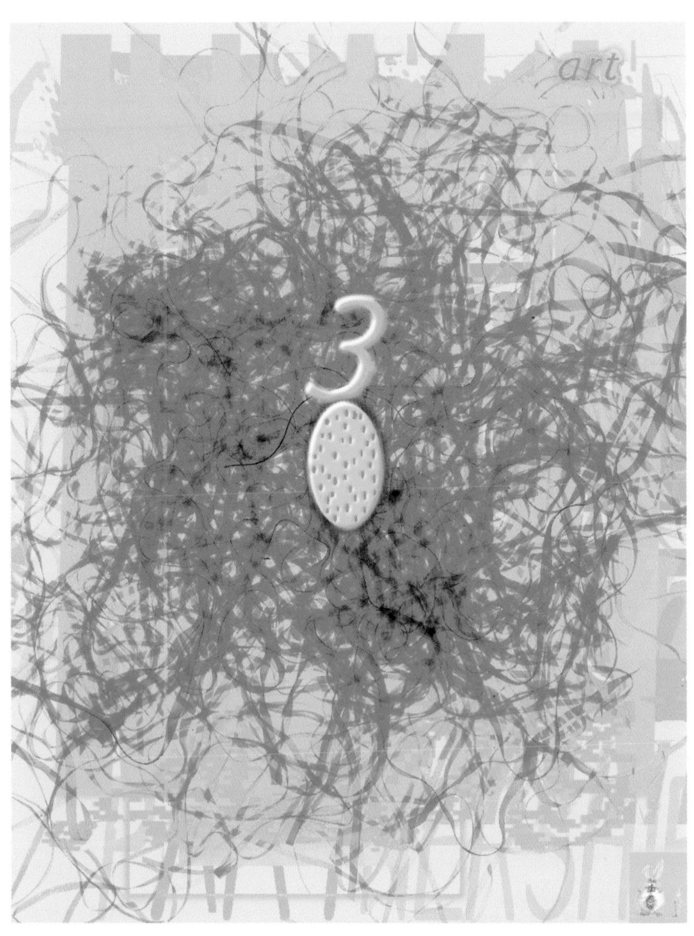

4

5

4 Cover for monthly publication ART 30 Easter issue

5 Cover for ART 30 Summer issue

6 Logo and packaging for Nimbus Brewery

7 Logo for *AOPA Pilot* magazine

8 Logo for Acid Rain awareness

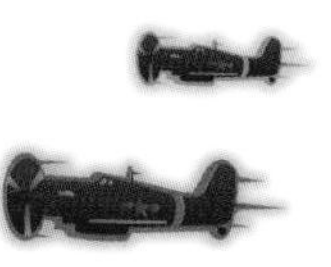

7

8

6

Tim Fuller

9

10

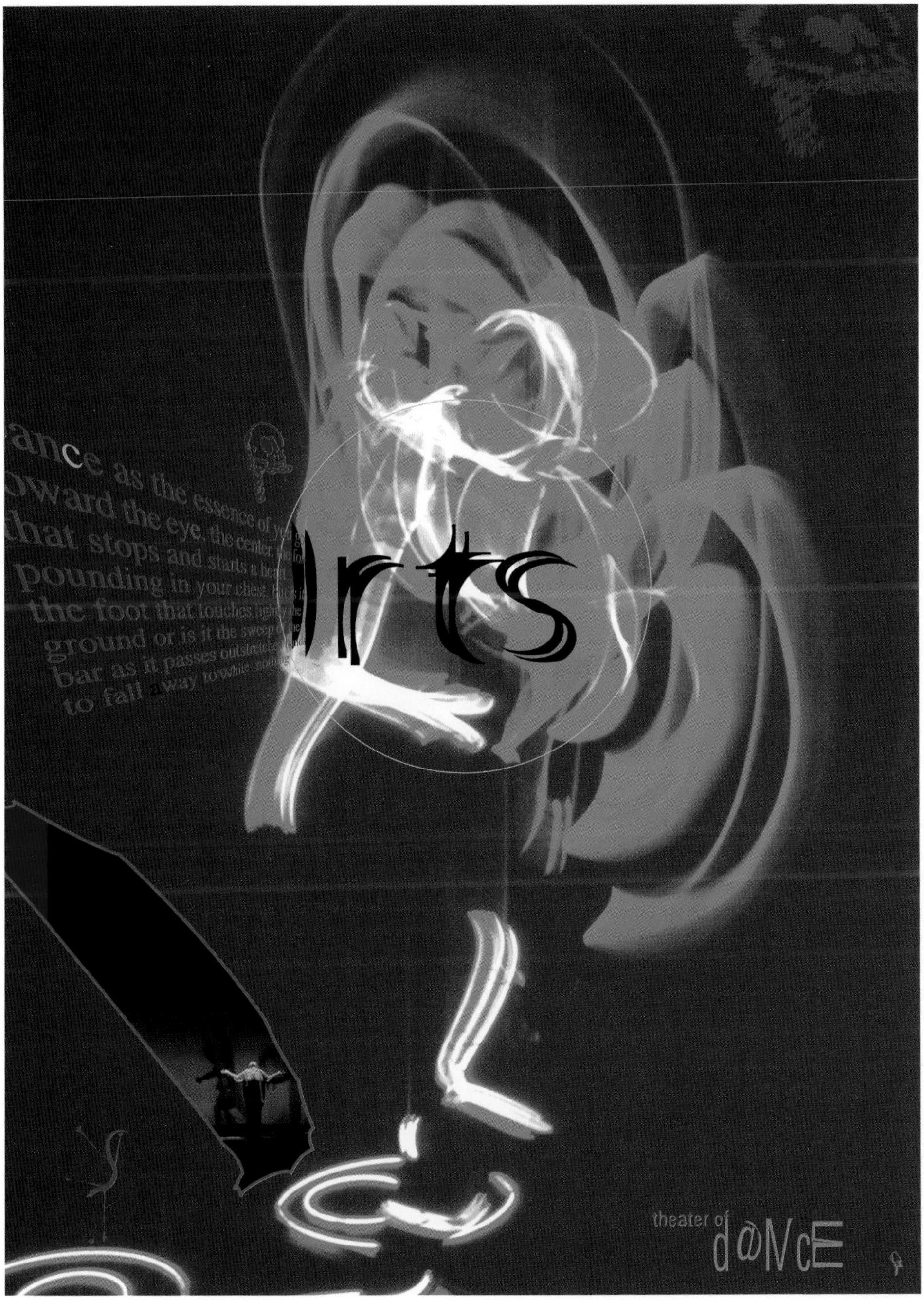

11

9 Logo for cable television promotion

10 Logo for Tucson Housing Authority

11 Poster/logo for ORTS Theater of Dance

13

14

12

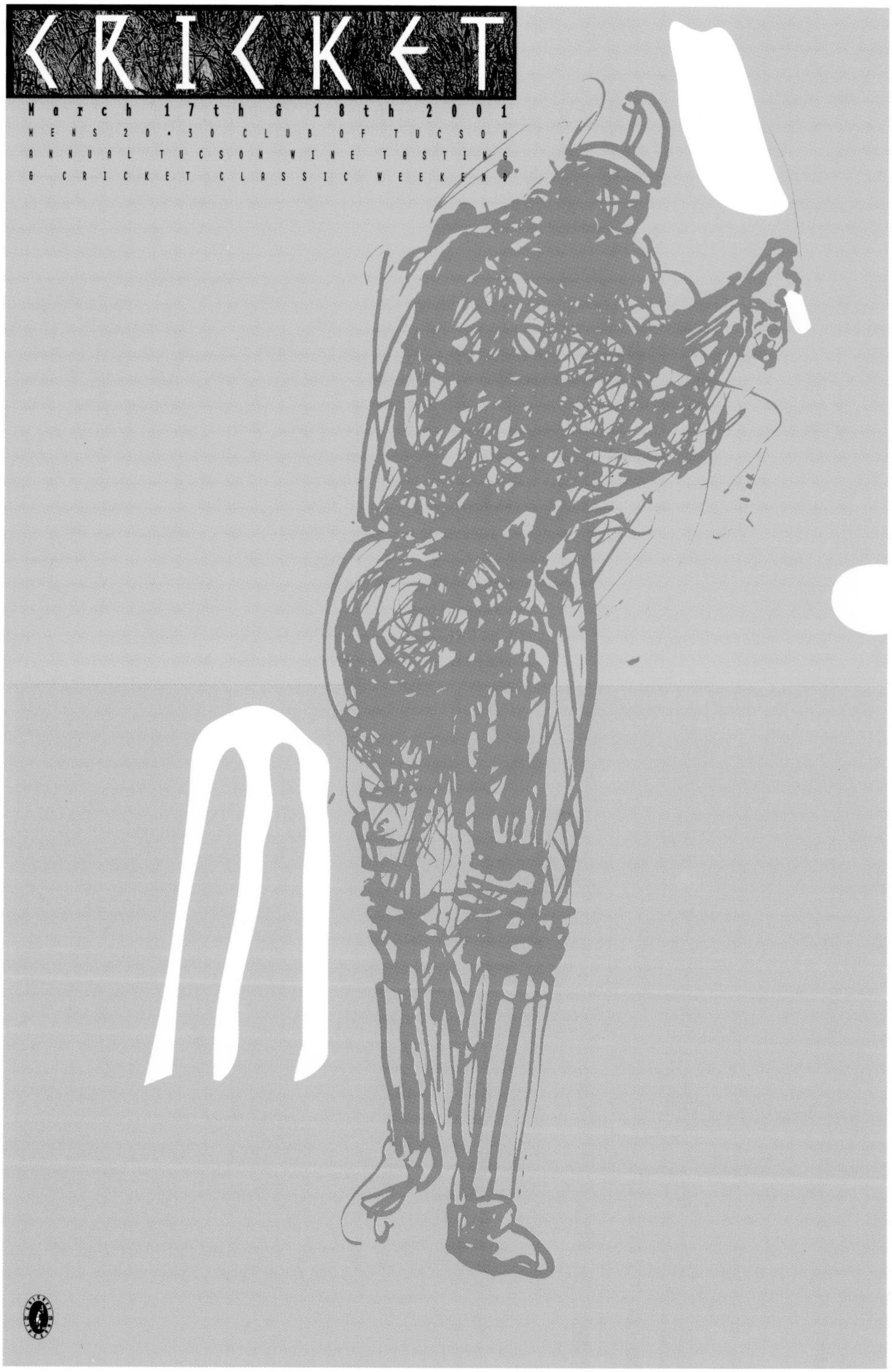

CRICKET

March 17th & 18th 2001

MENS 20 • 30 CLUB OF TUCSON

ANNUAL TUCSON WINE TASTING

& CRICKET CLASSIC WEEKEND

12 Logo and poster for cricket event

13 Logo for SIREN Public Relations

14 Logo for volleyball championship

15

16

15 Logo and poster for Colorado Dance Festival

16 Logo for Celestial Harmonies

COLORADO DANCE FESTIVAL IGNITING YOUR DANCE PASSIONS!
JUNE 25-JULY 22, 2001
WWW.CDF-DANCE.ORG COLODANCEFEST@EARTHLINK.NET
OLMYRA AMIRA, JOAQUIN PENA, JOSE FRANCISCO BARROSO, ROSEANGELA SILVESTRE, DOUG VARONE, KIM EPIFANO, TERE O'CONNOR, GABE MASSON, ROXANE BUTTERFLY, RICHARD MOVE, MOUMINATOU CAMARA, SHIREEN MALIK, DANELLE HELANDER, KEN JIMENEZ, MICAYA, ALEXANDRA OGSBURY, NANCY SMITH, ELLIE SCIARRA, SUELLEN EINARSEN, AMELIA RUDOLPH, CHRIS KERMIET, ALICE DIAMOND, PAT CONNELLY, AND MORE TO COME...

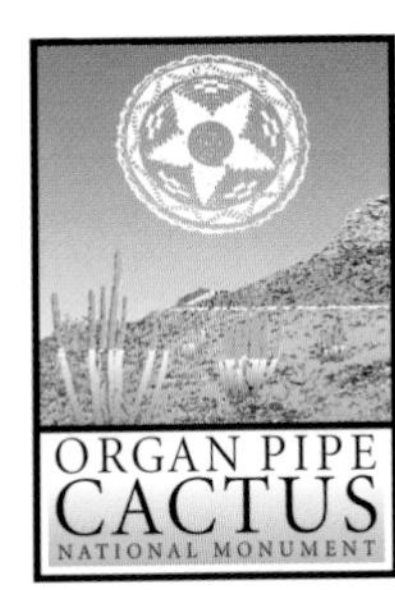

17

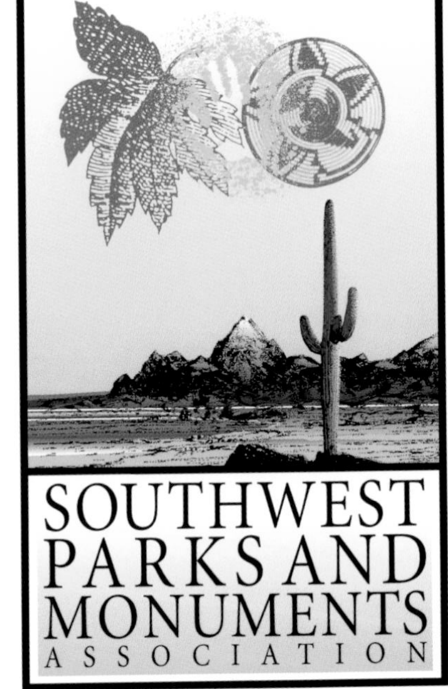

JOHN MUIR
NATIONAL HISTORIC SITE
AZTEC
RUINS
NATIONAL MONUMENT

GOLDEN
SPIKE
NATIONAL HISTORIC SITE

17 Logos in a series of 50 for the Southwest Parks and Monuments Association

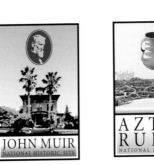

CommArts
1112 Pearl Street
Boulder, Colorado 80302
303.447.8202
info@commarts-boulder.com
www.commarts-boulder.com

COMMARTS

Whenever you're catching Shaq at Staples Center, Destiny's Child at Madison Square Garden, departing the new JFK International Terminal 4, shopping the Mall of Georgia, vacationing Disney's Grand Californian Hotel, skiing Vail, checking out the U.S. Ski Team at the 2002 Olympics or watching the last release of Star Trek - you're plugged into another branded environment created by Communication Arts, Inc.

Tracing our roots to the Office of Charles and Ray Eames, CommArts has applied their inventive, humanistic and collaborative process into dynamic projects worldwide. Sixty designers offer an array of integrated, strategic design services from urban, architectural, interior, environmental, graphic, marketing, branding and interactive web design.

CommArts goes deep to connect people, places, cultures and markets by weaving project stories that entice peoples' curiosity and invite their participation.

CommArts studio is on the Downtown Boulder Mall, which is one of our projects that has set a national standard for downtown revitalization. Here, we work on projects in Dubai, Tokyo, Los Angeles, New York, London, Barcelona - and jog the Rockies during lunch. "Get a life" is more meaningful and achievable in Boulder.

Beyond the recognition, awards and publications, CommArts' people are motivated by incredibly challenging projects that have the potential to change peoples' worlds, add meaning and beauty to their lives and help make this place a bit better for all of us. Yes.

1. The Block at Orange

1

2

3

4

1. Westminster Promenade
2. Light and Story Pylons
3. Entry Sign
4. Water Feature

1

2

3

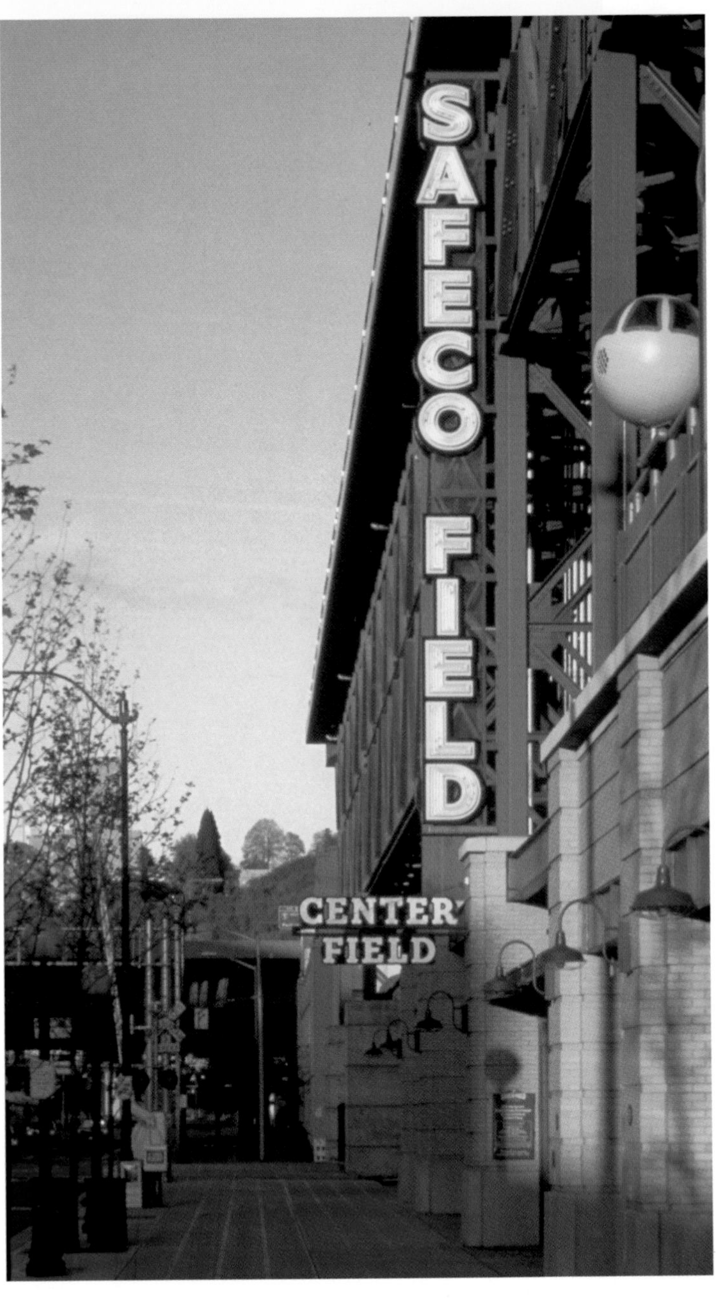

4

1. SAFECO Field, Seattle, WA
2. Food Concession Signage
3. Food Court Sign
4. Entry Signage

1

2

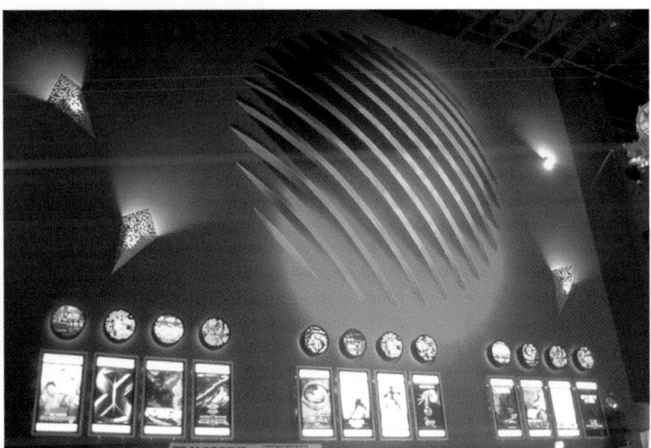

3

1. Famous Players Cinema, Canada
2. Feature Elements
3. Wall Sculpture

1

2

3

4

5

1. GO Boulder Transit
2. The Jump
3. The Hop
4. The Skip
5. The Bound

1

NANTUCKET
GOLF CLUB

2

3

4

5

6

7

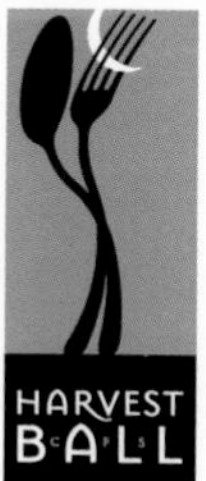

8

9

>LOST
>FOUND...
>RETURNED!

10

11

1. Spyder
2. Nantucket Golf Club
3. United Artists Cinemas
4. Percepta
5. Embarcadero Center
6. Rocky Mountain College of Art and Design
7. JFK International Arrivals Terminal 4
8. Harvest Ball
9. Rendezvous
10. StuffBak
11. TransBrasil Airlines

1

2

3

1. STAPLES Center Environmental Design
2. Entry Signage
3. Mall of Georgia Environmental Design

Dennis | Konetzka | Design Group, LLC
Suite one Floor two
1230 Thirty-first street NW
Washington, DC 20007
202.338.1164
info@denniskonetzka.com
www.denniskonetzka.com

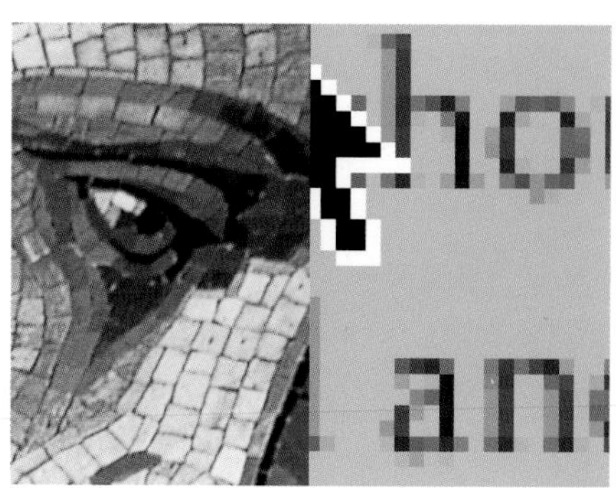

DENNIS | KONETZKA | DESIGN GROUP

Our focus is on the design and implementation of business communications and branding programs for corporations, institutions, and governmental organizations.

Our strengths are our design expertise, our thorough production knowledge of both print and digital media, and a clear understanding of how they work together.

Our approach is rooted in analysis.
Before we design anything, we dissect, digest, add, delete, and reassemble to ensure that the material makes sense.

Our results are a product of creativity and collaboration.

We understand not only what various technologies are capable of achieving, we also understand how to plan and purchase the production of various technologies for maximum efficiency and economy.

We have access to a wide network of creative professionals, including programmers and interactive media producers, architects and exhibition designers, and understand how to maintain branding programs across disciplines and media.

SHARKS!
The Mysterious Killers
Dresden
Treasures from the Saxon State Library
THOMAS
GENIUS O
NTRODUCT
THE JAMES MADISON COUNCIL OF THE LIBRARY OF CONGRESS 2000 ANNUAL REPORT
capitalve
Meyer Foundation 1999 Annual Report The Power of Partnerships

Annual Report back cover–front cover and editorial spreads, 1999-2001. Client: Meyer Foundation

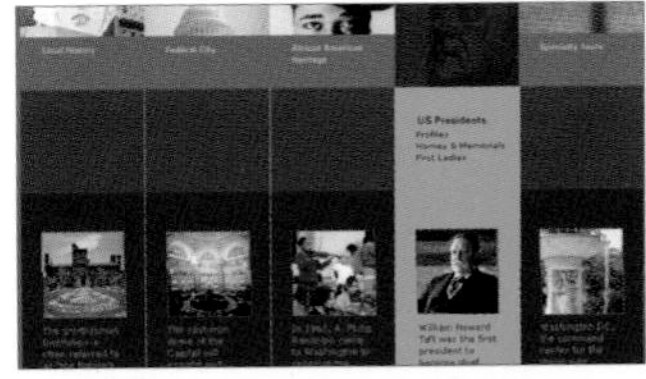

[1

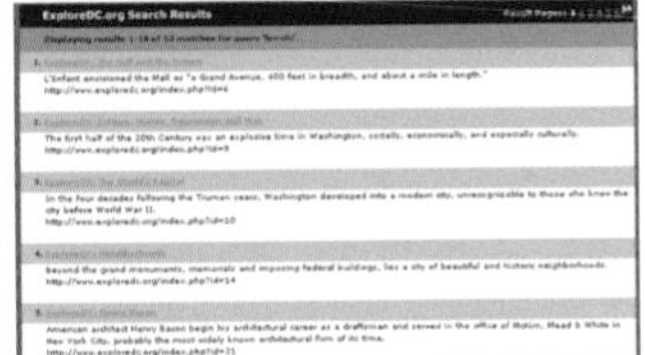

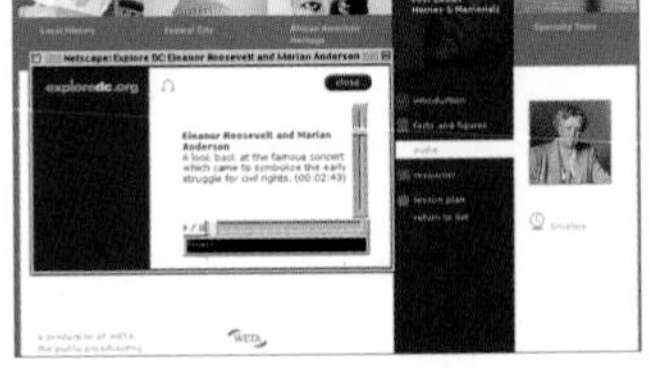

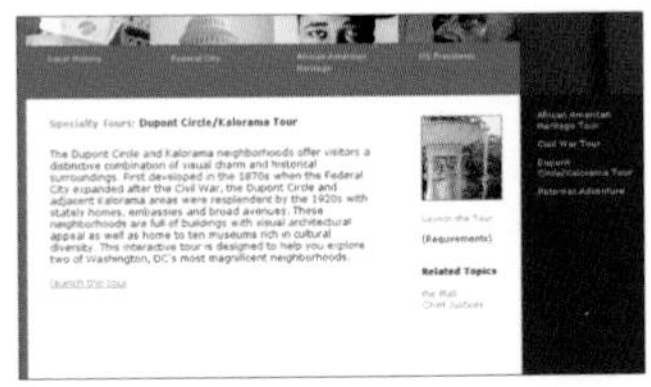
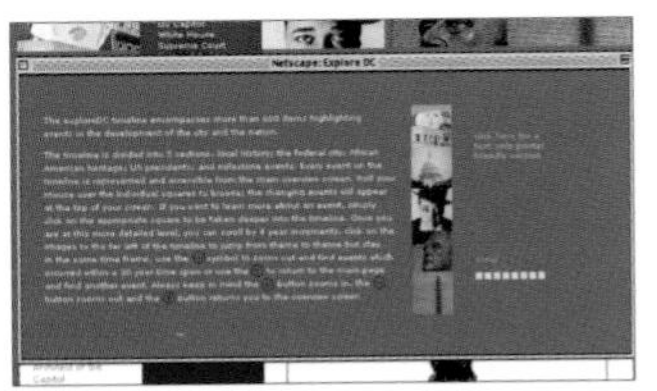
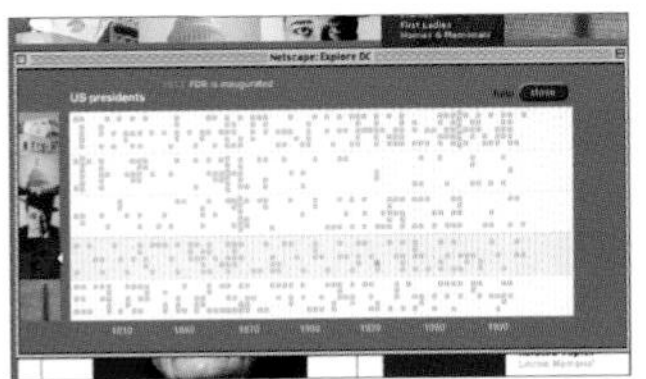
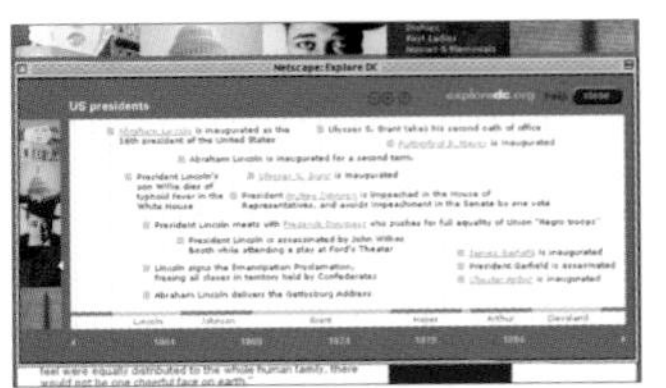
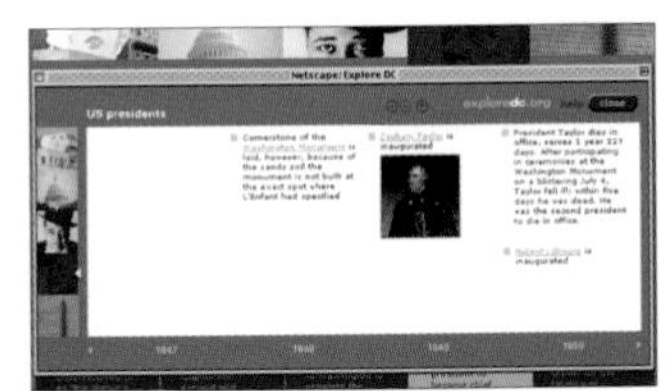

1]

[2

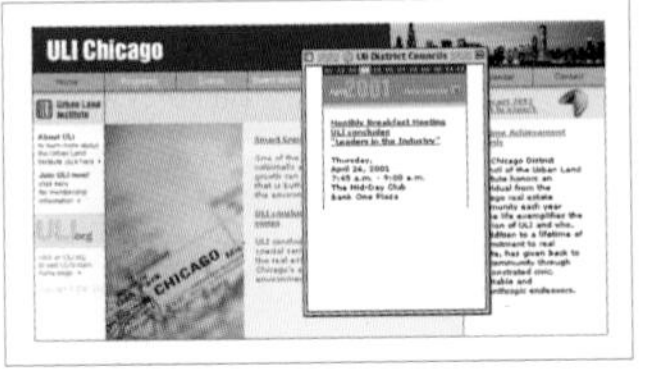

2]

1. www.exploreDC.org, 2001. Client: WETA Public Television **2.** www.uli.org, 2001. Client: Urban Land Institute

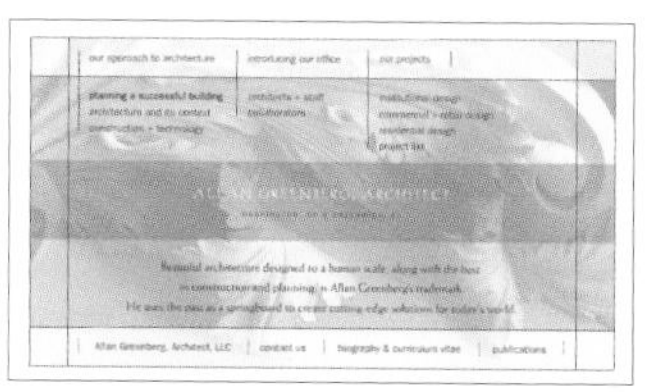
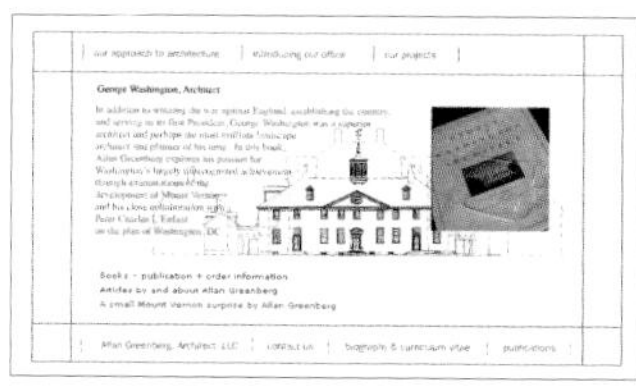
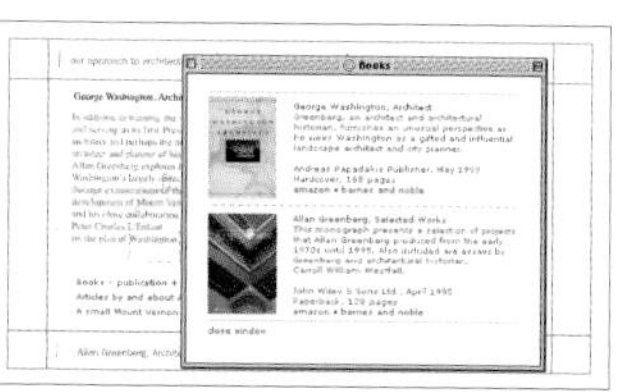
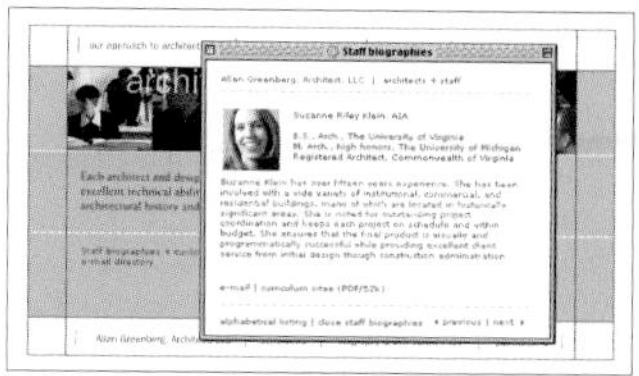
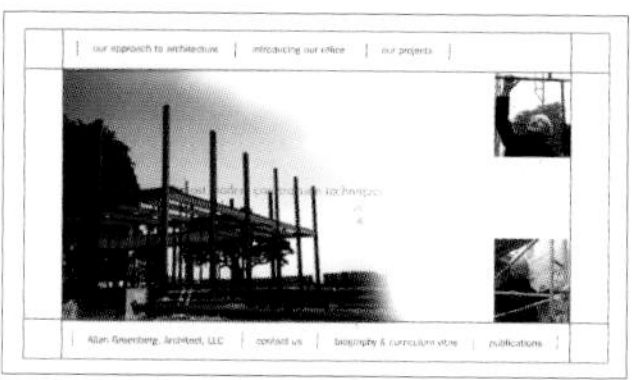

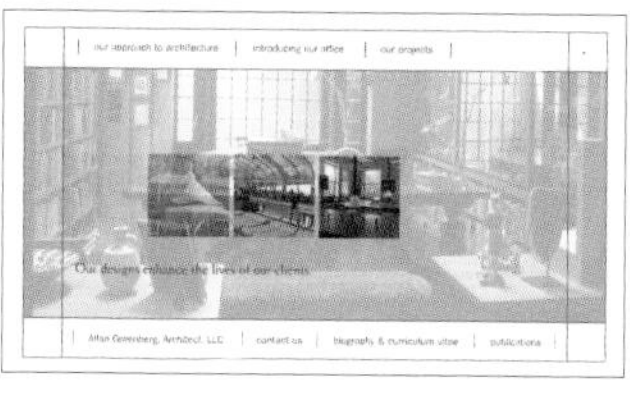

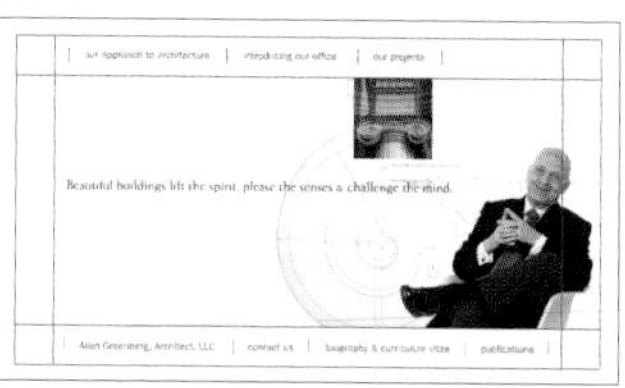

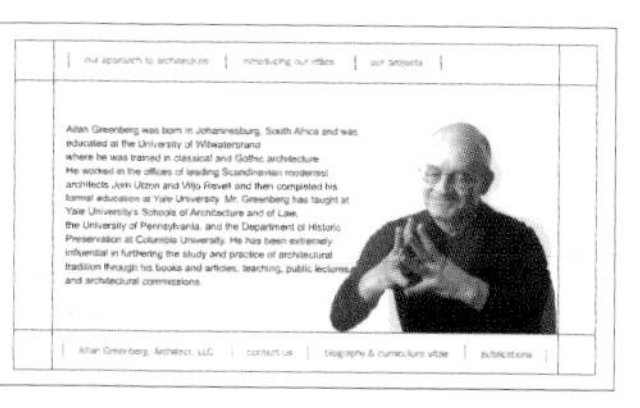
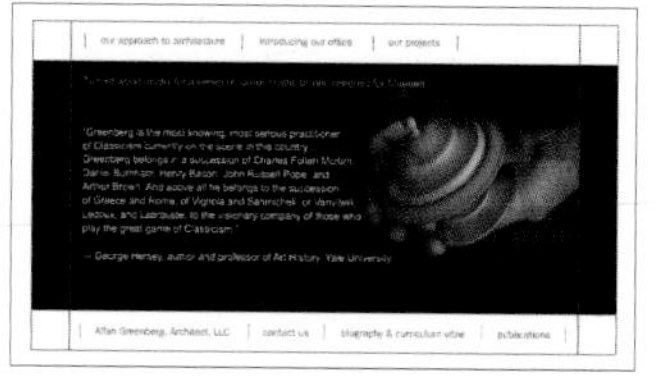
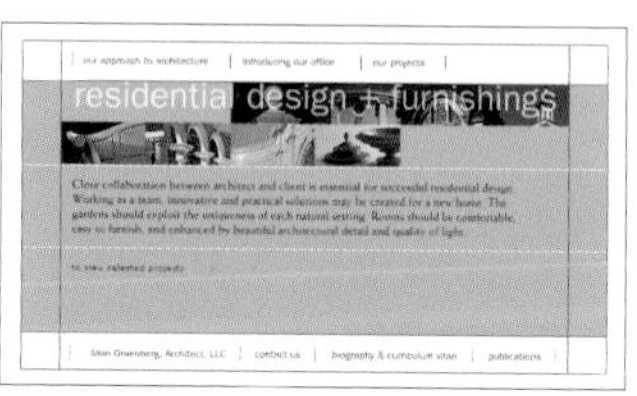

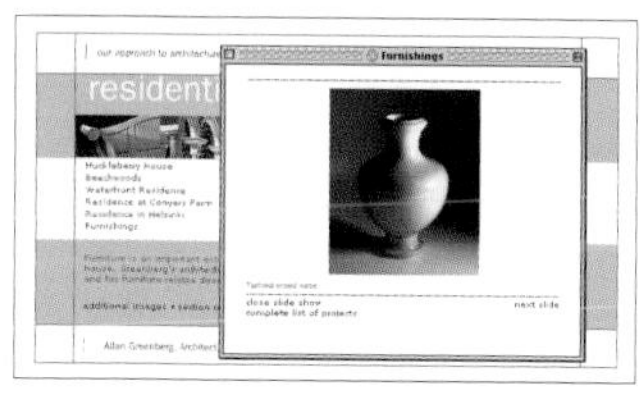
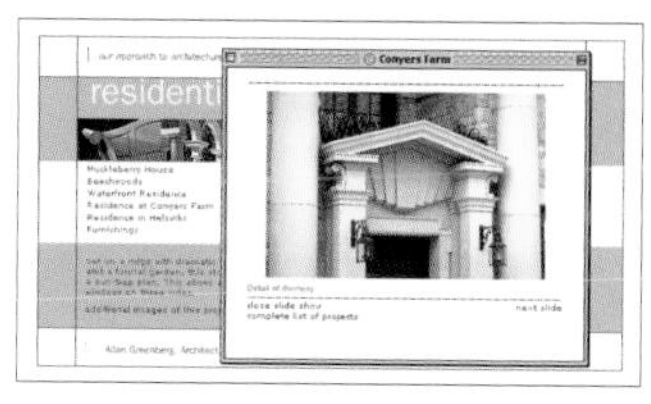

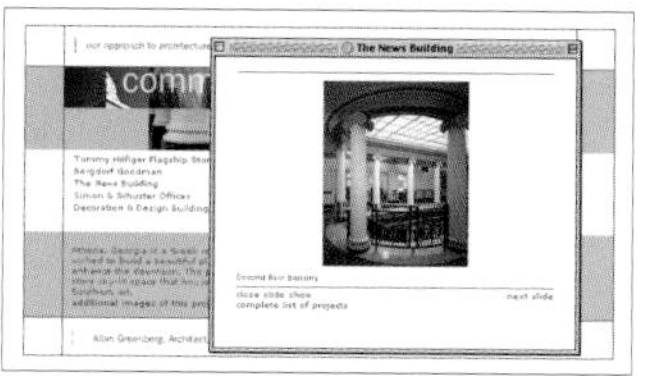

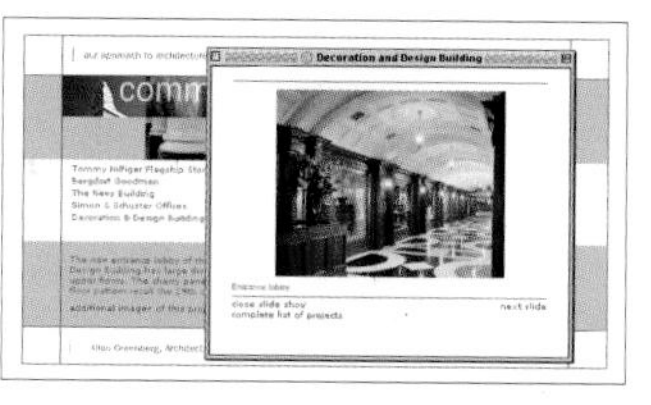
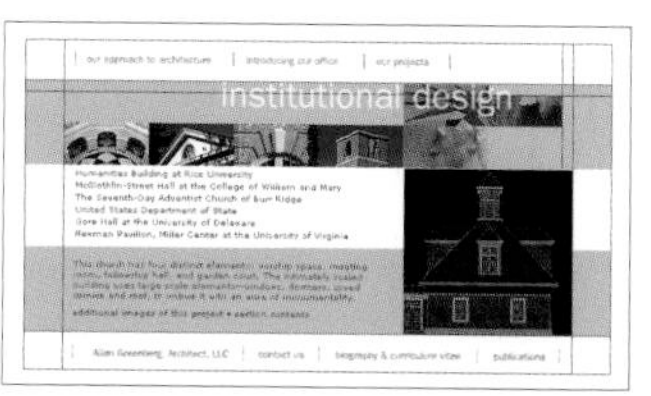

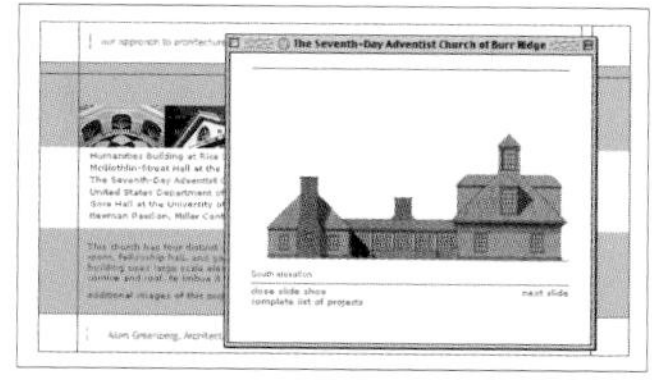
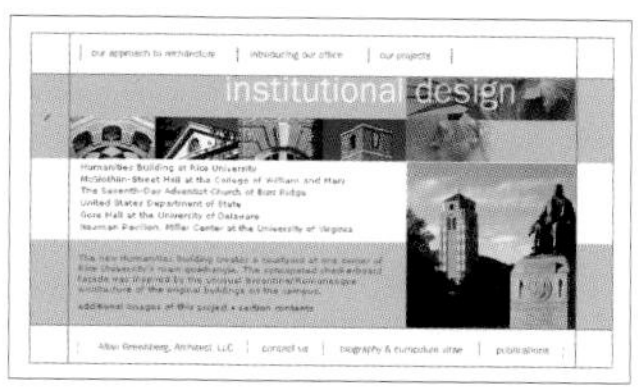

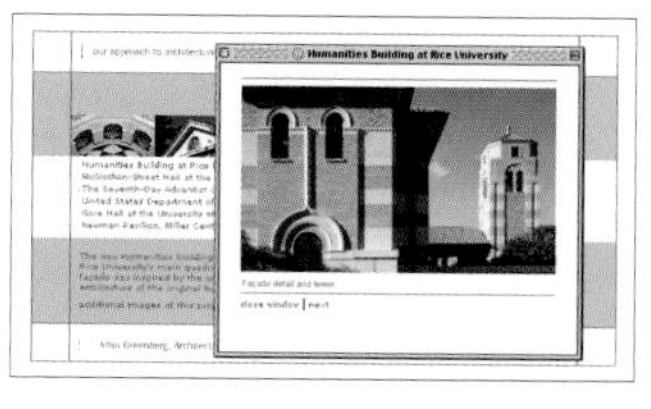
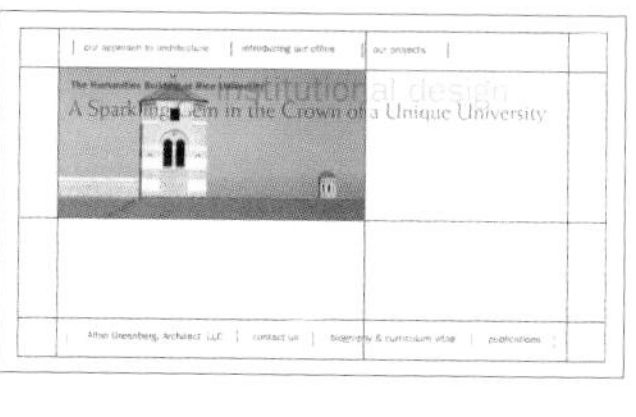
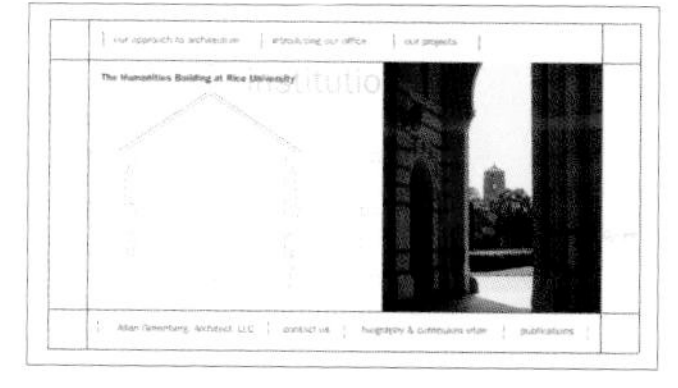
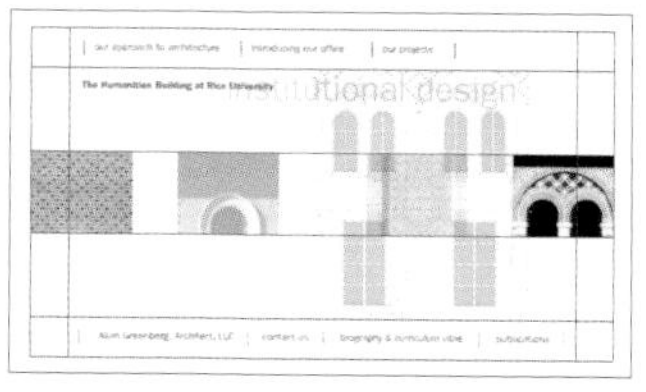
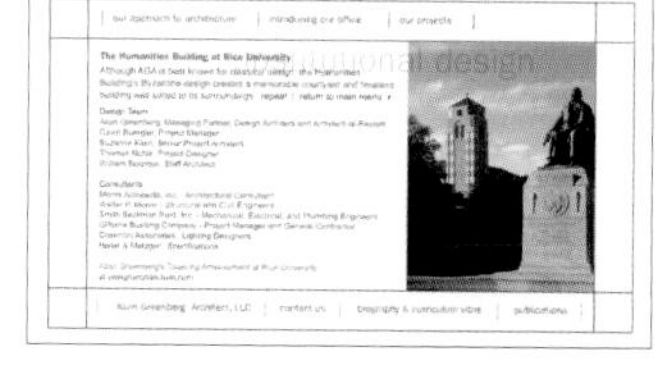
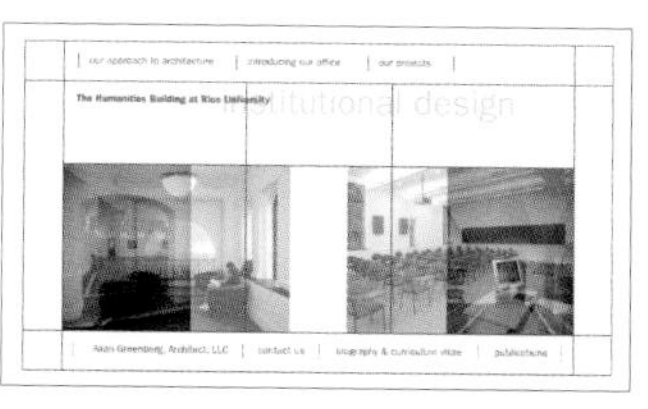

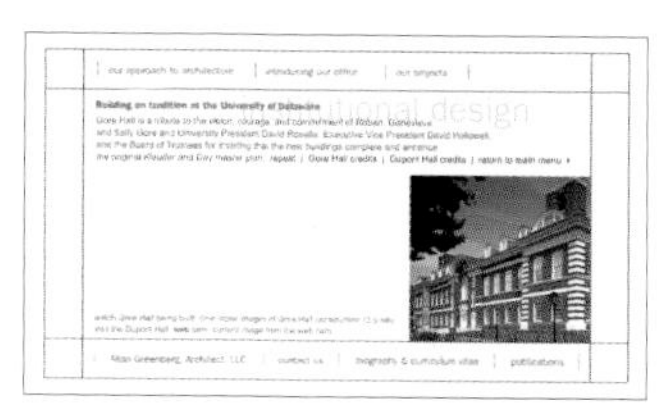
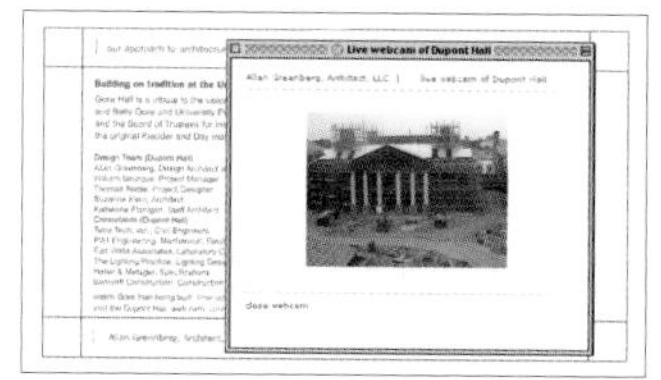

3]

3. www.allangreenberg.com, 2001. Client: Allan Greenberg Architect

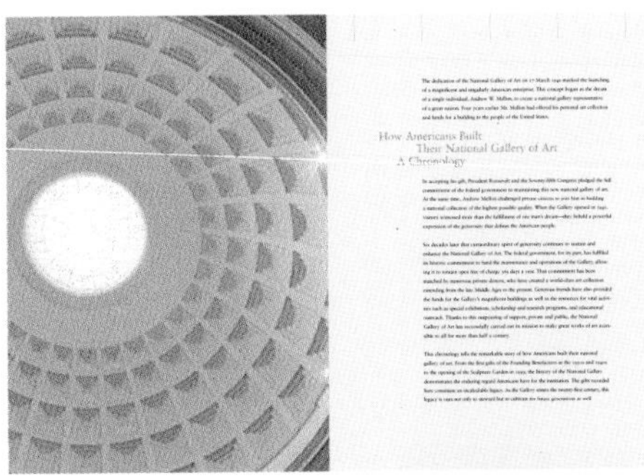

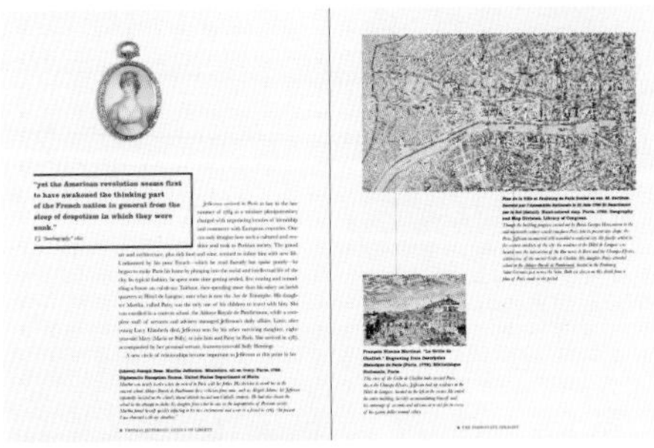

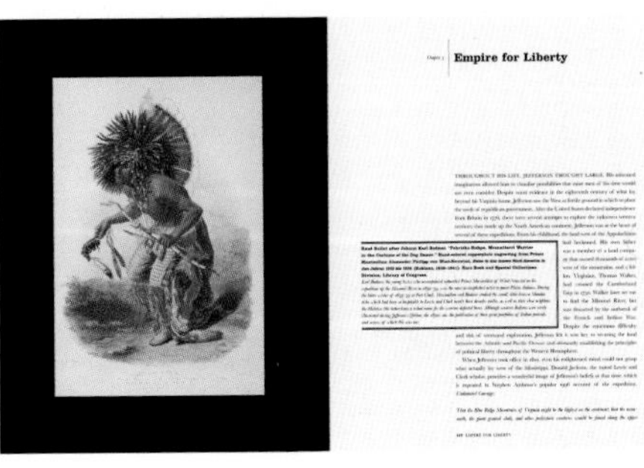

Chronology, 2001
Client: National Gallery of Art

Thomas Jefferson: Genius of Liberty
Client: Library of Congress

USGS
science for a changing world
USGS Visual Id
Management Policies 2001
NATIONAL PARK SERVICE
italventure
A new generation of nonprofit leaders
ERICANS BUILT
THEIR NATIONAL GALLERY OF ART
A Chronology
EVOHE
poemas eróticos | erotic poems
Cristina Peri Rossi
ONE · LIGHT · STREET
NEW ISRAEL FUND 1999 AN
The New Israel:
A Pro

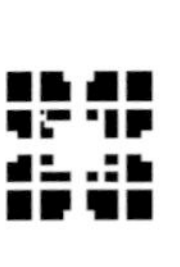

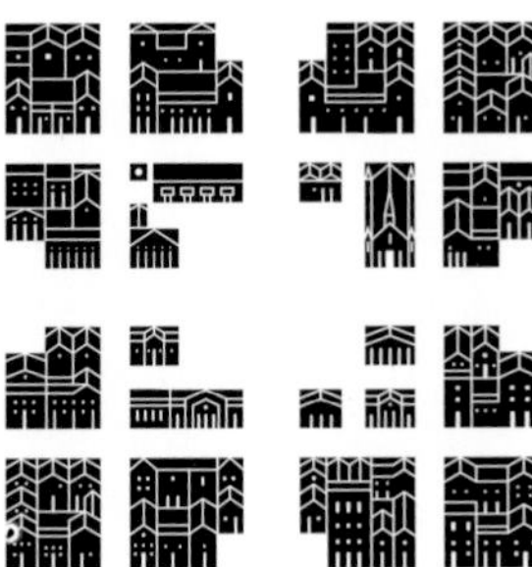

Logotype for Washington DC-based philanthropic foundation, 1999
Client: Meyer Foundation

Refined suite of symbols, 2000
Client: National Park Service

Symbol, 1998.
Client: U.S. Geological Survey

Symbol for Architectural and Urban Planning firm, 1999
Client: Torti Gallas and Partners CHK

Ema Design Inc.
1546 South Clarkson Street
Denver, Colorado 80210
303.825.0222
303.825.2800 fax
www.emadesign.com

EMA DESIGN INC.

"As our work evolves, we seem to be more involved in communicating positive ideas to and about people and how they interface with places and things. Hopefully, we can instill positive stimuli into our environment that inspires the human spirit in us all," states firm principal Thomas Ema.

Ema Design's work has won numerous local and national awards and is published in Graphic Design: America, The work of 28 leading edge design firms from across the United States and Canada (c.1993) and Graphic Design America 2, The work of many of the best and brightest design firms from across the United States (c.1997).

Thomas Ema is a graduate of the Kansas City Art Institute and a founding member and first Vice President of the Colorado Chapter of the American Institute of Graphic Arts (AIGA). In 1982, he started Ema Design in Denver, Colorado.

"Having grown up in Williamsburg, Virginia, I have a deep appreciation for history and enduring quality," states Ema. Thomas Ema believes the secret to creating great work is, "You have to listen to your client's needs with one ear. With the other ear you have to listen to your own heart."

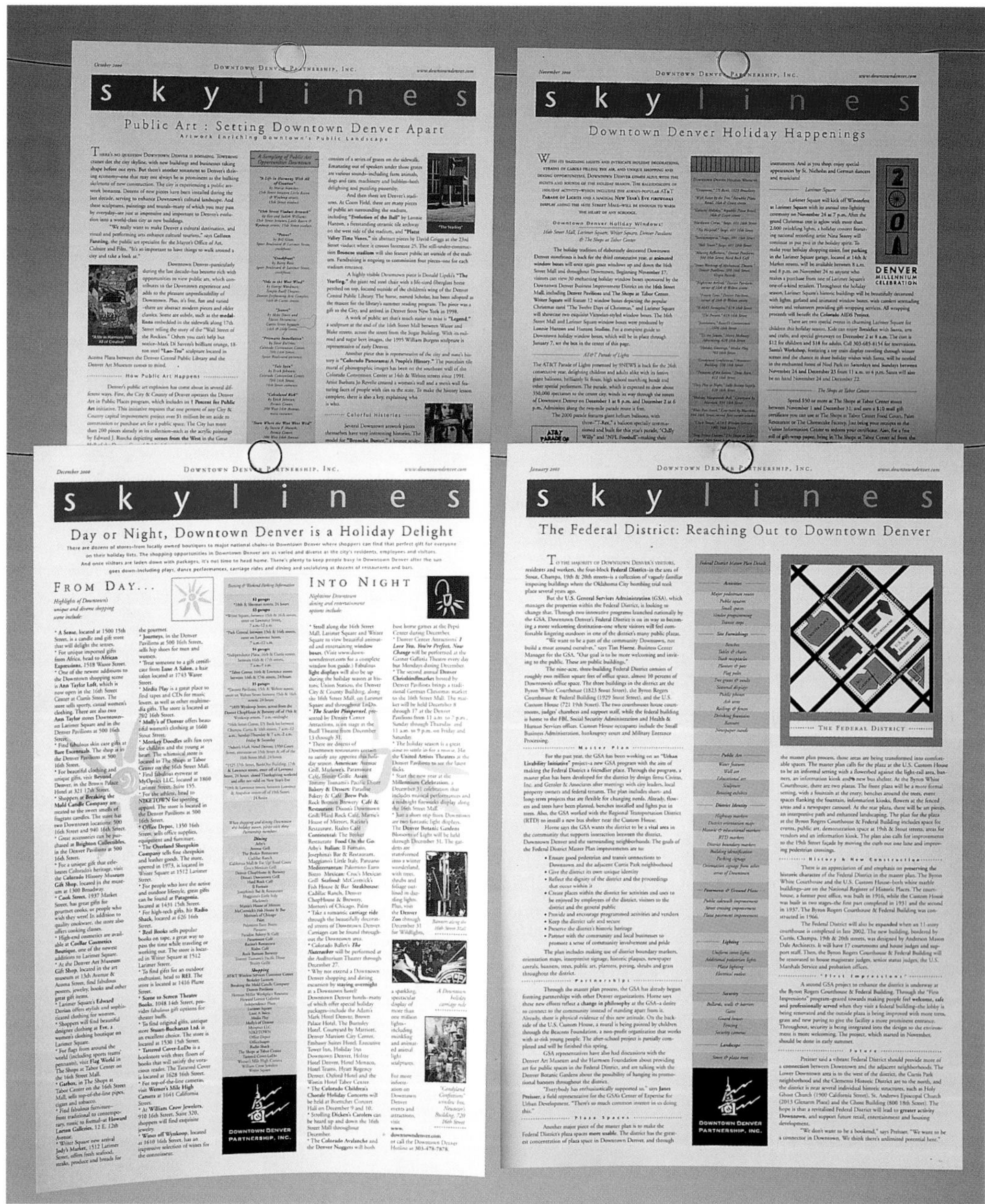

Downtown Denver Partnership, Inc.

skylines

Public Art: Setting Downtown Denver Apart

Downtown Denver Partnership, Inc.

skylines

Downtown Denver Holiday Happenings

Downtown Denver Partnership, Inc.

skylines

Day or Night, Downtown Denver is a Holiday Delight

From Day...

Into Night

Downtown Denver Partnership, Inc.

Downtown Denver Partnership, Inc.

skylines

The Federal District: Reaching Out to Downtown Denver

The Federal District

Downtown Denver Partnership, Inc.

Four issues of the monthly newsletter SKYLINES for the Downtown Denver Partnership Inc.

1

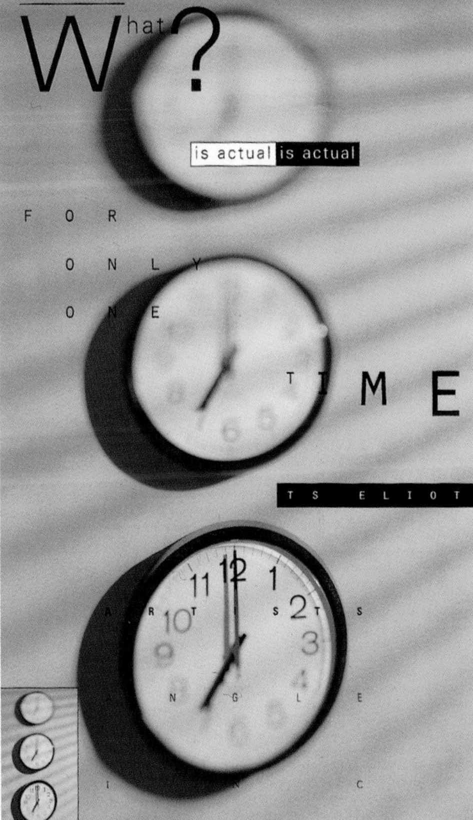

2

1. Post card for a graphics support company promoting its computer services

2. Post card for a graphics support company promoting its fine line comps

best *adj.* most excellent, finest, superior, choice, highest quality, top-notch,unrivaled,unequalled

No Match

1999 ANNUAL SHOW

CALL FOR ENTRIES

ART DIRECTORS CLUB OF DENVER

Deadline: March 31, 1999

1

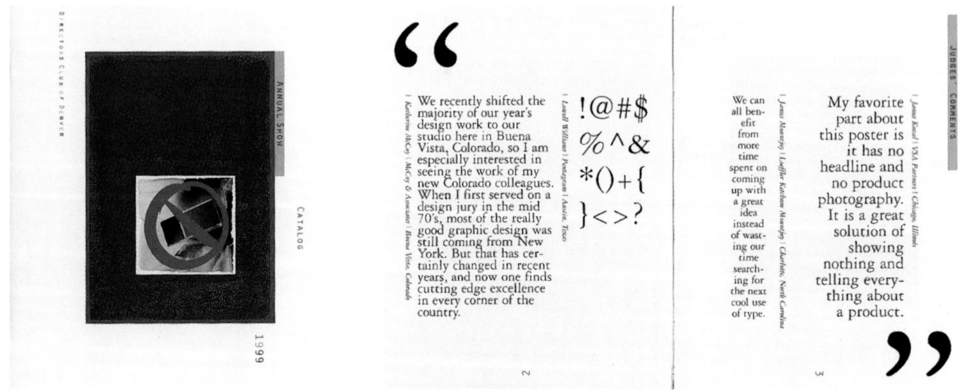

2

1. Poster for the Art Directors Club of Denver 1999 Annual Show Call for Entries

2. Catalog cover and spread for the Art Directors Club of Denver 1999 Annual Show

1

2

3

1. Cover and two spreads for OMI, Inc.'s Annual Report

2. Logo for a Blues Music Festival and Barbeque cook-off event

3. Product brochure for Hewlett-Packard's line of Intelligent Test equipment

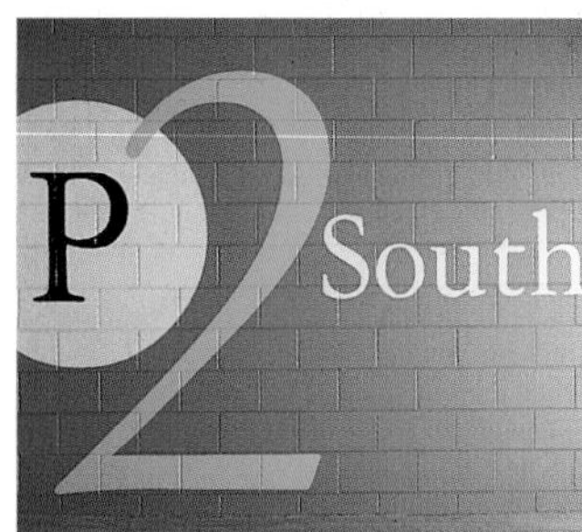

1

2

3

1. Detail of Parking Garage Wall Graphics at Denver Pavilions
2. Detail of Maggiano's Wall Sign at Denver Pavilions
3. Denver Pavilions Wayfinding Signage
4. Denver Pavilions Shopping Bag
5. Thomas Ema oversees the installation of Maggiano's Little Italy Wall Sign at Denver Pavilions in Downtown Denver
6. Maggiano's Little Italy three story tall, two-sided permanent Outdoor Banners at Denver Pavilions
7. Maggiano's Blade Sign on the 16th Street Mall in Downtown Denver
8. Corner Bakery Signage on the 16th Street Mall

4

MAGGIANO'S
LITTLE ITALY
UpRight
MX 19

5

MAGGIANO'S
LITTLE ITALY

6

MAGGIANO'S
cornerbakery
LITTLE ITALY

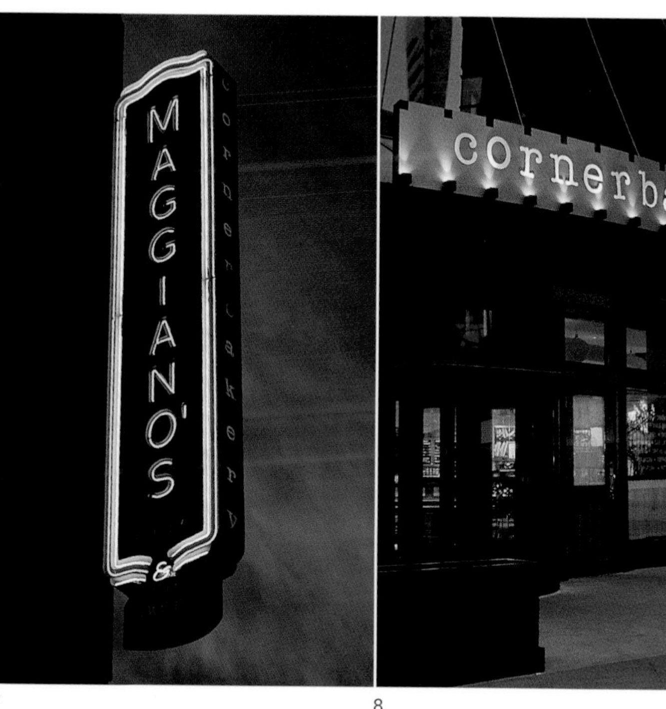
MAGGIANO'S
cornerbakery
cornerbakery

7

8

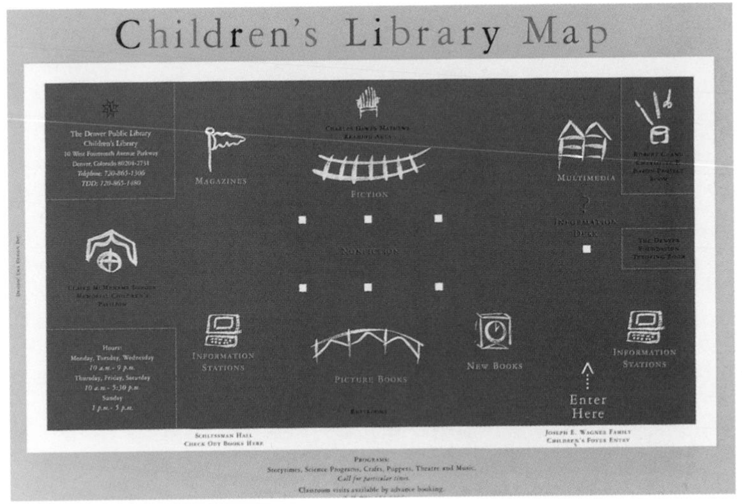

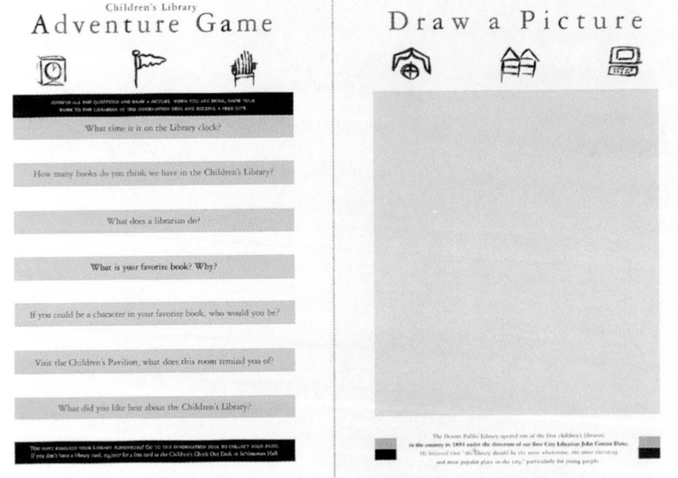

Children's Library Map for the Denver Public Library including Adventure Game, Draw a Picture and Landmark Icons

EM2
121 Church Street
Decatur, Georgia 30030
404.370.6050
www.em2design.com

EM2think.2create.2inspire.

Who do you want 2 be? Answer that question and everything else falls into place. That's the philosophy of EM2, the Atlanta-based creative agency who embrace the concept of individuality in their work – building brand personalities for national clients in high-image categories – and in their business – assembling a diverse staff with differing talents.

"Companies are like people," explains Creative Director Maxey Andress. "It's the quirks that define our character. Why act like Ginger if you're really Mary Ann? Just be yourself. Be honest. Promote the core qualities that make you different from the rest. When you do, it creates a more soulful, meaningful expression. It's communication that centers around what's true and real, and that makes for powerful – and memorable – connections with whomever you want to reach."

This philosophy has helped EM2 forge long-standing relationships with clients, such as Neenah Paper and UPS, as well as attract aesthetically-driven companies, like Beaulieu Commercial Carpets and Johnston & Murphy. "What we do best," says Managing Director Chris Martin, "is integrate ourselves with the brand personality. Not only do we give it a face and a voice across an array of media, we look after it, nurture it, make sure it evolves so our clients remain current in the marketplace. You could say we're brand stewards."

With such a focus on individuality and an ensemble of creative talent with different perspectives, EM2's work doesn't follow a standard format. "The companies are diverse. Our people are diverse. The projects are diverse," Maxey concludes. "So, naturally, our solutions are too. Each is as unique as the client. That's what makes it all work."

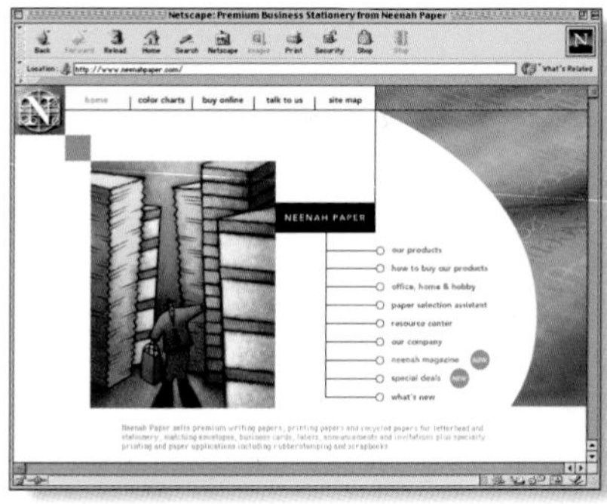

1.

2.

3. 4. 5. 6.

1. Neenah Paper web site (www.neenahpaper.com)
2. Neenah Paper CLASSIC COTTON™ swatchbook spread
3. Neenah Paper CLASSIC COTTON™ swatchbook
4. Neenah Paper ENVIRONMENT® swatchbook
5. Neenah Paper CLASSIC COLUMNS® swatchbook
6. Neenah Paper CLASSIC® Laid swatchbook

1.

2.

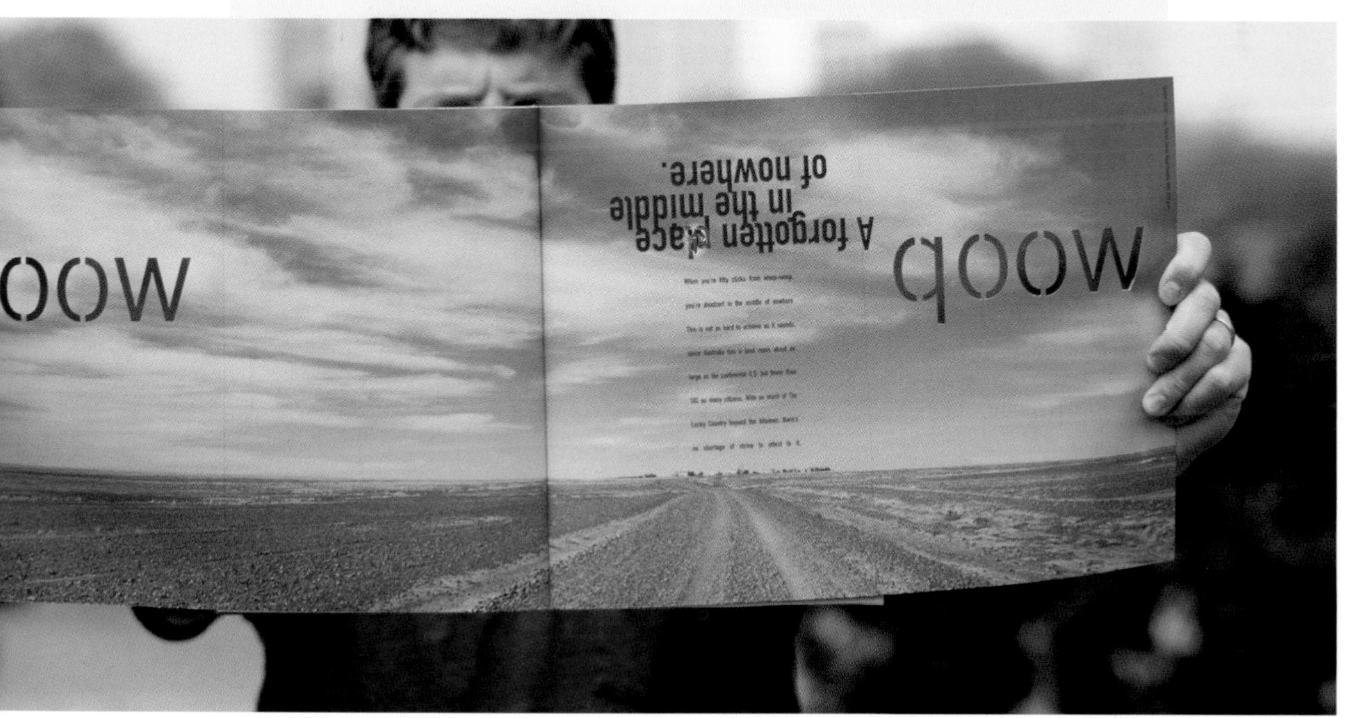

3.

1. Neenah Paper tradeshow exhibit
2. & 3. Neenah Paper Australia paper promotion

1.

2.

3.

4.

1. & 2. Johnston & Murphy retail packaging
3. Johnston & Murphy seasonal window display
4. Johnston & Murphy wholesale catalog

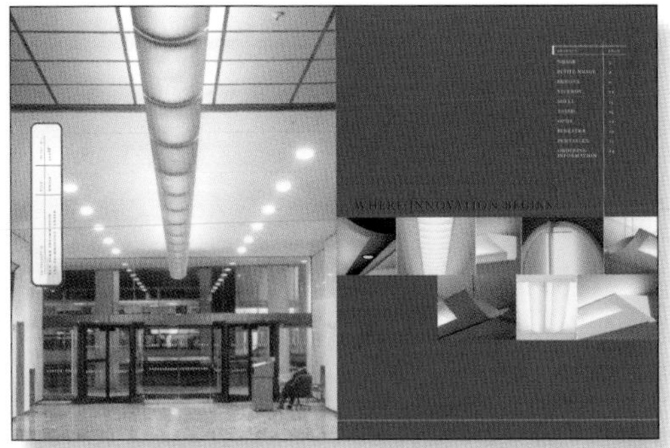

1.

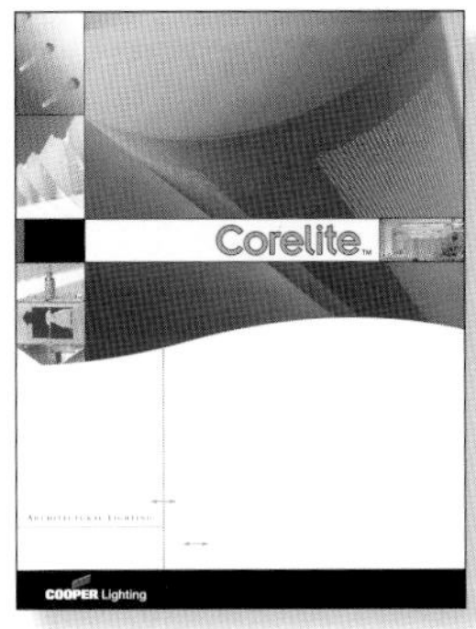

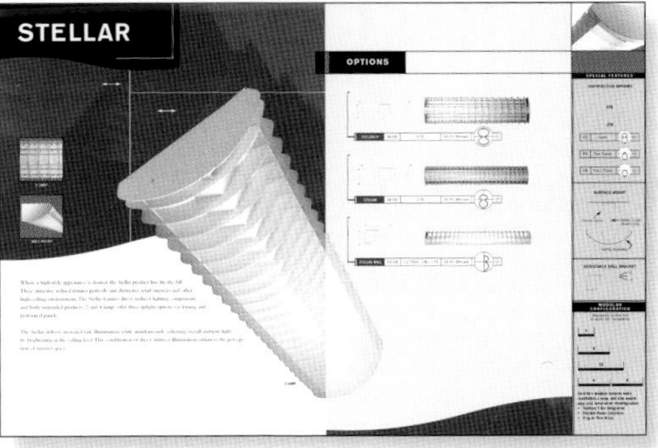

2.

1. Cooper Lighting Neoray product catalog
2. Cooper Lighting Corelite product catalog

1.

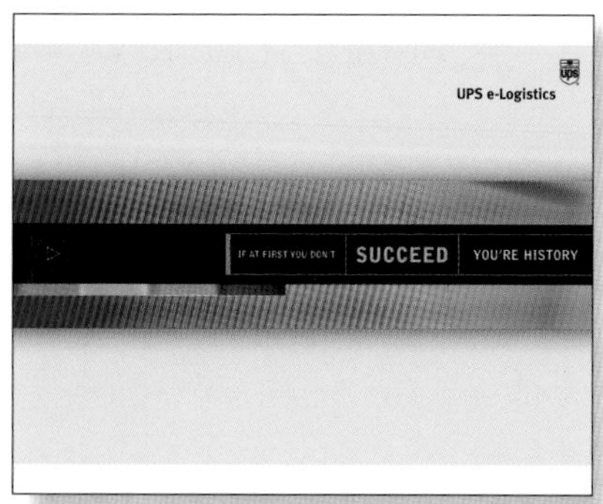

2.

1. UPS Envoy product packaging
2. UPS e-Logistics capabilities brochure
3. UPS ClickUPS publication

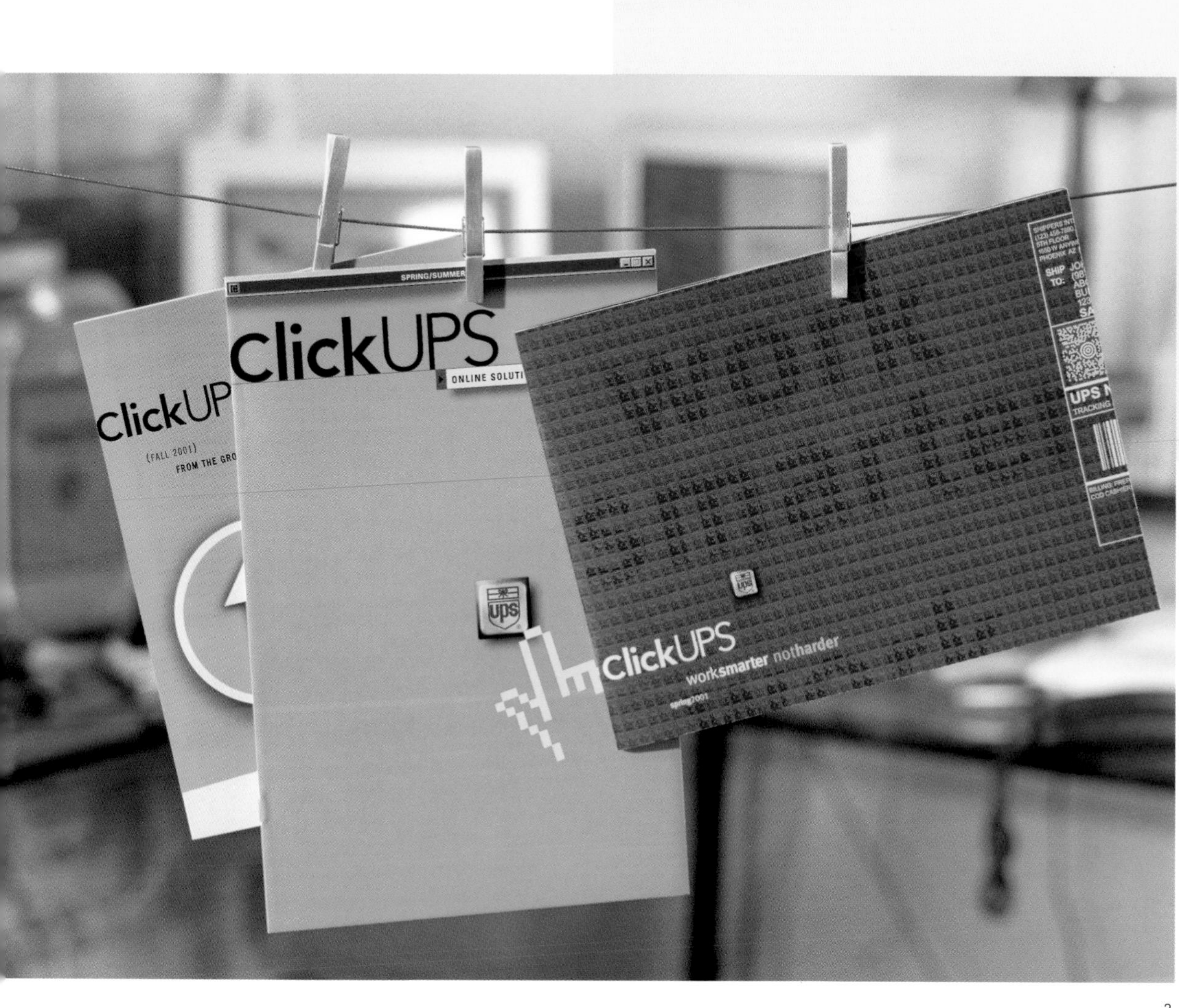
(FALL 2001)
SPRING/SUMMER
ClickUPS
clickUPS
worksmarter notharder
spring2001

3.

5.

6.

7.

1.

2.

3.

4.

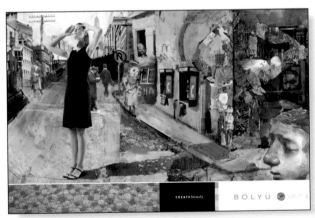

1. Avado corporate identity
2. Neenah Paper CLASSIC COTTON™ product identity
3. Sage restaurant identity
4. WebInservice corporate identity
5.- 7. BOLYU Carpet advertisements

Frankfurt Balkind
244 East 58th Street
New York, NY 10022
212.421.5888
www.frankfurtbalkind.com

FRANKFURT BALKIND

Take a group of exceptionally talented, bright people from all creative and strategic disciplines, let them work to the highest standards for clients with unique marketing challenges, and you have the business organism known as Frankfurt Balkind.

Founded in 1972, we're an innovative agency that specializes equally in five key areas: Strategy, Identity, New Media, Advertising, and Marketing Communications.

Three qualities distinguish us in the marketplace.

First, we work in cross-functional teams integrated at the highest strategic level. This allows us to create *brand coherence* across all media without having to impose lots of creatively inhibiting executional rules that freeze the brand in time and conform to the lowest common denominator.

Second, we have extensive client experience in technology, information, and entertainment—today's major cultural drivers. This gives us a deeper understanding of the very areas that have the strongest *resonance* with today's target audiences.

Third, we're equally committed to and *equally strong in all media*. This frees us to think outside the box to give you the smartest return on your investment.

Frankly, we're not for everybody. But for companies who need to succeed in fast-changing, challenging markets, we know how to build uniquely powerful brands.

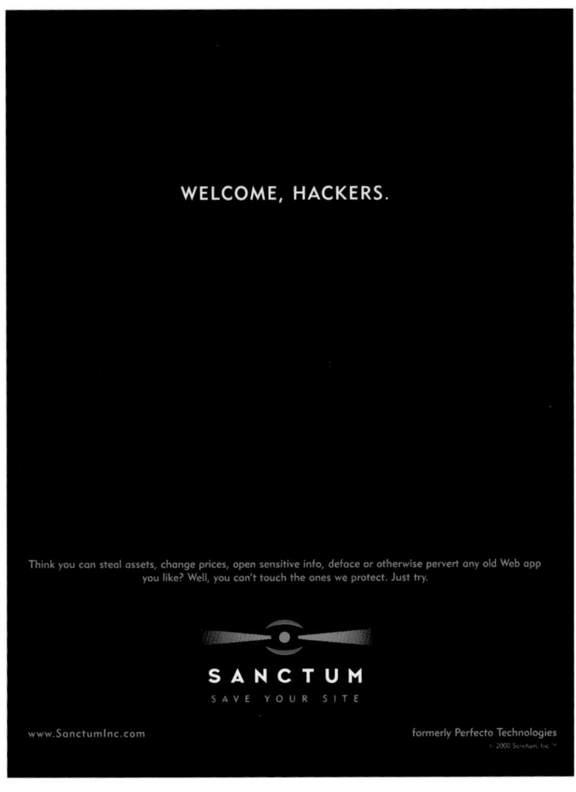

WELCOME, HACKERS.
Think you can steal assets, change prices, open sensitive info, deface or otherwise pervert any old Web app you like? Well, you can't touch the ones we protect. Just try.
SANCTUM
SAVE YOUR SITE
www.SanctumInc.com
formerly Perfecto Technologies

1

3

2

4

SANCTUM As integrated agency of record for Sanctum, a Web security software company, Frankfurt Balkind developed the brand strategy, including changing the name from Perfecto Technologies and creating a new identity (**2**). In repositioning the brand, a new category—"Web Perversion"—was established for a product that keeps hackers from defiling a site. Web perversion was highlighted on the Sanctum Web site (www.sanctuminc.com), as were the four categories of perverts: Type A steals assets; Type B alters prices; Type C steals customer information; Type D defaces sites (**4**). The direct mail brochure reinforced key and support messages (**3**). Advertising directed to senior executives and IT decision-makers demonstrated Sanctum's confidence by issuing a challenge to hackers. The product benefit is summarized in the tagline: "Save Your Site" (**1**).

No sad faces.
Sellers get more money. Buyers get more car.
Selling it yourself with StraightAway is just plain better than dealing with a dealer. Plus, we offer financing, warranty, inspection and more. Everyone's happy. See for yourself at the StraightAway Center at Pep Boys.
StraightAway
The easy way you buy and sell.

5

6

STRAIGHTAWAY For StraightAway, a company that helps car buyers and sellers do a direct deal, we created the brand strategy, then launched the new entity. As integrated agency of record, Frankfurt Balkind created the name (formerly Auto2Auto), identity, and tagline: "The easy way to buy and sell." Advertising ran in print (**5**), on radio, and outdoor (**9**); signage appeared on StraightAway retail kiosks in Pep Boys locations (**7**); and marketing collateral and point-of-purchase rack brochures (**8**) explained the proposition. Sunscreen windshield visors (**6**) were a unique outdoor promotion.

7

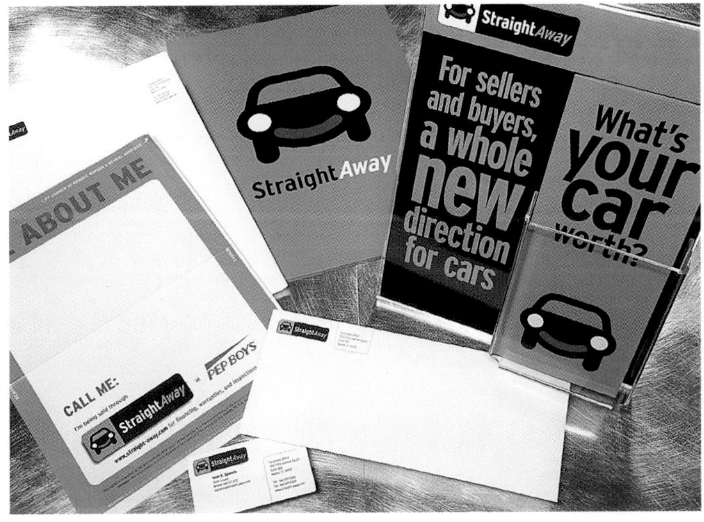

8

Why trade in when you can cash in?

StraightAway at PEP BOYS

9

1. MBRANE www.mbrane.com
A B2B marketing site for a wireless infrastructure company. Frankfurt Balkind created the brand strategy, name, identity, and marketing vehicles.

2. SUI GENERIS www.suigeneris.com
A consumer site for luxuries targeted to high-net-worth individuals. We also created the brand identity.

3. PITNEY BOWES www.pitneybowes.com
A marketing site that provides users with a broad understanding of and quick access to solutions, products, and services, and presents Pitney Bowes as one unified global brand.

4. J&J E-PHARMA intranet
An intranet where sales and marketing executives can share best practices, understanding, and intelligence across divisions, countries, products, and services.

5. SCHERING-PLOUGH www.freebreather.com
Created as a community site for asthma sufferers and their caregivers to receive and share information and lifestyle advice. Name and identity were also created.

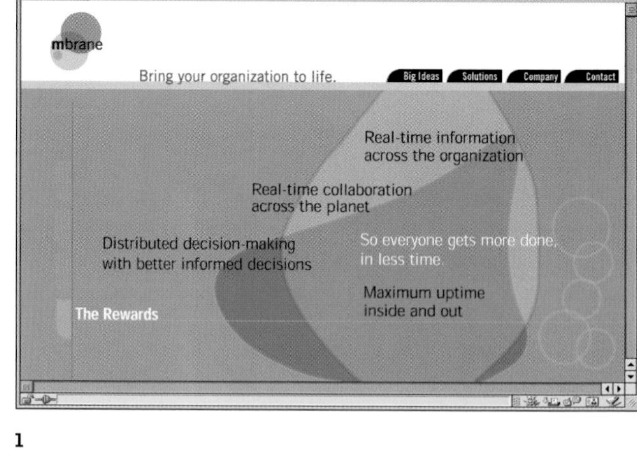

1

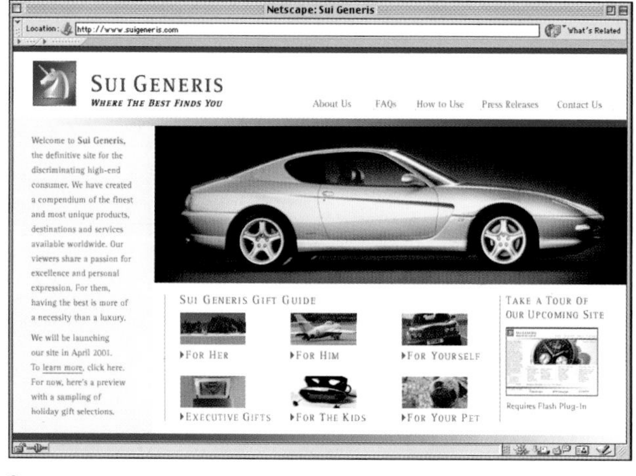

2

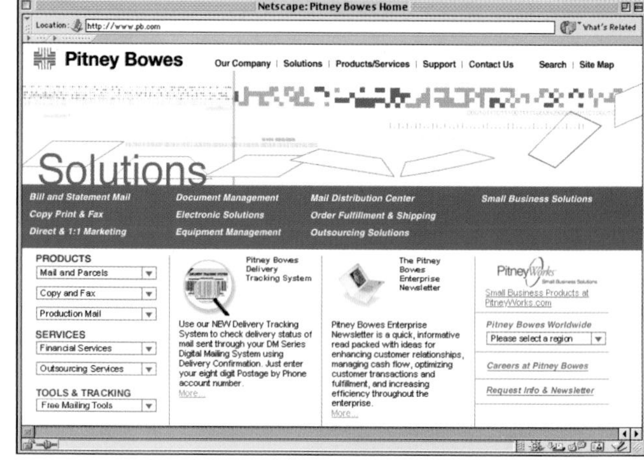

3

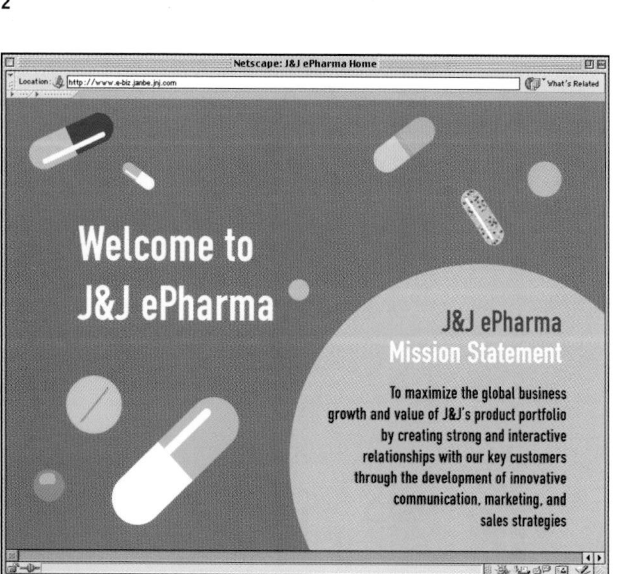

4

5

1. INFORMIX The multimedia global campaign for this international software company, including TV commercial (top) and outdoor (bottom), helped reposition the company as a player in Web development. Identity was also redesigned.

2. TELEDOTCOM MAGAZINE Read by high-level executives at communication service providers, the campaign was directed to both readers and media buyers. The magazine identity and masthead were also redesigned.

3. HOWIWORK The tagline "Work Online, Live Offline" launched a new online workspace for technologists with some 20 different trade ads. Name and identity were also created.

1

2

GO TO: www.informationweek.com/howiwork

9. REVIVING CFO AFTER PRESENTING BUDGET

1. Log on to online workspace (howiwork)
2. Select Benchmark tool
3. Compare your IT budget to industry benchmarks
4. Convey IT budget rationale to CFO
5. Consider taking dance lessons

FIG. 3A

CFO BUDGET REACTION

EXPERT TIP
THERE ARE SEVERAL TYPES OF DANCE YOU MAY WISH TO STUDY (FIGS. 3B, 3C, 3D). CHOOSE THE ONE MOST SUITED TO YOUR FITNESS LEVEL.

FIG. 3B FIG. 3C FIG. 3D

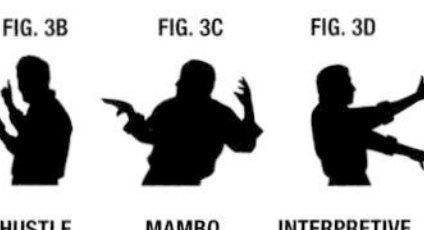

HUSTLE MAMBO INTERPRETIVE

WORK ONLINE. LIVE OFFLINE.

3

1

About.com

2

Radio Central

3

>KNIGHT RIDDER>

4

5

Novell

6

7

8

9

10

1. Name and identity for Adobe Acrobat
2. Name and identity for About.com
3. Identity for Radio Central
4. Corporate identity for Knight Ridder
5. Name and identity for Mbrane (formerly Centura Software)
6. Identity for Novell
7. Identity for Informix
8. Identity for The Station@sony.com
9. Identity for NetGenesis
10. Identity and shopping bag for Sony Style retail stores

1

2

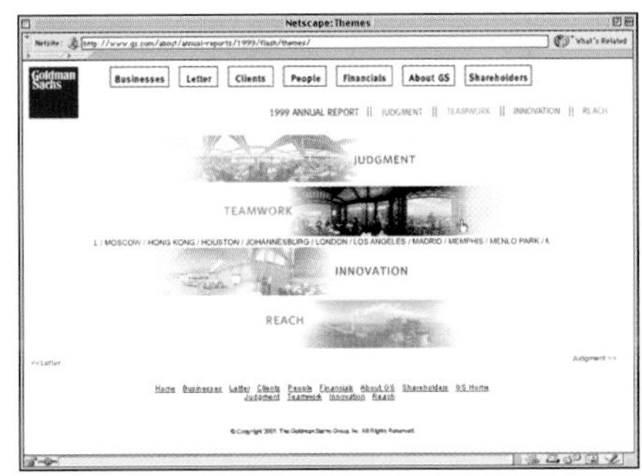

3

4

5

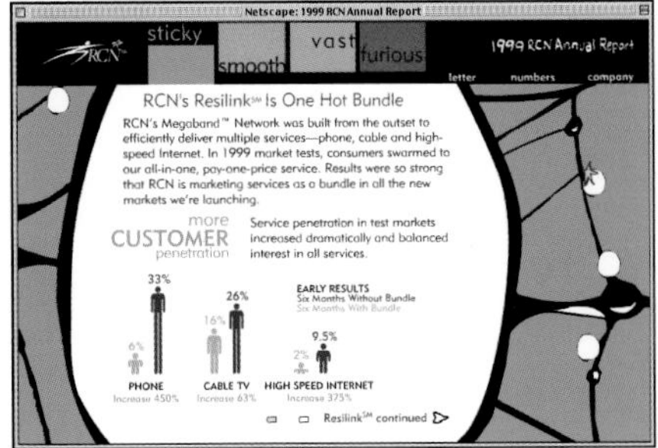

6

GOLDMAN SACHS The print and online annual reports for Goldman Sachs help to strengthen the firm's position as the premier brand in financial services (**1**). The online annual is animated and specifically designed for the Web (**3**). Frankfurt Balkind also created www.gs.com, the corporate marketing site (**2**).

RCN The RCN annual was created to position the company and give it a distinctive share of voice in the crowded telecom environment (**4,5**). The annual is brought to life online using sound and animation (**6**).

1

2

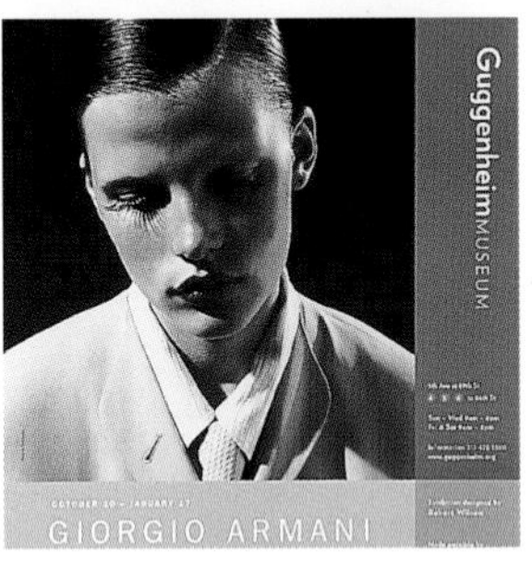

3

4

1,2. MOVIE POSTERS Examples from the many motion picture campaigns created each year for U.S. and global markets.

3. THE GUGGENHEIM Guggenheim Museum exhibit advertising appearing in newspapers, outdoor, and on subway trains.

4. ANTHONY LOGISTICS FOR MEN The brand strategy, name, identity, copy, and packaging for a new line of men's skin care products sold in upscale retail stores.

GouthierDesign, Inc
2604 Northwest 54 Street
Fort Lauderdale, Florida 33309
Ph . 954 739 7430
Fx . 954 739 3746
www.gouthier.com

GOUTHIERDESIGN

Classic innovation, a combination of traditional good taste with a concept-driven approach to a company's marketing strategy is the hallmark of GouthierDesign's work. The visual solutions created by our firm ensure that each client's unique personality rises above the plethora of competing messages to claim a powerful position.

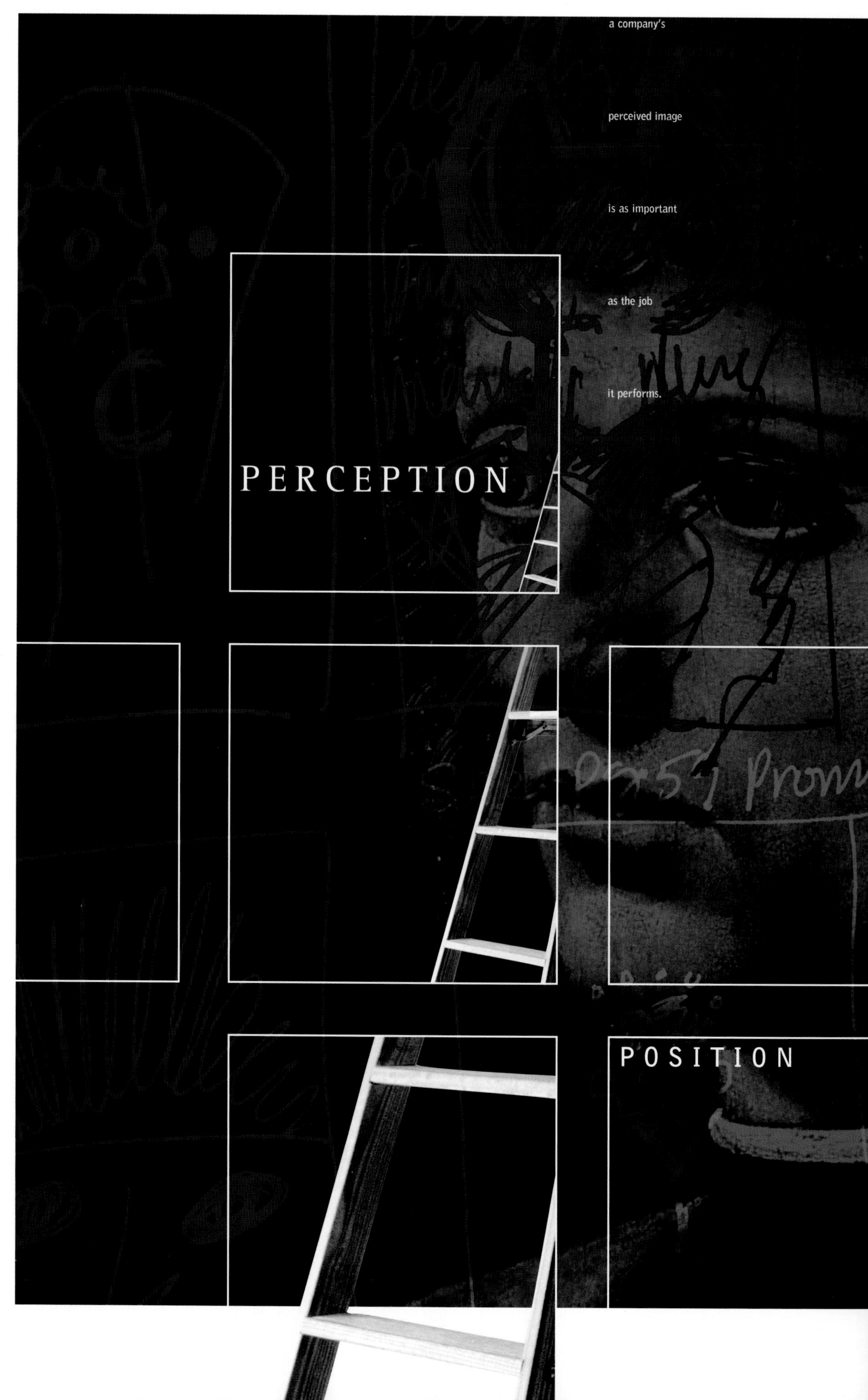
a company's
perceived image
is as important
as the job
it performs.
PERCEPTION
POSITION

1

2

3

4

1. DaVinci Systems product brochures

2. The AGES Group corporate brochure
(in collaboration with: Pinpoint Communications)

3. Kellstrom Industries annual report
(in collaboration with: Curran & Connors)

4. Isotag Technology security product brochure

MAYO
FLAVORED MAYONNAISE
MAN!A
Roasted Garlic
Sun-Dried Tomato
Sun Dried Tomato

1

2

3

4

5

6

7

8

9

10

1. Goodie Jar Foods product label
2. CRW Medical Productions
3. ViSonic Systems, Inc.
4. Good Shepherd Methodist Church Fund
5. B4B Partner
6. Strategic technology Group, Inc.
7. Nemschoff Sports, Ltd.
8. Grapevine Gourmet Catering
9. Senior Life Resource Institute
10. Global Telecast & Communications, LLC

1

2

3

4

5

1. Unisource Paper Company open house invitation
2. Marco Island Marriott Hotel direct mail promotion
3. LifeScan corporate identity and marketing package
4. Levinson Jewelers annual product catalog
5. Paramount Hotel Group corporate identity and brochure

ideas start as fragmented thoughts
whose message, when in the hands
of a professional graphic design
firm is built upon and transformed
into visual communication that
informs and persuades a specific
audience.
CON
CEPT
CONTENT

Tom Graboski Associates, Inc.
Design
4649 Ponce de Leon Blvd.
Suite 401
Coral Gables, Florida 33146
305.669.2550
tgadesign@mindspring.com
www.tgadesign.com

TOM GRABOSKI ASSOCIATES, INC. DESIGN

The year 2000 marked the twentieth anniversary of Tom Graboski Associates, Inc. Design. Founded in 1980, we are an internationally recognized Graphic Design studio located in Coral Gables, Florida, specializing in wayfinding and environmental graphic design and brand identification.

Our diverse strengths enable us to provide consistently innovative and effective graphic solutions to complex environments and situations. We are proud of our long-term relationships with our clients, and remain committed to the formation of solid business relationships built upon trust and unsurpassed customer satisfaction. A few of our valued clients include Royal Caribbean International, Celebrity Cruises, Universal Studios Florida, Disney Development Company, American Classic Voyages, The Graham Companies, Arvida, CMC Group, Baptist Health Systems, Mt. Sinai Medical Center, Marriott, Ritz-Carlton and Inter-Continental Hotels.

While Environmental Graphic Design is our specialty, our knowledge and skill in a variety of design disciplines allows us to provide expert solutions to almost any challenge. We have designed award winning brand and corporate identity programs, signage systems, exhibits, interiors and industrial designs across a broad spectrum of projects and clients, and successfully operate internationally with projects in Finland, France, Germany, Spain and Central America. Our versatility affords us the ability to provide "the total package" to our trusted clients—from a new identity to a new environment. Our recent success stories include new brand identity programs for United States Lines, Miami City Ballet, Beacon Council and the Miami Centennial. Urban design programs for the City of Miami, Ocean City Maryland, City of Coral Gables have been award winning solutions to complex public sector situations. We also recently worked as the Design Directors for the internationally renowned Miami Film Festival.

Today we face the challenge of new and emerging technologies that are changing the language of "visual communication". We welcome the exciting new opportunities and possibilities this affords our clients—as well as the growth and evolution of our design studio. We will continue to provide our clients with the latest design innovations and technologies, building upon our twenty years of excellence, integrity, design philosophy and client satisfaction.

1

Royal Caribbean International
"Voyager of the Seas"

1 - 4. Design of a 9-hole miniature golf course on the ship involving signage, architectural embellishments and decorative elements.

5 - 11. Complete interior and exterior wayfinding, directional and identity, life safety and theme signage systems for ship.

Celebrity Cruises
"Millennium"

12. Suite sign.

2

3

4

5

6

7

8

9

10

11

12

P6
P5 BRIDGE
P4
P3 BRIDGE
TARGET
Michaels
P2
P1
BEST BUY
GROUND LEVEL
IN CASE
OF FIRE
DO NOT USE
ELEVATORS
USE STAIRS

1

DADELAND STATION
BED BATH &
BEYOND

2

DADELAND STATION
BED BATH &
BEYOND
SPORTS
TARGET
BEST BUY
Michaels

3

P
90 SW 1 ST
G2
MUNICIPAL
PARKING

4

P

5

P
CITY OF
CORAL GABLES
MUNICIPAL
PARKING
24 Hours · 7 Days
Permit Parking Only
Lot 30

6

1-3. Retail center - Miami, Fl.
4. City of Miami (FL) parking system.
5,6. City of Coral Gables (FL) parking system.
7,8. Boardwalk identity (with WRT) - Ocean Ciy, Maryland.
9,10. City of Miami (FL) downtown neighborhood identity signage system.
11. City of Miami Beach (FL) neighborhood identity signage.

9

7

10

8

11

Universal's Islands of Adventure, Port of Entry
Universal City Development Partners - Orlando, Fl.

Universal's Port of Entry Design Team:
Mark Woodbury, Vice President/Design
Steve Leff, Graphics Manager
Adrian Gordon, Art Director
Wayne Clark, Graphic Designer
Mary Mingin, Project Coordinator

Graphic Design:
Tom Graboski Associates, Inc.

UNIVERSAL STUDIOS
ISLANDS
OF
ADVENTURE
TRADING COMPANY

Olive
Oil

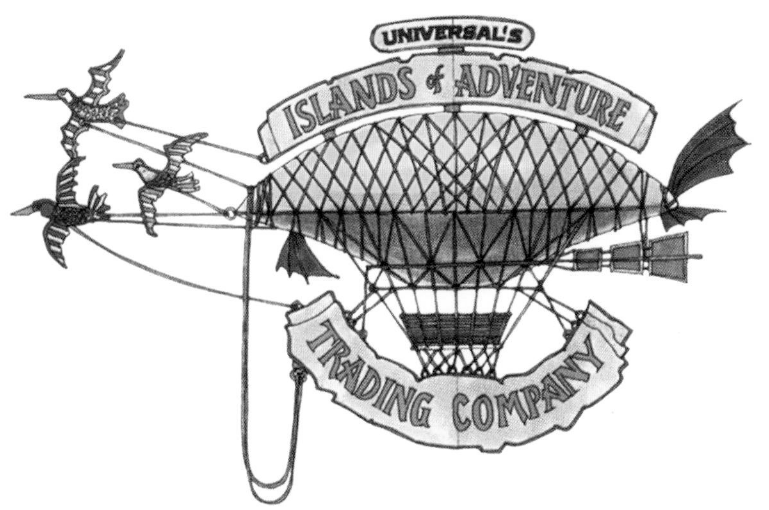
UNIVERSAL'S
ISLANDS of ADVENTURE
TRADING COMPANY

LUCKY
MONKEY

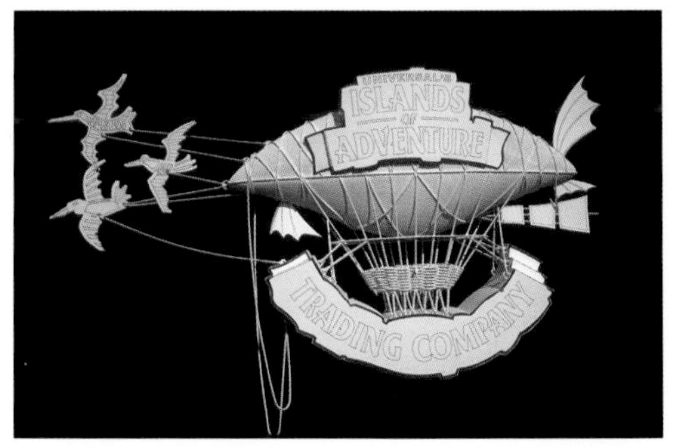
ISLANDS
ADVENTURE
TRADING COMPANY

1. Summit of the Americas.

2. Miami Centennial Celebration.

3. Ballet company.

4. Steamboat cruise line.

5. Internet phone service.

6. Ship color scheme & cruise line logo for first U.S. built cruise ship in over forty years.

1

2

3

4

5

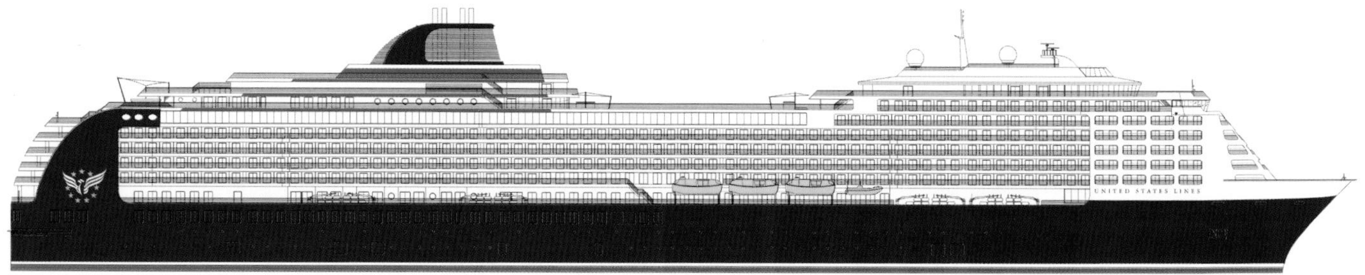

6

5 Prospect Street
Hanover, NH 03755-1906
harp@valley.net
harpandcompany.com
603.643.5144
fax 603.643.2048

HARP AND COMPANY

Good design results from listening, understanding, and interpreting. It is based on ideas, not trends.

Harp and Company's award-winning work has been published in books and design journals internationally. It covers a broad spectrum: from corporate identities, brochures and school publications, to posters and banners for not-for-profit organizations.

Their work can be found in the collections of the Reinhold Brown Gallery in New York; the Museum für Kunst und Gewerbe in Hamburg; the Lahti Poster Museum in Lahti, Finland; Maison du Livre et de l'Affiche in Chaumont, France; and the Library of Congress in Washington, DC. They were one of two studios in the United States invited by the Berliner Ensemble to design a poster commemorating the 100th anniversary of Bertolt Brecht's birth.

Harp and Company's work fits no particular style. However, people seem to recognize it when they see it. It's clean, simple, colorful and energetic.

And it's fun.

1 Tuck School of Business at Dartmouth admissions materials
2 Tuck School Resource Guide
3 Spreads from the Tuck School bulletin
4 University Photography at Cornell identity
5 Identity for woodworker, William Braasch
6 The Howe Library identity

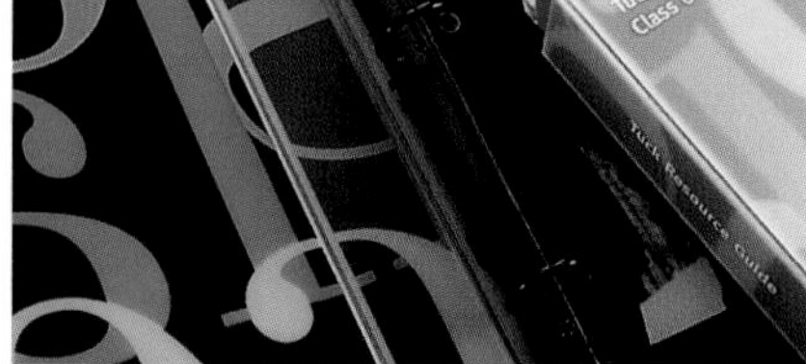

1

2

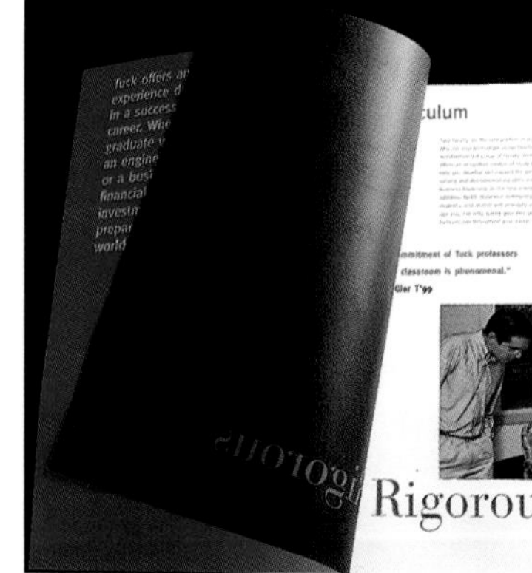

3

University Photography
at Cornell

4

WILLIAM BRAASCH

5

THE HOWE LIBRARY

6

1

2

3

4

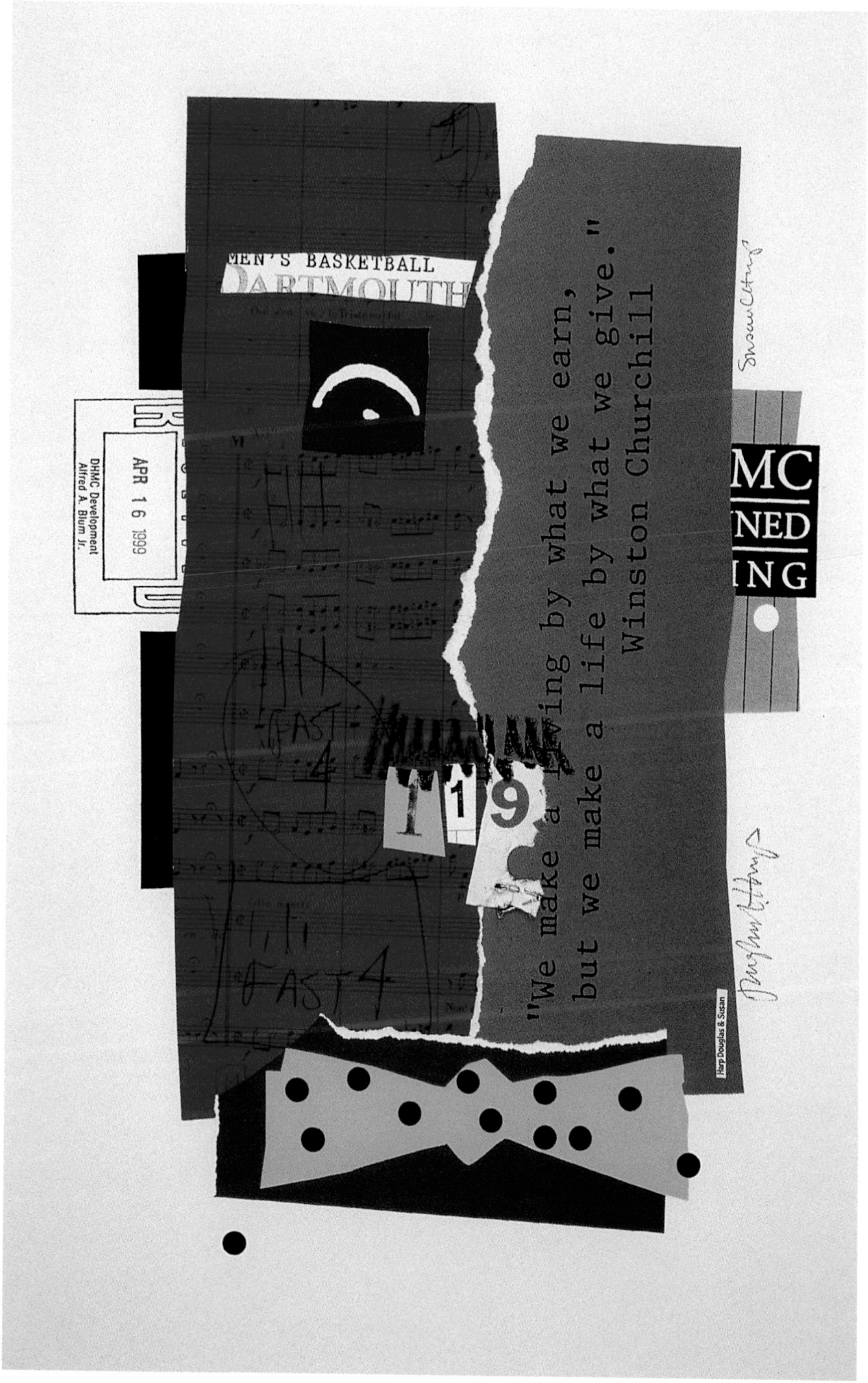

5

1 New Canaan Country School Annual Fund identity

2 Dartmouth Donor Advised Fund identity

3 Identity for Kleiser-Walczak Construction Company, a special digital effects film company

4 Corporate brochure for software company, Tally Systems Corp.

5 Commissioned portrait of Alfred A. Blum, Jr.

1

Cayuga
Medical Center
at Ithaca

2

3

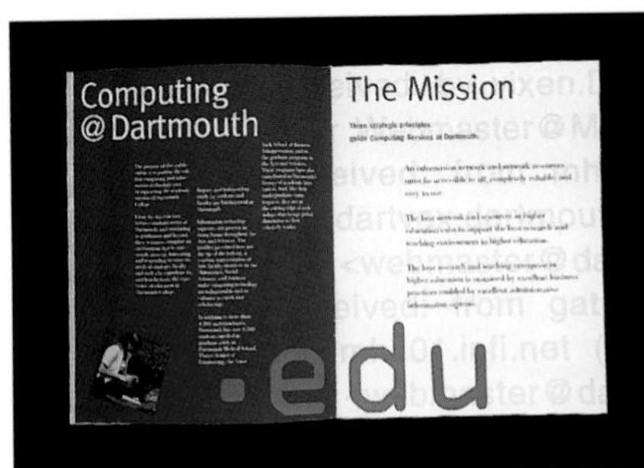

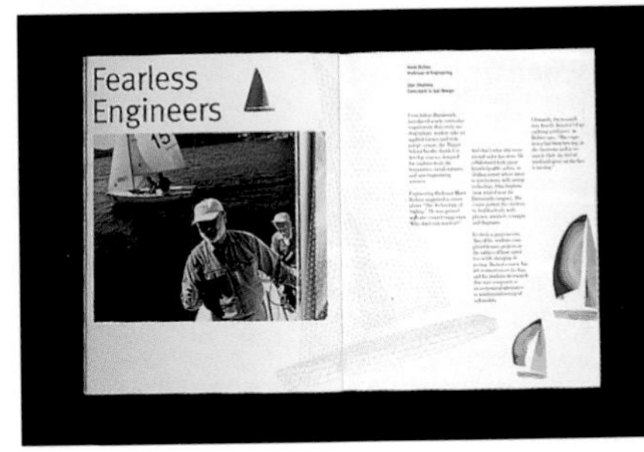

4

1 Annual Report for Cayuga Medical Center at Ithaca

2 Cayuga Medical Center identity

3 Cover and spreads from *Computing at Dartmouth* brochure

4 Identity for New England Ski Team

1

2

1 Catalogue for *Crossroads Alaska*, a Smithsonian National Museum of Natural History exhibition

2 Identity for New Hampshire's participation in the Smithsonian Folklife Festival

3 Banners for the entry gates to the National Zoo in Washington DC

3

1

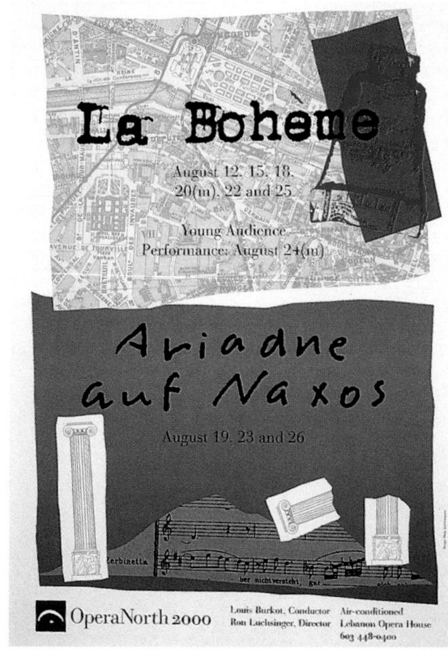

2

3

4

1 Poster for Opera North
2 Poster for Opera North
3 Identity for Opera North
4 Brand identities and packaging for software company, Tally Systems Corp.

1

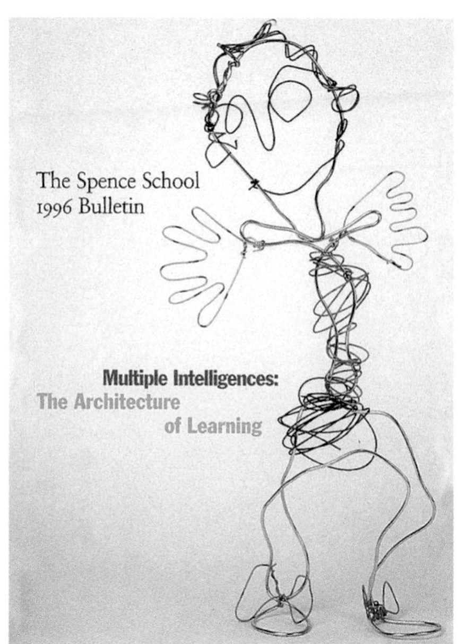

2

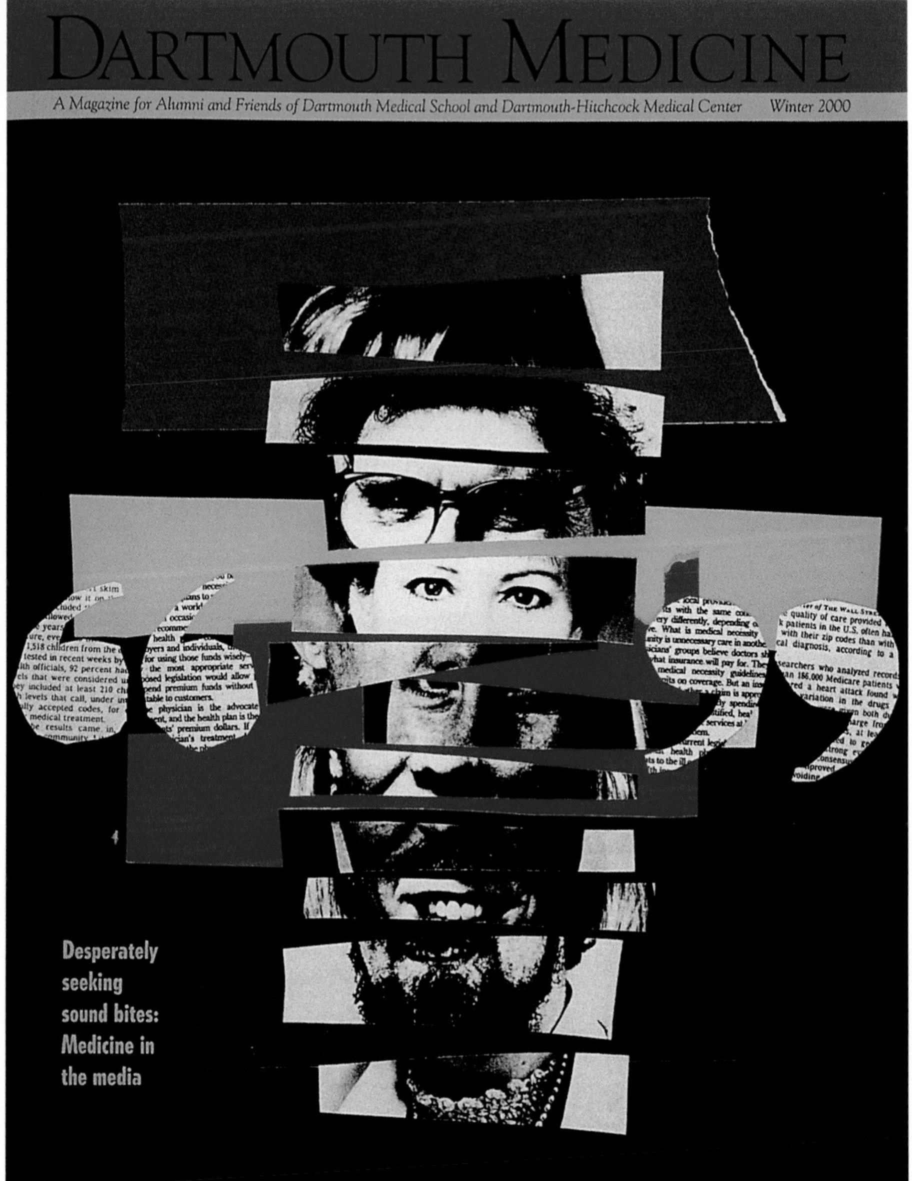

5

3

4

1 Identity for an on-line service provided by the Tuck School at Dartmouth

2 Cover for The Spence School bulletin

3 Identity for fund-raising consultant, Kenneth P. Spritz

4 Identity for The Friends of Hopkins Center and Hood Museum of Art, Dartmouth College

5 Cover illustration for an article on medicine in the media for *Dartmouth Medicine*

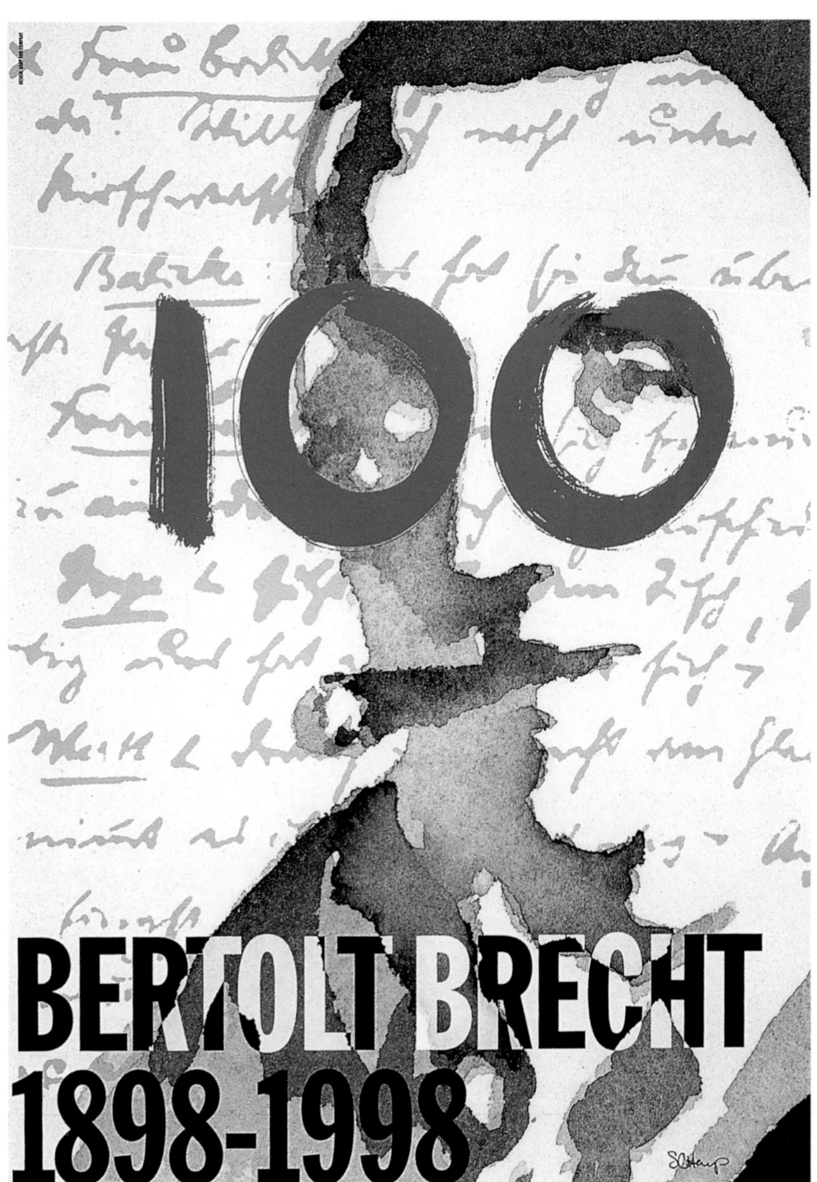

1

2

FERRATELLA'S LAWN GROOMING

3

4

5

1 Poster celebrating the 100th anniversary of the birth of Bertolt Brecht

2 Identity for World Kitchen Inc., formerly Corning Consumer Products Company

3 Identity for Ferratella's Lawn Grooming

4 Valley Montessori School identity

5 Case Statement for Boston Latin School's capital campaign

1008 Western Ave.
Suite 600
Seattle, WA 98104
206.467.5800
www.hadw.com
info@hadw.com

HORNALL ANDERSON DESIGN WORKS

FACE TO FACE. In any interaction, there's a space between. Hornall Anderson Design Works operates in that space. Our goal is not just to turn heads with great design, but to create a meaningful interaction that brings our clients face to face with their audience.

At Hornall Anderson Design Works, we have always had two main goals: first, to give our clients design solutions in tune with their marketing objectives; and second, to do the best work in the business, striving to elevate every job above the ordinary. The plan has succeeded. Our firm has become one of the largest, most respected design firms on the West Coast.

Rather than follow an inflexible process, we employ a fresh but consistent approach to each project. We have a wealth of talent--a deep bench---and we are relentless in the pursuit of the right idea. Through a diverse span of disciplines, Hornall Anderson is able to blend technology know-how with artistic talent.

Thanks to our staff's variety of talents and depth of experience, adaptability and versatility are among our strongest assets. Our clients range from Fortune 500 companies with worldwide markets, to small businesses just getting started. Our work falls within an extensive scope of disciplines including integrated online and print branding; corporate, brand and product identity; print collateral; online media and web site design; packaging design and merchandising displays; and environmental graphics and tradeshow exhibits.

1.

S b P a Λ s C e E

2.

1. Corporate logo and sub-brands within the Space Needle Vertical Village.
2. Space Needle identity program including t-shirts, packaging, and stationery.

1.

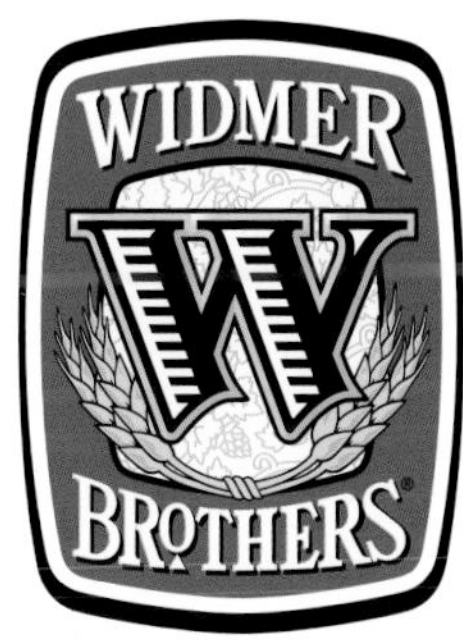

1. Widmer Brothers identity program including packaging and promotional sign applications.
2. Ghirardelli Chocolates packaging.

2.

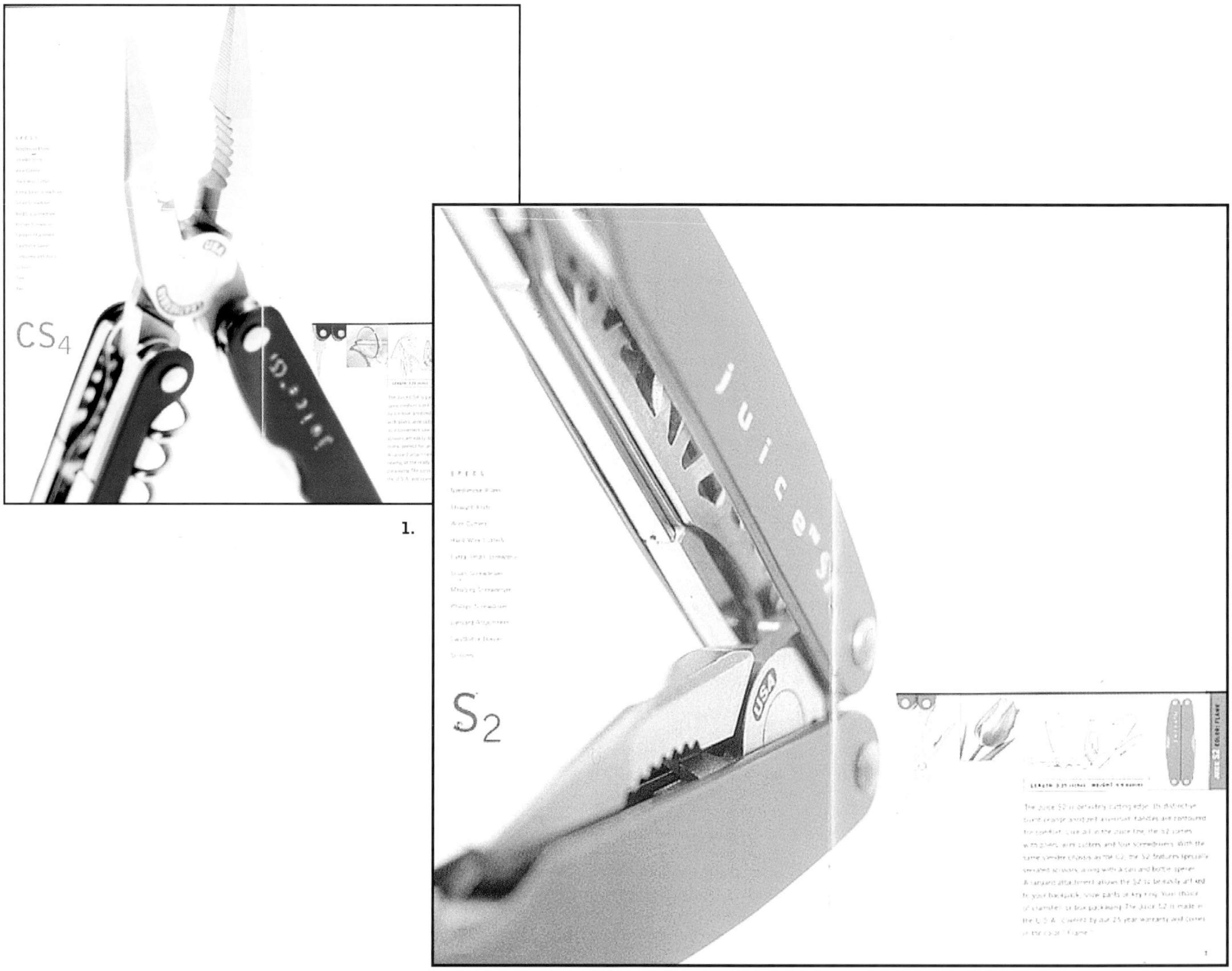

1.

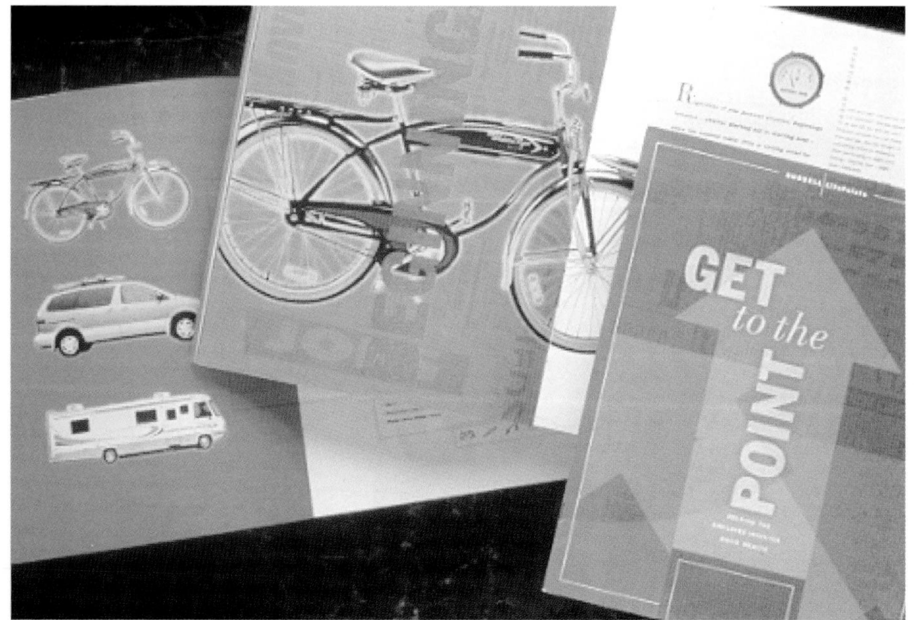

2.

1. Leatherman Tools product brochure spreads.

2. Frank Russell Company LifePoints brochure.

1.

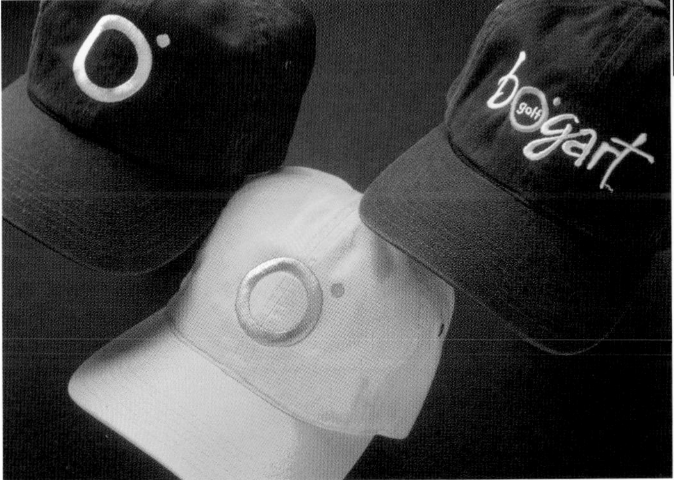

1. Bogart Golf capabilities brochure and promotional merchandise.
2. Impli identity including marketing folder and CD.

impli

2.

1.

2.

3.

1. XOW! identity and promotional flyer.
2. Grapefinds identity and promotional stickers.
3. Guittard Chocolates packaging.

1. InnoVentry identity and brochure spreads.
2. Heavenly Stone identity and stationery.

innoVentry

1.

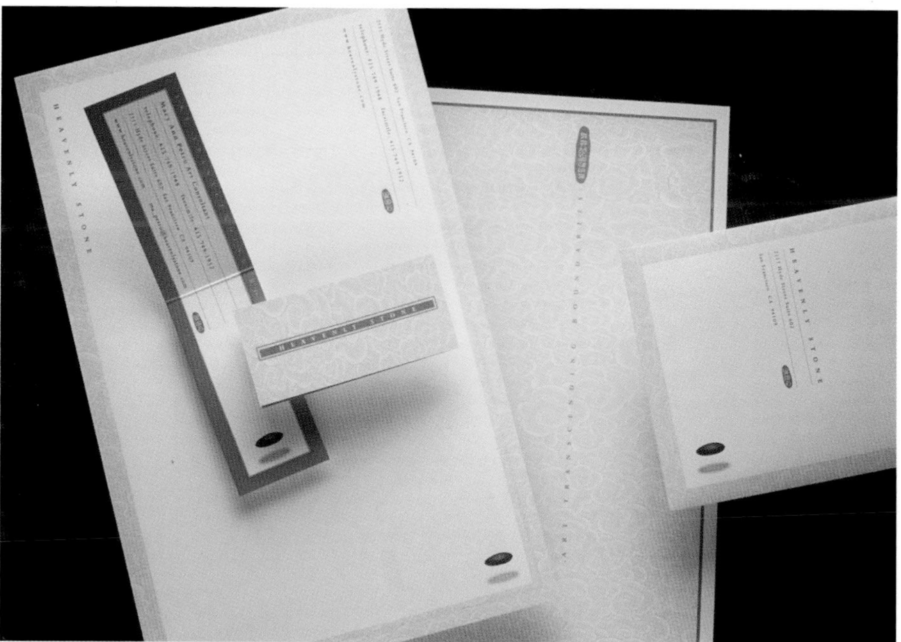

2.

Provider of wireless Internet service, office space, work stations, and technical support to business travelers

Provider service for improving corporate communications by deploying print literature more effectively, using the Web in concert with printing on demand

maveron

Venture capital company

Manufacturer of educational software that runs over the Internet

RECHARGE

Corporate special events planner

Rapid Paying Machine for retail consumer check cashing and self-banking

the image designers group
1913 SW 3rd Avenue
Miami, Florida 33129
T 305.858.1420
F 305.858.1421
studio@imagedesignersgroup.com

Rosario Martínez-Cañas and Maggy Cuesta started The Image Designers Group 10 years ago in Miami.

While working together for a local design firm, they realized that they had much in common: their cuban heritage, their love for design and their involvement with teaching.

The Image Designers Group's approach to design is to work on jobs the studio enjoys and finds challenging, and to create conceptual work that its clients are excited about and pleased with.

Rosario and Maggy's approach to life is... to enjoy it.

Their commitment toward design has led them to become involved with New World School of the Arts where they teach design and typography courses.

The design studio's work has been recognized in various competitions and graphic design publications.

1

2

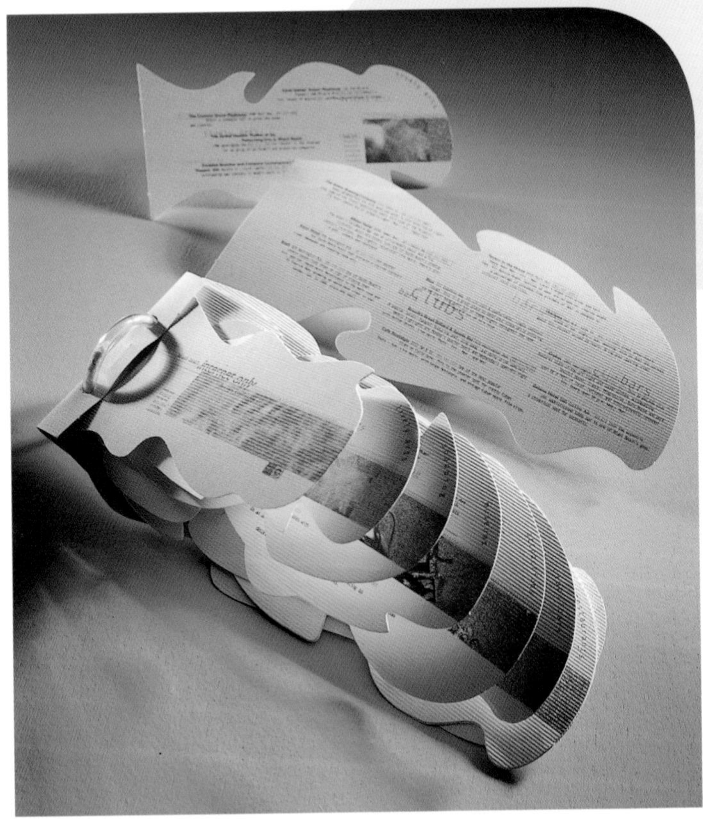

3

Associated Printing Productions inc.

4

5

THE GARAGE

6

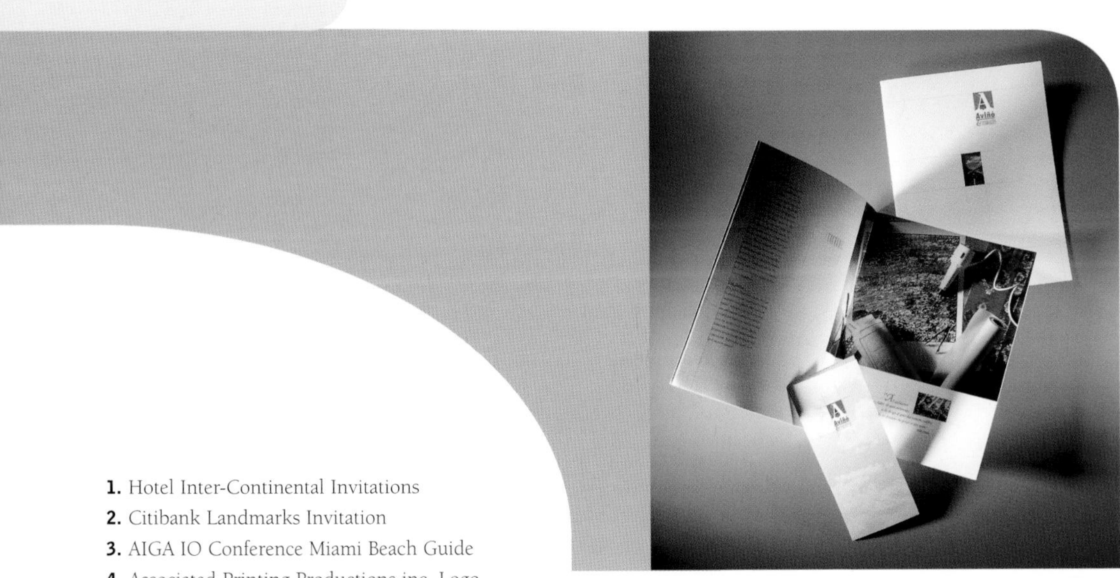

7

1. Hotel Inter-Continental Invitations
2. Citibank Landmarks Invitation
3. AIGA IO Conference Miami Beach Guide
4. Associated Printing Productions inc. Logo
5. AIGA Steff Geissbuhler Event Invitation
6. The Garage Automobiles Logo
7. Aviño & Associates Corporate Materials

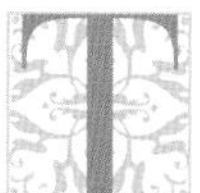

1

2

3

1. Design Transformations Inc. Logo
2. Villa Vizcaya Development Marketing Brochure
3. AIGA Xposed Exhibition Invitation
4. María Martínez-Cañas Stones Exhibition Catalog
5. Julie Fuchs Announcement
6. The School of Entertainment Technologies Logo
7. Perez Trading Company Corporate Brochure

4

6

5

7

1

2

3

4

1. Parc Plaza Development Marketing Materials
2. Parc Plaza Development Logo
3. The Anchorage Development Logo
4. María Martínez-Cañas Shadow Gardens Exhibition Catalog
5. Sphere Foods Stationery Package
6. Sphere Foods Logo
7. Gwen Austin Interior Design Stationery Package
8. Ann Yonover Backdrops Stationery Package

sphere foods
sphere foods
sphere foods

5

6

GWEN AUSTIN
GWEN AUSTIN
GWEN AUSTIN

7

ANN YONOVER
11950 N. Bayshore Studio 4C
North Miami Florida 33181
ANN YONOVER
11950 N. Bayshore Studio 4C
North Miami Florida 33181
ANN YONOVER
11950 N. Bayshore Studio 4C
North Miami Florida 33181
ANN YONOVER
11950 N. Bayshore Studio 4C
North Miami Florida 33181

8

1. BTCB Corporate Brochure

2. Coral Paper Swatchbooks and Awards Certificate

3. Coral Paper Logo

PHOTOGRAPHY:
DOMINIC MARSDEN STUDIOS

Alexander Isley Inc.
9 Brookside Place
Redding, Connecticut 06896
Phone (203) 544-9692
Fax (203) 544-7189

580 Broadway, Suite 709
New York, New York 10012
Phone (212) 941-7945
Fax (212) 226-6332

info@alexanderisley.com

www.alexanderisley.com

ALEXANDER ISLEY INC.

Alexander Isley Inc. was founded in 1988 to do work that communicates with intelligence, sensibility, and a point of view. Over the years, our experienced team of designers has earned the trust of a diverse range of clients, while establishing an international reputation for innovative, influential, and effective work.

Our expertise lies in the design and development of promotional materials, corporate communications, and publications. Alexander Isley Inc. is also well known for award-winning work in the areas of architectural signage, retail merchandising, packaging, and exhibition graphics.

With offices in New York and Connecticut, we provide all services relating to research and design while overseeing all aspects of implementation. We form design and support teams for each of our clients in order to provide attentive collaboration and service over the course of every assignment.

We come from different design, marketing, and technical backgrounds. In addition to the staff design group, Alexander Isley Inc. has in-house account, project-management, and marketing support as well as alliances with research, writing, and production firms.

We attribute the success of our company's work to our history of collaborating with clients who have a strong belief in the value of their own products and services. We begin each assignment by thinking about what a design should do rather than focusing on what it should look like. More than anything else, however, what sets Alexander Isley Inc. apart is the stubbornly unusual way in which we approach our assignments: We assume that our audiences are smart.

Our work is represented in the permanent collections of the Cooper-Hewitt Museum, the Smithsonian Institution's National Design Museum, and the YCS Design Library in Japan. Our projects have been exhibited at the Georges Pompidou Center and the New York Art Directors' Club and have been featured in *Time*, *Communication Arts*, *I.D.*, *Print*, *Entertainment Weekly*, *Metropolis*, *Blueprint*, and *Architectural Record*.

Prior to establishing the firm, Alexander Isley was senior designer at Tibor Kalman's influential M&Co. and art director of the fearless, much-missed, and much-imitated *Spy* magazine.

1

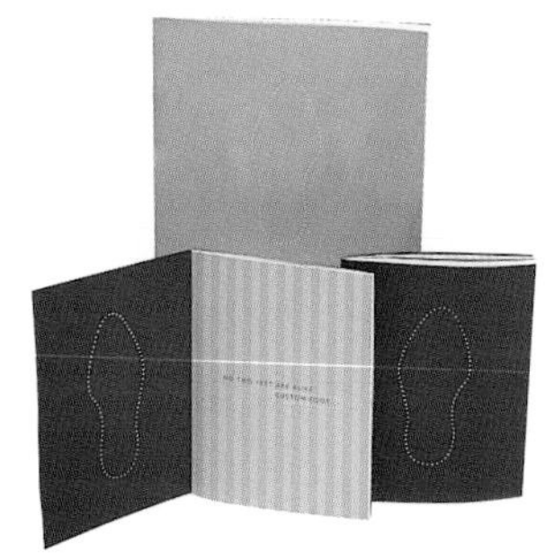

2

1 **The Children's General Store**
New York, NY
Retail merchandising, identity, and packaging program for a toy store chain. The signs were designed to be easily updatable and the tissue paper contains hidden messages such as "share your toys" and "no fair peeking."

2 **Custom Foot**
Westport, CT
Our responsibilities included developing the overall brand personality, including graphic identity, marketing materials, packaging, and advertising for this chain of shoe stores.

3 **Linens N Things**
Clifton, NJ
Alexander Isley Inc. was charged with developing new positioning for the Linens N Things Gift and Bridal Registry program. We created a unique personality for the program through the development of in-store environments, signage, printed materials, and advertising. The program's identity is designed to incorporate various products sold within the stores and can be modified seasonally.

3

4 **Animal Planet**
Discovery Communications
Bethesda, MD
We designed an "attitude guide" for use as the basis for development of a new consumer products line for Animal Planet. As part of our assignment, we developed guidelines establishing the products' brand personality along with editorial and visual guidelines for in-house, retailing, and licensee use.

5 **Toys "R" Us**
Paramus, NJ
Development of a packaging program for Animal Planet products, based on the brand personality we designed. Our responsibilities included naming the products and writing, designing, and producing packages for over 100 different toys. The introduction of the line was a great commercial success, and Toys "R" Us recognized us for our contribution with their Vendor of the Year Award for consumer products.

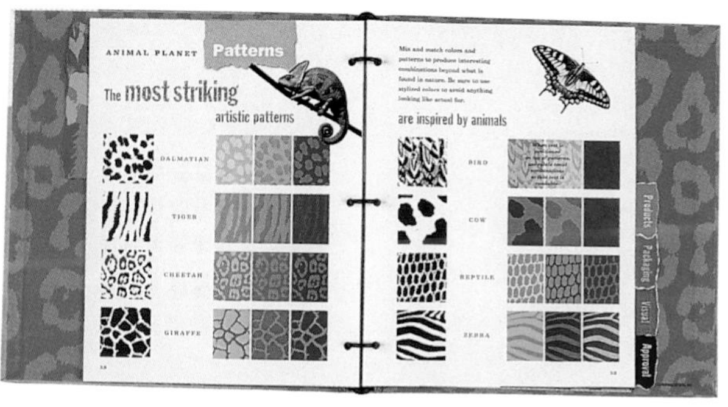

4

5

1

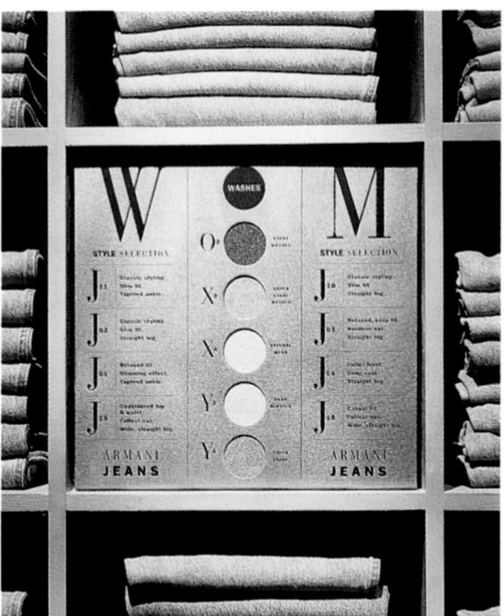

1 **A/X: Armani Exchange**
New York, NY
Development of visual identity and merchandising system for A/X stores. We designed packaging, signage, fixturing systems, and the Armani Jeans logo and oversaw the national rollout of the program. Elements of the design are included in the permanent collection of the National Design Museum, Smithsonian Institution.
Architect: Naomi Leff and Associates
Agency: Weiss, Whitten, Carroll, Stagliano Advertising

2 **John G. Shedd Aquarium Gift Shop**
Chicago, IL
Development of a retail interior program. We created fixture designs, informative signage, and wall murals to fashion an educational undersea retail environment. The program received an AIA honor award.
Architect: Frederic Schwartz Architects

3 **BlueBolt Networks**
Durham, NC
Development of a comprehensive identity and marketing program for a company providing specification products and services to the architectural and interiors communities. Alexander Isley Inc.'s responsibilities included product naming and the development of a brand personality, marketing platform, graphic identity, sales materials, interface design, trade show booths, and advertising.

2

3

4 ***How* Magazine**
Cincinnati, OH
Redesign of *How*, a publication targeted to the graphic design industry. We gave the magazine a top-to-bottom overhaul and developed a style guide for *How's* designers and production artists.

5 **Equity Marketing**
Los Angeles, CA
Identity program for a manufacturer and distributor of licensed toys. We created the logo and sales and marketing materials with an eye toward reflecting the playfulness of the client's products.

6 **The Hearst Corporation**
New York, NY
Design of *@hearst*, a quarterly publication for employees of The Hearst Corporation.

7 **Lend Lease Corporation**
New York, NY
Publication system for Lend Lease, an international financial services company. We developed booklets, informational pieces, and printed and electronic presentation materials with a consistent sensibility reflecting the nature of the client's business.

4

5

6

7

1

1 **Reebok International**
Stoughton, MA
Creation of an annual report for Reebok. We established an editorial approach based on that of a magazine to reflect the exuberance and design-forward sensibility of the company. Alexander Isley Inc. collaborated with writer Tom Parrett to position, write, and design both the 1995 and 1996 annual reports.

2 **Toys "R" Us/Scholastic**
Paramus, NJ
Creation of a promotional video introducing a new product line for Scholastic. Alexander Isley Inc. conceived, wrote, and oversaw the casting and production of the video. Our work with Scholastic also included product naming along with the writing and design of companion activity booklets for over 40 products.
Director: Monica Hayes Anderson, Black Watch Productions

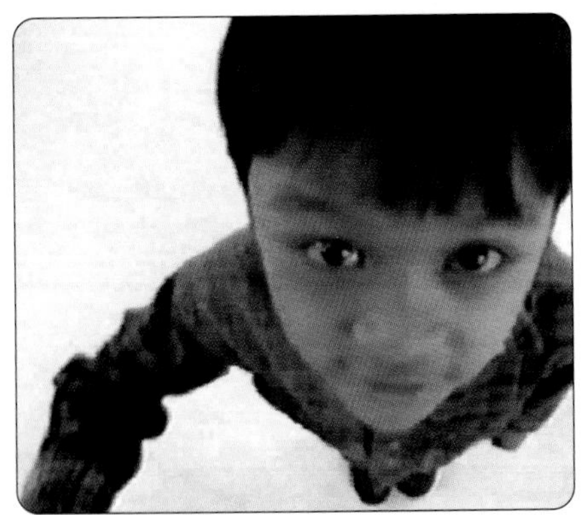

2

3

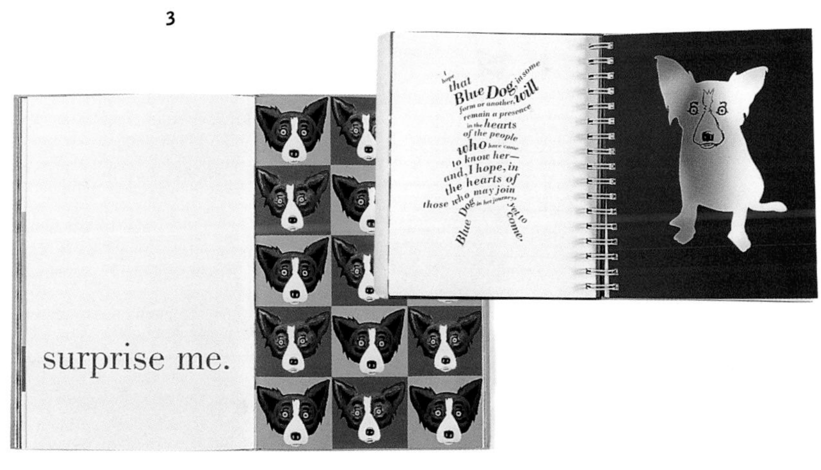

3 **Stewart, Tabori and Chang**
New York, NY
Design of a series of books and products featuring the Blue Dog paintings of artist George Rodrigue. Over the years, the line has expanded to include gift books, calendars, note cards, journals, and sketch books. The products are unified by their spirit of fun, warmth, and surprise. Most incorporate engaging interactive pieces such as postcards, holograms, masks, and foldouts, making them as much objects as they are books.

4 **Modem Media**
Norwalk, CT
Design of the 1999 annual report for Modem Media, an e-business advertising and consulting firm. We focused on the theme of growth with a series of foldout illustrations demonstrating employee, financial, client, and worldwide growth. The simple nature of this solution is in contrast to the approach of most annual reports. Our experience in developing books and magazines has given us the knowledge and ability to create simple, direct, and compelling communication materials, designed with intelligent readers in mind.

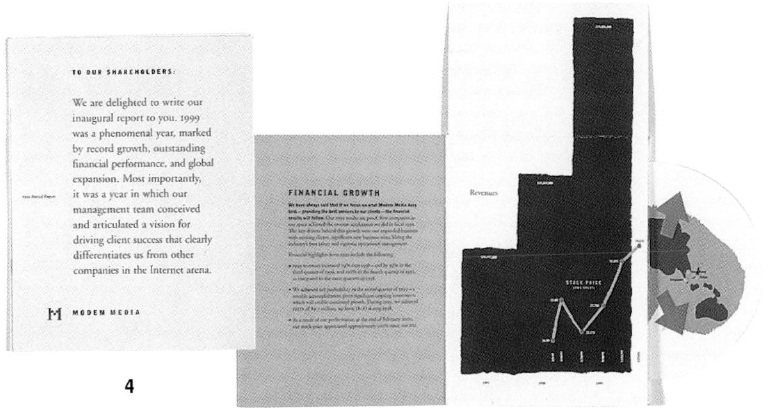

4

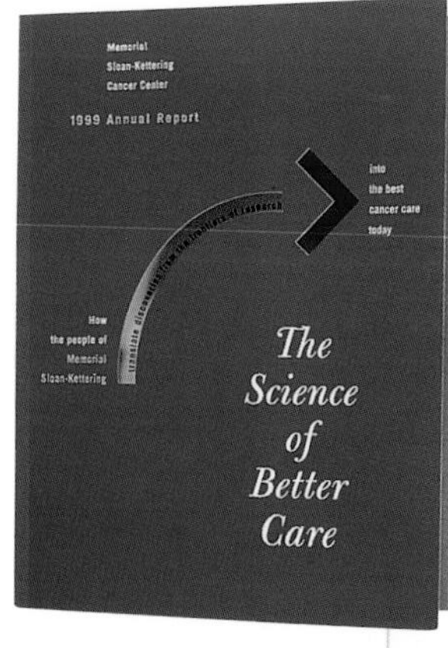

1

1 **Memorial Sloan-Kettering Cancer Center**
New York, NY
Alexander Isley Inc. designed Memorial Sloan-Kettering's award-winning 1999 annual report to address multiple objectives. It had to provide general information, report on fundraising, list staff members, and illustrate case studies of doctors doing important research. The format was based on the look and approach of a traditional book, and the die-cut cover conveyed the sense of discovery and surprise that is inherent to the Cancer Center's work.

2 **New Times, Inc.**
Phoenix, AZ
Redesign of all newspapers within the New Times chain. Alexander Isley Inc. established overall design formats to create unique looks for twelve publications located throughout the country. This design framework provides enough latitude to allow individual editors and designers to imbue each publication with its own personality.

2

Selected Clients

American Lung Association
American Museum of the Moving Image
Animal Planet
AOL Time Warner
A/X: Armani Exchange
Brooklyn Academy of Music
Canon USA
City of New York
Cooper-Hewitt National Design Museum
CSFBdirect
Discovery Communications
Forbes FYI
Hearst Corporation
iVillage
John G. Shedd Aquarium
Lend Lease Corporation
Liberty Science Center
Linens N Things
Memorial Sloan-Kettering Cancer Center
Modem Media
MTV Networks
National Endowment for the Arts
New Times, Inc.
Nickelodeon
Polaroid
Polo/Ralph Lauren
Reebok International Ltd.
Revlon
Rock and Roll Hall of Fame and Museum
Scholastic
ScreamingMedia
Sony Wonder
Sports Illustrated
Texaco
The Limited
Time
Timex Corporation
Toys "R" Us
Van Kampen Funds
WHSmith Ltd.

M.A. Winter Building
1436 U Street NW
Suite 404
Washington DC 20009
www.kinetikcom.com
www.kitchenk.org

KINETIK was founded in 1988 by three young designers sharing two drawing tables in one very small room. Since then, the studio has evolved into a 12-person firm in a light-filled loft in Washington, D.C.'s hip and historic U Street corridor. What has not changed, however, is KINETIK's passion for design and our confidence in its ability to shape perceptions and be a powerful, positive influence on society. We believe that design is both a journey and a destination: a creative, collaborative process that leads to excellence. Our spirit of teamwork comes through in everything we do. From the moment we pick up pencils and sketch to the day a project delivers, we're committed to helping our clients create and convey their messages in fresh and original ways.

tropical express
PBS
enhanced
DIGITAL TELEVISION
THE FUTURE OF ENHANCED DIGITAL TELEVISION
IMAGINE
PBS ENHANCED DIGITAL TV DEMONSTRATION CD

1

2

3

1. Tropical Express Identity System
2. Eclipse Coffee Promotion
3. PBS Digital Television Press Kit
4. ELINK Communications Brochure Cover
5. ELINK Communications Brochure Interior
6. ELINK Communications Logo
7. ELINK Communications Identity System
8. ELINK Communications Marketing Kit

4

5

6

7

8

1. JNG Communications Identity System
2. PEAKE Printers Promotional Calendar
3. AIGA DC Design Camp Marketing Materials
4. AIGA DC Design Camp Souvenirs
5. Broad Run Technology Park Marketing Kit
6. Broad Run Technology Park Logo
7. Nature of Reston Book Package
8. Prospective Inc Web Site

5

BROAD RUN
TECHNOLOGY PARK

6

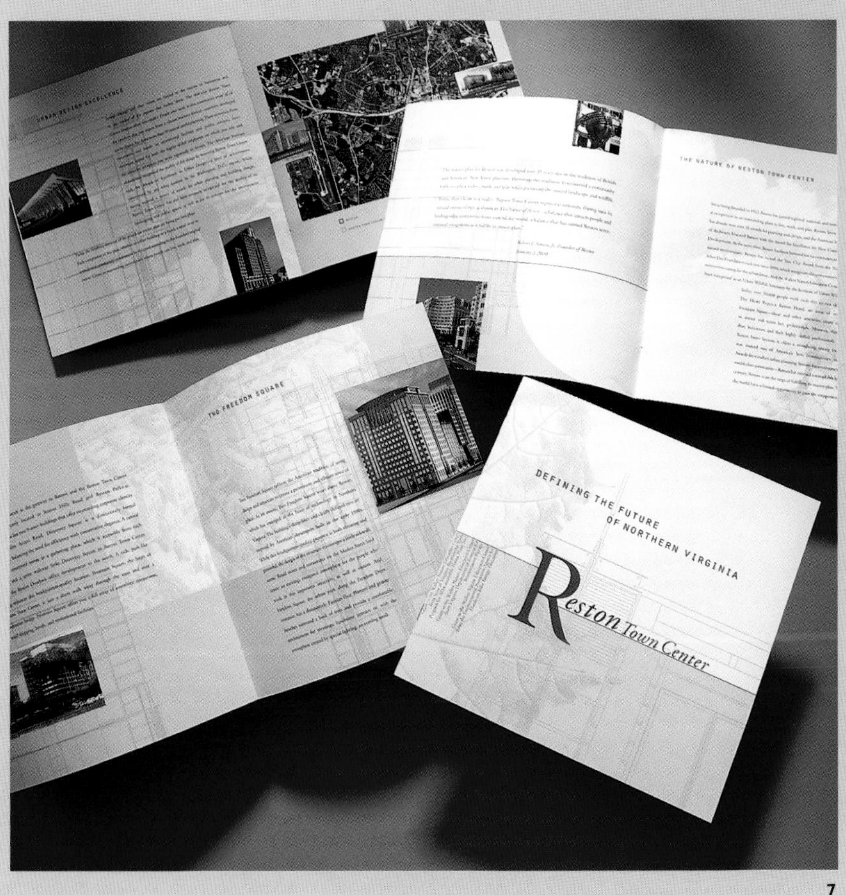
DEFINING THE FUTURE
OF NORTHERN VIRGINIA
Reston Town Center
THE NATURE OF RESTON TOWN CENTER
TWO FREEDOM SQUARE
URBAN DESIGN EXCELLENCE

7

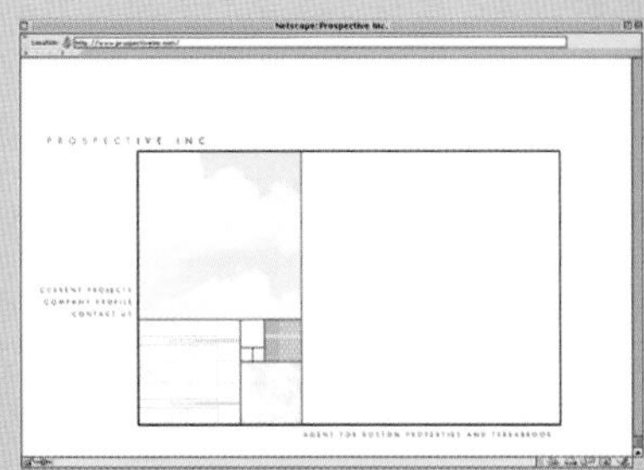
PROSPECTIVE INC

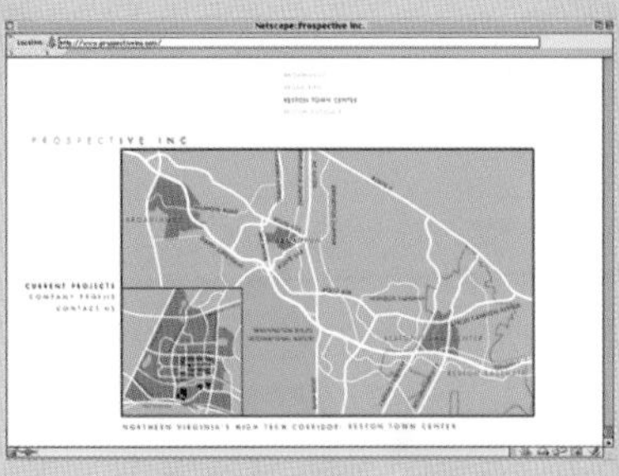
PROSPECTIVE INC

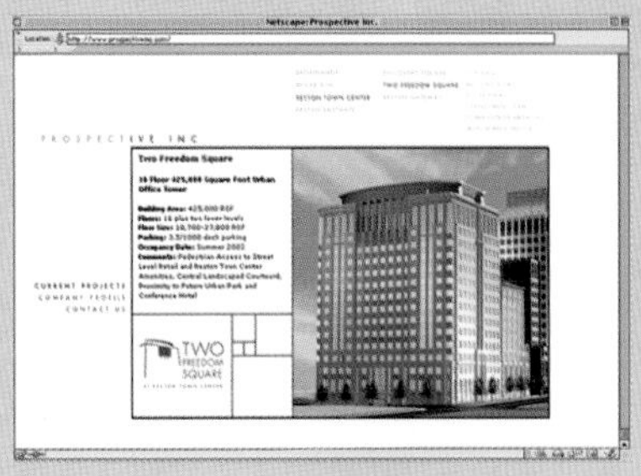
PROSPECTIVE INC
Two Freedom Square
TWO
FREEDOM
SQUARE

8

CRITICAL
ECOSYSTEM
PARTNERSHIP
FUND
INVESTORS
CEPF PHOTO GALLERY
FOCUSED ENERGY
POWERFUL RESULTS
PROGRESS
CONSERVATION INTERNATIONAL
THE EMERALD
CIRCLE

1

2

3

1. Critical Ecosystems Partnership Fund Web Site
2. Conservation International 1999 Annual Report
3. Emerald Circle Logo
4. Shaqab College of Design Arts Viewbook
5. Making Connections Card Set
6. American Council of Life Insurers 1999 Annual Report

4

5

6

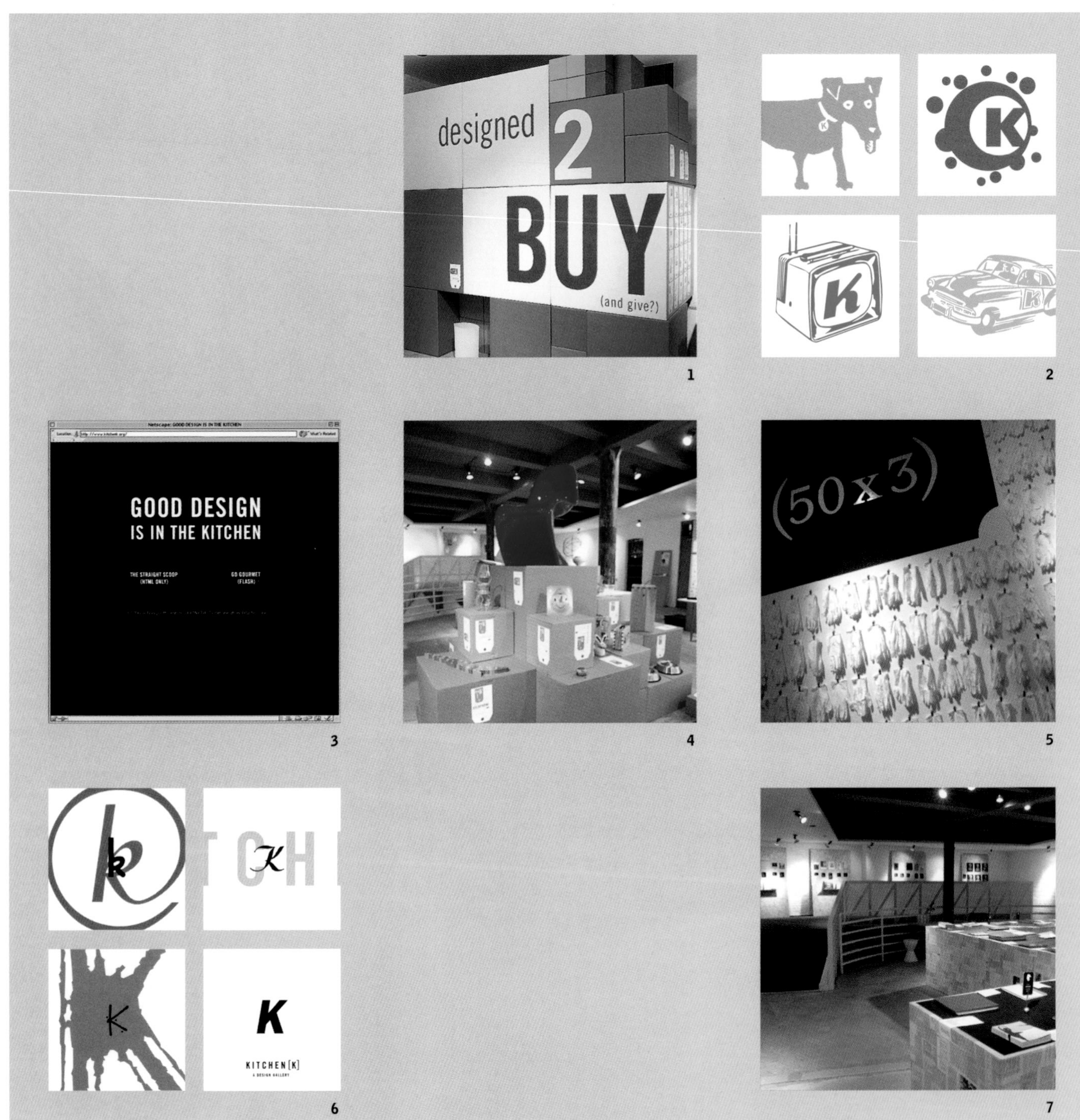

1. *Designed 2 Buy* Exhibition Space
2. Details of KITCHEN [K] Identity System
3. KITCHEN [K] Web Site
4. *Designed 2 Buy* Exhibition Space
5. *(50 x 3)* Exhibition Space
6. Flash Introduction / KITCHEN [K] Web Site
7. *(50 x 3)* Exhibition Space

644 Eden Park Drive
Cincinnati, OH 45202
513.961.6225

666 Dundee Road
Northbrook, IL 60062
847.291.0500

747 Third Ave. 35th Floor
New York, NY 10017
212.486.3090

1130 Main Street
Napa, CA 94559
707.265.1891

www.laga.com

LIPSON ALPORT GLASS & ASSOCIATES

Shaping visions. Listening closely to consumers. Moving potential into performance. Driving client profitability. These are the touchstones of our approach to developing successful strategic solutions for marketers and their brands.

Lipson Alport Glass & Associates is one of the world's leading brand marketing and design consultancies, providing our clients with a range of cross-disciplinary marketing expertise that includes brand strategy and identity, market research, packaging, e-branding, and integrated communications.

Founded in Cincinnati in 1947 by Sam W. Lipson, the firm has grown steadily over the years to now include offices in Chicago, New York, and Napa, with a total professional staff of over 200 individuals.

In 1994, the company created International Design Partnership®, a global marketing and design resource operating in nine countries, and servicing a diverse client base.

Whether for established one hundred year old brands or newly created ones, poised for market introduction, we offer our clients fresh, innovative, market-driven thinking in the context of a true partnership.

LAGA...moving brands deep into the hearts and minds of consumers.

1. Coca-Cola Signage System
2. Coca-Cola Signage System
3. Coca-Cola Signage System
4. Coca-Cola Fleet Graphics
5. Coca-Cola Packaging

4

1

2

3

5

1

2

1. Poland Spring Packaging
2. Loriva Gourmet Oil Packaging
3. Campbell Soup Packaging
4. Colombo Yogurt Packaging
5. Life Savers Packaging
6. Benjamin Moore Packaging

3

4

5

6

1. Smucker's Magic Shell Packaging
2. Athenos Mediterranean Spreads Packaging
3. California Pizza Kitchen Packaging
4. Carando Bread Packaging
5. Hanes Premium Packaging

1

2

3

4

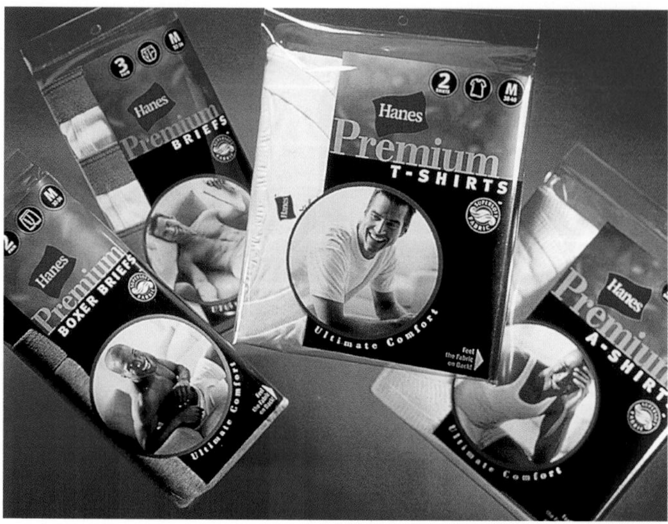

5

1. Sunrise Cereal Packaging
2. Perrier Packaging
3. McCormick Spice Blends Packaging
4. Green Giant Packaging
5. Boston Market Frozen Entrees Packaging
6. Heinz Nature's Goodness Baby Food Packaging

1

2

3

4

5

6

1

2

3

4

1. Spring Dot Brand Identity
2. Spring Dot Fleet Graphics
3. Spring Dot Signage
4. Spring Dot Collateral
5. Spring Dot Web Site

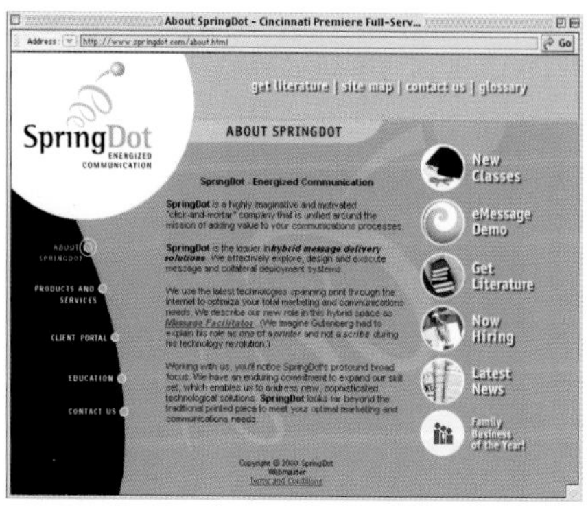

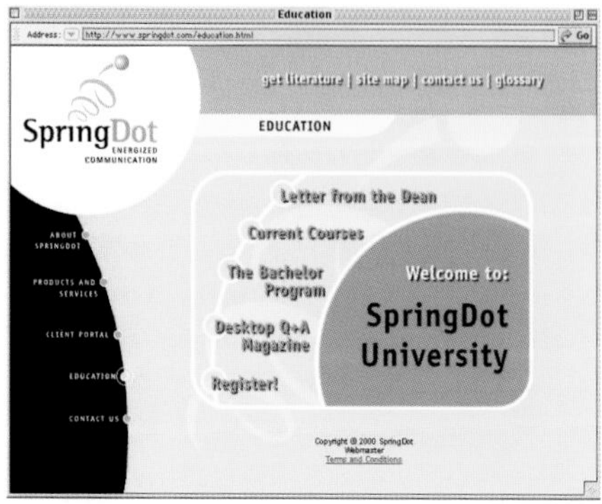

5

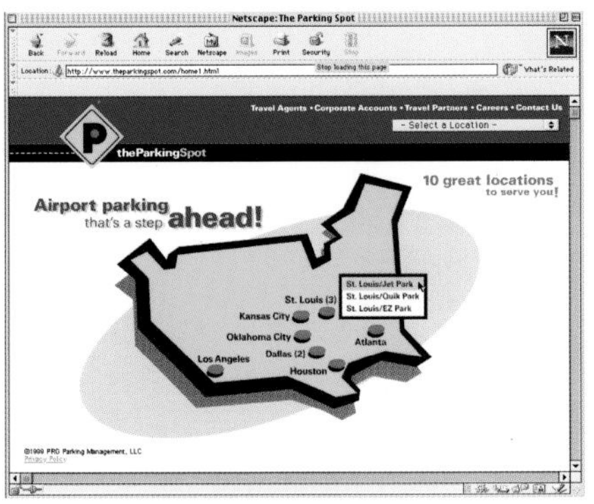

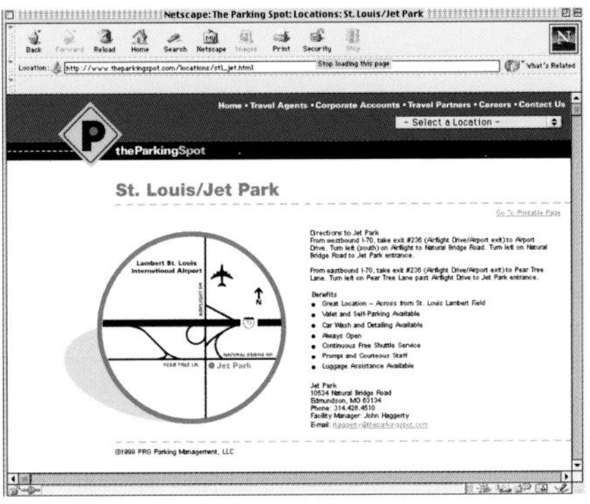

1

2

1. The Parking Spot Web Site
2. The Parking Spot Brand Identity
3. The Parking Spot Fleet Graphics
4. The Parking Spot Collateral
5. The Parking Spot Signage

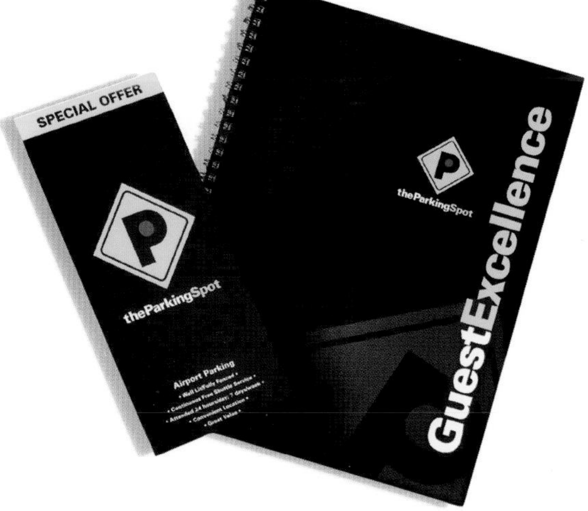

3

4

5

1

2

3

4 

5 

6 

7 

8 

1. Ha-Lo Industries Annual Report
2. Keebler Company Annual Report
3. USG Sheetrock Cafe Exhibit
4. Pritzker Realty Group Brand Identity
5. Ameritech Clearpath Brand Identity
6. Allegiance Brand Identity
7. Sawtooth Brand Identity
8. Store Your Things Brand Identity

LORENC+YOO DESIGN
109 Vickery Street
Roswell, GA 30075
770.645.2828
jan@lorencyoodesign.com
www.lorencyoodesign.com

LORENC+YOO DESIGN

Lorenc+Yoo Design has endeavored to become a multiple-disciplinary design studio since our inception in 1978. Currently LYD is comprised of a dozen designers with backgrounds in industrial design, graphic design, architecture, interior design, furniture design, and journalism. The diversified cultural backgrounds of the staff, including Polish, Korean, Thai, and Columbian, have enabled us to respond to the various creative challenges we are faced with today. LYD works with a variety of clients, ranging from small regional firms to large international corporations, from individual entrepreneurs to Fortune 500 companies. Strategic alliances throughout the U.S. and Korea allow the firm to stay small, but also to be involved in a variety of design areas simultaneously. Projects range from signage to furniture to sculpture to exhibits and other environmental communication design challenges.

Context for design is an important consideration in the LYD design process. Architecture, landscape, interior design, materials and finishes, and lighting must all be taken into account. The goal of each project is to create an integrated, seamless design approval that directly reflects the overall project intent. This approach results in projects that are far stronger in design significance and longevity. LYD gains knowledge of an overall project, the goal of the team, and conceives a project that responds to historical or existing context.

1

2

3

4

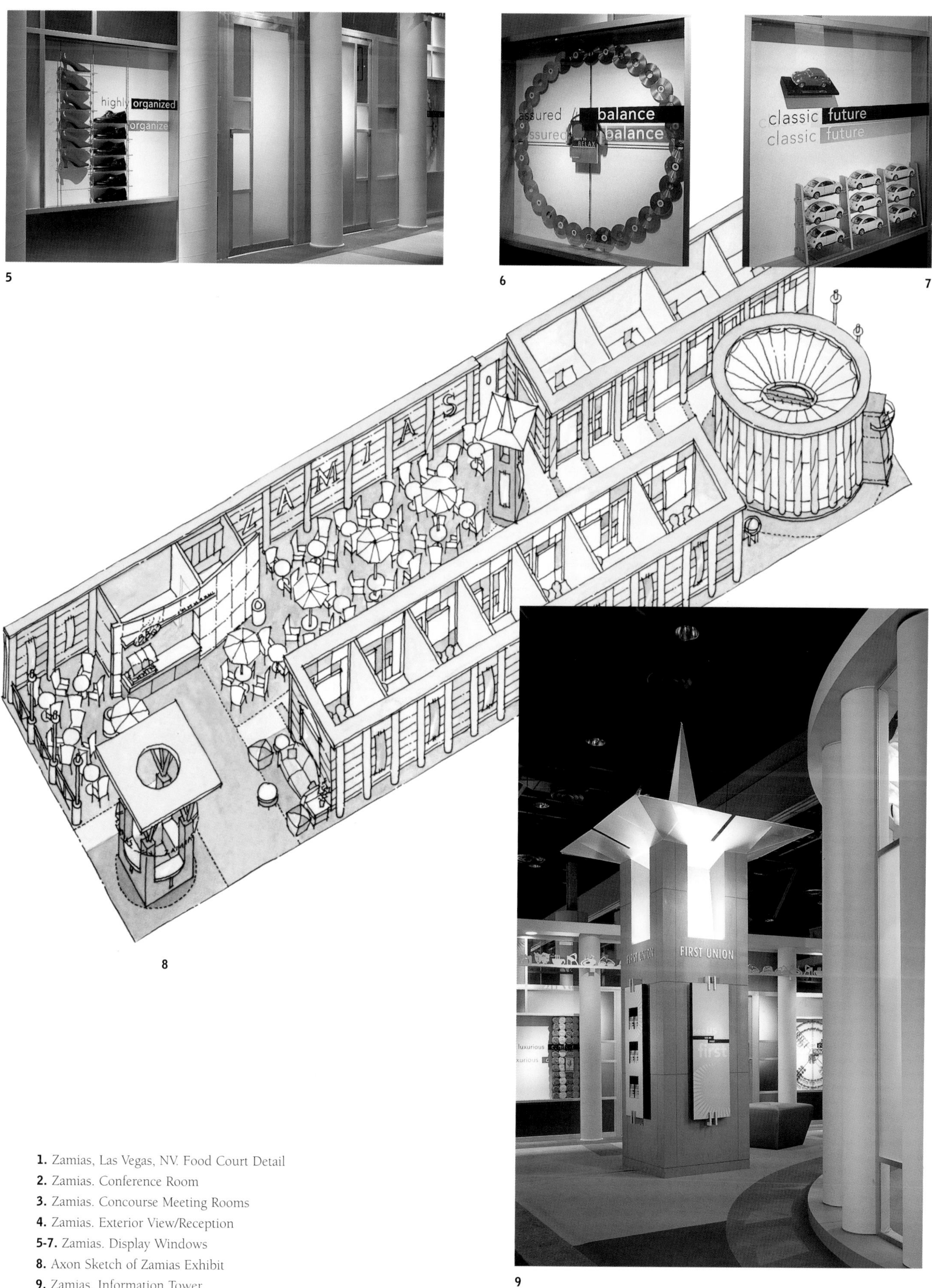

5

6

7

8

9

1. Zamias, Las Vegas, NV. Food Court Detail
2. Zamias. Conference Room
3. Zamias. Concourse Meeting Rooms
4. Zamias. Exterior View/Reception
5-7. Zamias. Display Windows
8. Axon Sketch of Zamias Exhibit
9. Zamias. Information Tower

1

TEAM
Pennsylvania
Creative
Approach
Real Estate
Investm
Discipline
Trust
Instinct
Stability
2

3

4

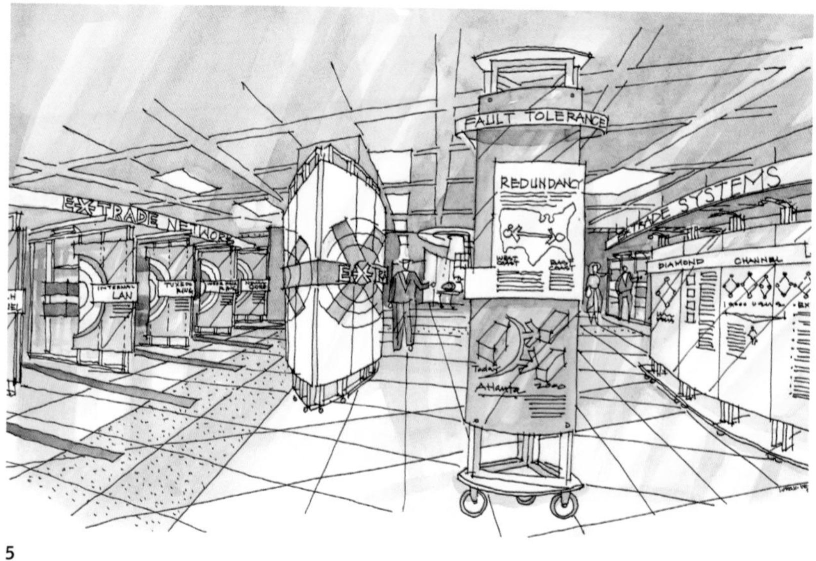

5

6

1. Preit, Las Vegas, NV. Exhibit Reception
2. Preit. Conference Room Sketch
3. Continuum, Las Vegas, NV. Conference Room.
4. Perimiter Summit, Atlanta GA- sculpture
5. E-Trade. Control Room
6. Continuum. Conference Room and Gallery.
7. Phillips Edison, Las Vegas, NV. Exhibit Reception

7

1

2

3

5

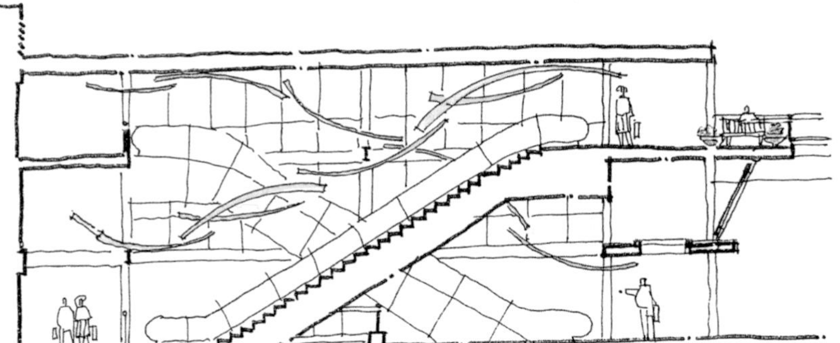

4

1. Oakbrook Center, Oakbrook, IL. Vertical Directional
2. Oakbrook. Canopy, Sign, & Escalator Enclosure Graphics
3. Oakbrook. Color Accent Panels
4. Oakbrook. Escalator Accent Section
5. Oakbrook. Logo Panel, Directory, Canopy & Lighting
6. Westshore Plaza, Tampa, FL. Food Court Light Feature Sign & Tracery Graphic Panels
7. Westshore. Food Court Entry Sequence
8. Westshore. Secondary Entrance Feature

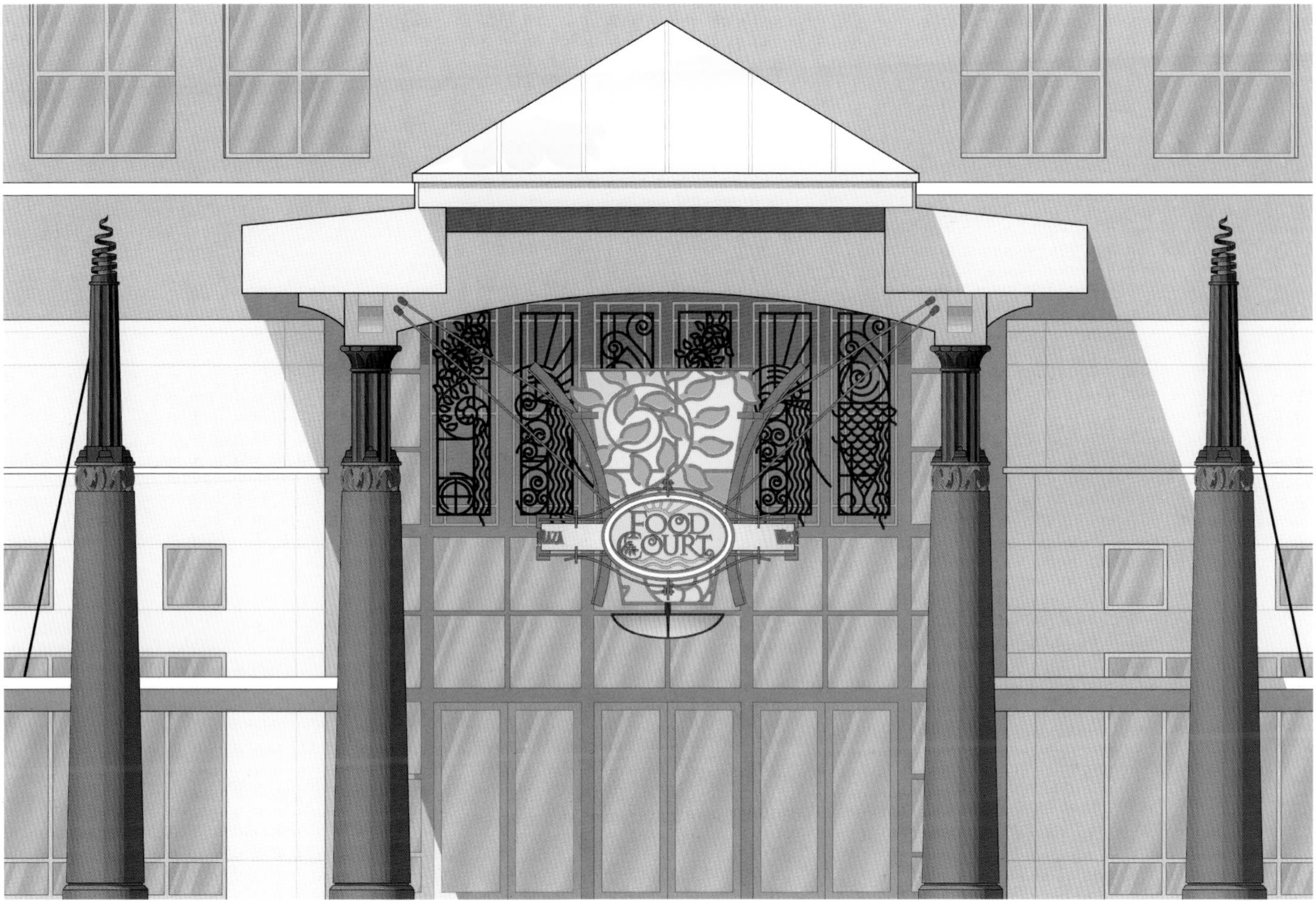

6

8

7

1

2

3

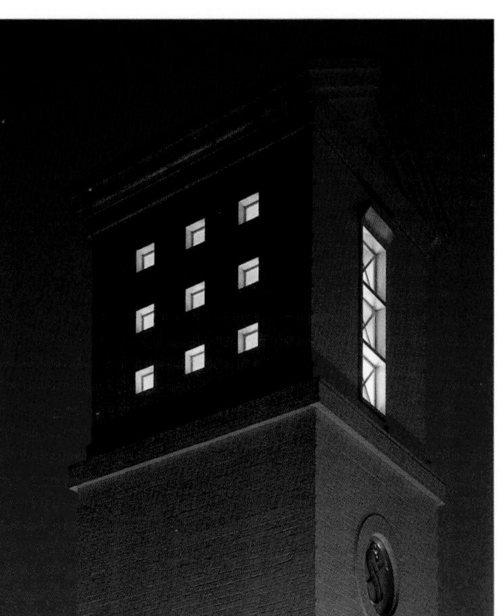

4

5

1. World Golf Village, St. Augustine, FL. Landmark Sign

2. WGV, King & Bear. Tower Detail

3. WGV, King & Bear. Entry Tower and Fence

4. Schilling Farms, Collierville, TN. Icon Tower

5. WGV, King & Bear. Rotary Windmill Sketch

CREATE A DISTINCT VOICE.

Miriello Grafico
419 West G Street
San Diego, California 92101
v. 619.234.1124
f. 619.234.1960
pronto@miriellografico.com
www.miriellografico.com

MIRIELLO GRAFICO

IDENTITY, PRINT AND WEB COMMUNICATIONS FOR EMERGING COMPANIES.

"Thanks for calling Miriello Grafico. Identity, print, and web communications for emerging companies. How can we help you?"

"We've been bkjh need help mnrps lqzfkjsj structure dk kjhsdk impact hhpm fast."

..."I'm sorry, can you speak up? I'm having trouble hearing you."

"We're getting that response a lot and that's really why I'm calling. I saw you in several design books and directories and your work looks well thought out and exciting. Do you think you can help my company be heard?"

"Sure, we create a unique and distinct voice for every one of our clients."

"And how do you do that?"

"Well, we start by focusing on what you're trying to achieve. Are you launching a new product? Searching for a new position in your marketplace? Trying to change the way your audience thinks about your company? Announcing your plans for an exciting new vision? Knowing where you want to go — is the first step in knowing how to get there. Then we get to know your company... what it does...what it wants to stand for... what sets it apart... and we use that information as the foundation of our messaging. Whether it's printed materials, an identity standards program, packaging, or digital design, our approach is to make your communication dollars work toward a unified message and a distinct voice for your company. An honest voice, that stands apart from the noise your competition is making."

"What size companies do you work with?"

"We work regionally, nationally, and internationally with companies of various sizes in many different industries, including technology, entertainment, and consumer products. Some are evolving businesses and others are established corporations. But there's one thing they all have in common — they're smart. They understand the positive effect that distinctive, unified, design messaging can have on their bottom lines. They also appreciate the benefits that can come from an on-going relationship. Our criteria for selecting clients really comes down to a shared passion for quality, more than size, and whether we have the potential to increase their chances for success."

"Do I need to come to San Diego?"

"Only if you're looking for an excuse to get some sun in February or hit the links in December. Our process is streamlined, so we can usually discuss and define strategies using e-mail or conference calls, and work through the conceptual, design and production stages through a variety of technical wonders. But getting to meet in person — maybe over Rubio's Fish Tacos at the waterfront — is always better than e-mail."

"I'm ready to speak up!"

"Hey, we hear you loud and clear — now let's make sure the rest of the world does too."

FLASH EXHIBIT GRAPHICS

1 **QUALCOMM CDMA TECHNOLOGIES**

Help us communicate the power and potential of our new chip technology

NEW PRODUCT CONCEPTS

3 **QUALCOMM**

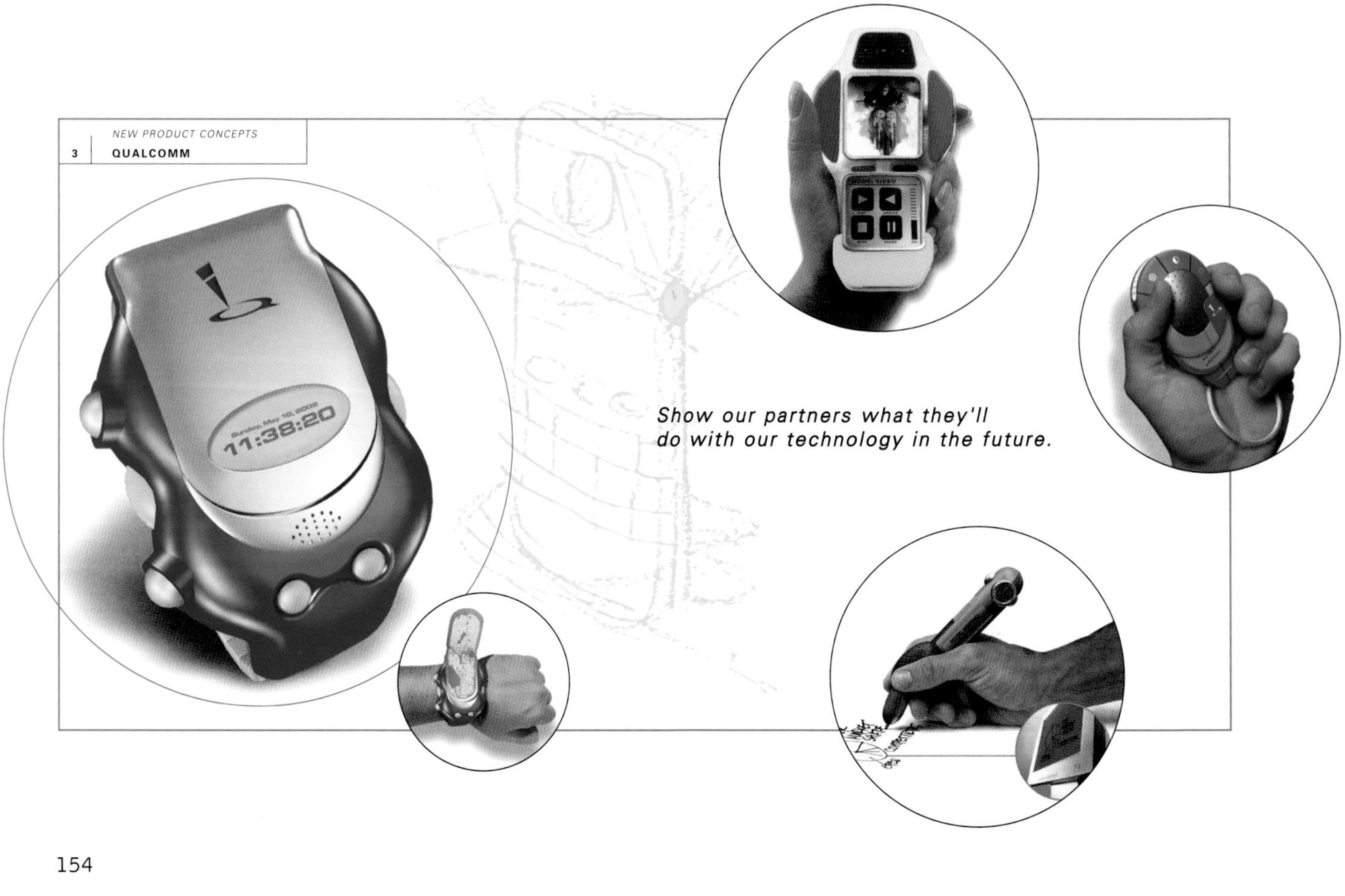

Show our partners what they'll do with our technology in the future.

NEW PRODUCT CD LAUNCH

2 **CARDIFF LIQUID FORMS**

start>>>>>>

DESIGN PUB

eFORMS

CARDIFF

<<<<<<end

PRODUCT PACKAGING

4 **CARDIFF LIQUID FORMS**

Help us launch a brand new concept—digital forms management.

We've got one chance to tell our compelling story in a crowded market sector.

1	WOMAN'S SPA CARE PRODUCTS LAUNCH **CREATIVE SPA**

In a world of change, how can I stay ahead? In today's marketplace, it's not enough to establish your brand. You have to differentiate it. Presenting your product o

Communication design can provide you with a distinct voice that will help position your company for success. At Miriello Grafico, our job is to help you develop that voice i

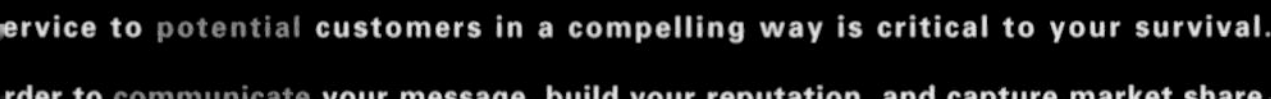

ervice to potential customers in a compelling way is critical to your survival.
rder to communicate your message, build your reputation, and capture market share.

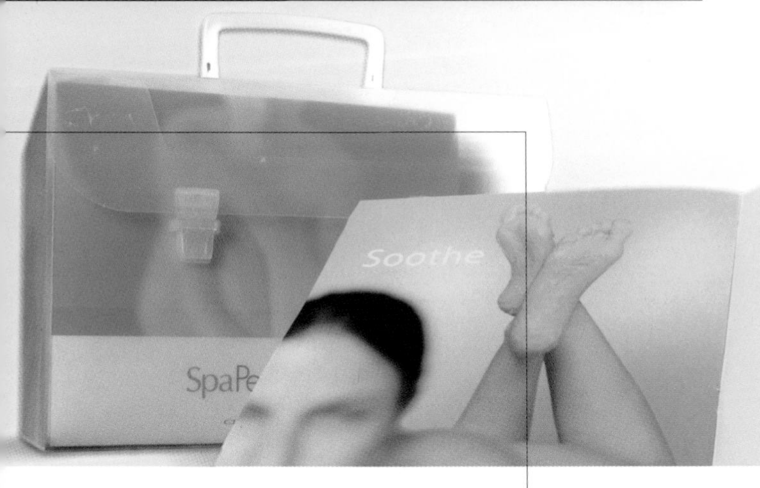

RETAIL STORE COLLATERAL

2 **LEGO GLOBAL ATTRACTIONS**

MATHEMATICS SERIES BOOK PACKAGING

3 **HARCOURT SCHOOL**

IDENTITY STUDIES

1 *HOLISTIC MEDICINE* **DR. VISSER**	2 *REAL ESTATE* **SHADY CANYON/THE IRVINE COMPANY**	3 *HEALTHCARE* **AGE CONCERNS**

DR. RICHARD VISSER

AGE CONCERNS

Dr. Richard Visser

Age Concerns
Begin Living Life

Age Concerns

IDENTITY FINALS

identity	signage	collateral

SHADY CANYON

age CONCERNS Assisted Living At Home

HOMECARE for the ELDERLY

4	*SOFTWARE TRAINING SYSTEMS* **TOTAL TRAINING**	5	*DESTINATION BRANDING* **SAN DIEGO NORTH**	6	*E-BUSINESS SOLUTIONS* **VELOCIGEN**

stationery system

standards guide

web

LEFT BRAIN/RIGHT BRAIN JOURNAL BOOK
1 **PROMOTIONAL BOOK**

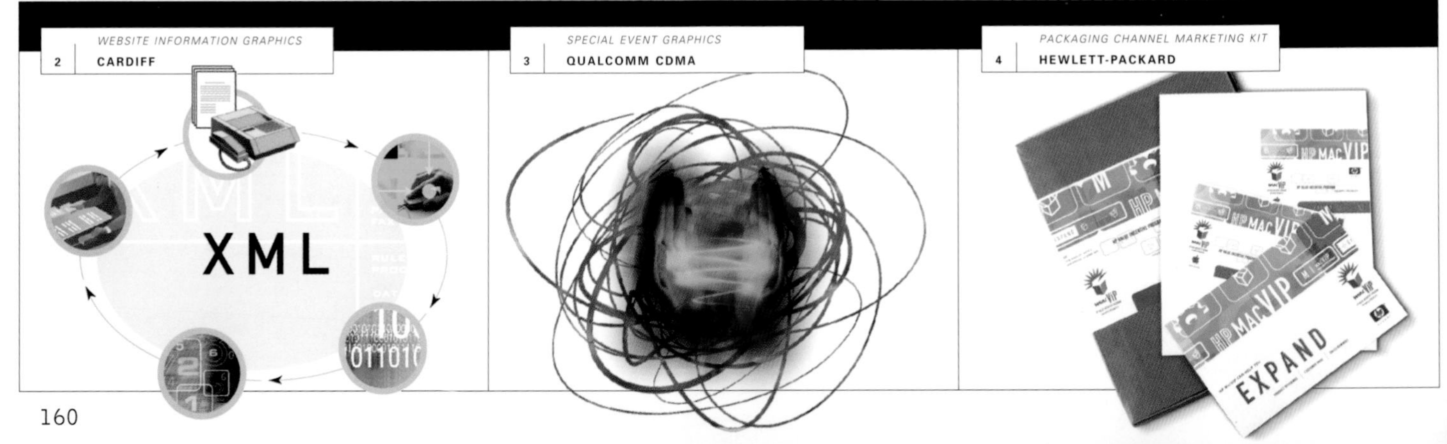

WEBSITE INFORMATION GRAPHICS
2 **CARDIFF**

SPECIAL EVENT GRAPHICS
3 **QUALCOMM CDMA**

PACKAGING CHANNEL MARKETING KIT
4 **HEWLETT-PACKARD**

10803 Magnolia Drive
Cleveland, Ohio 44106
216.791.7721

One Bond Street
New York, New York 10012
212.673.8888

511 King Street West
Toronto, Ontario M5Z 1K4
416.595.9950

NESNADNY | SCHWARTZ

www.NSideas.com

On the back of each Nesnadny + Schwartz business card you'll find one word: ideas.

It's the ideas that drove an inexperienced Mark Schwartz and Joyce Nesnadny to form their own business 20 years ago. Having no preconceived notions of real-world limitations, they broke down barriers they didn't know existed. Few guidelines were followed. No concept seemed too risky.

That irreverent disregard for the status quo helped to position Nesnadny + Schwartz as one of the world's preeminent design consultancies. With offices in Cleveland, New York and Toronto, the venture grew from a two-person partnership into a full service firm employing 15 creative professionals. With a strong emphasis on new technologies, their collective expertise is rooted in the seamless, cohesive, memorable and cost-effective integration of ideas across all forms of printed and electronic communication.

Innovation does not come without responsibility, however. The firm quickly learned that every risk it took meant giving a rationale in return: creativity grounded in logic, concepts backed by research, experience driven by results.

Mark Schwartz has been quoted as saying "I don't think you can do great work without great clients," a realization that informs every project the firm accepts. Their work includes a diverse portfolio of national and international clients from both the corporate and institutional sectors.

"We rarely look at design when we brainstorm," Schwartz states. "We encourage our staff to go to the art museum if they need inspiration." That artistic cross-pollination has led to numerous collaborations with fine artists, and has paid off creatively. To date, Nesnadny + Schwartz has won nearly 1,000 national and international awards in marketing, interactive media, recruiting, development, public relations, investor communications, photography, illustration and graphic design. Additionally, the firm's work has been featured globally in virtually every periodical devoted to visual communications.

It is clear that commitment is at work here. Commitment to the ideas — to the clarity of thinking — to the attention to detail — and ultimately, to exceeding expectations. For Nesnadny + Schwartz, it is through this commitment that the voice of each client and project reveals itself.

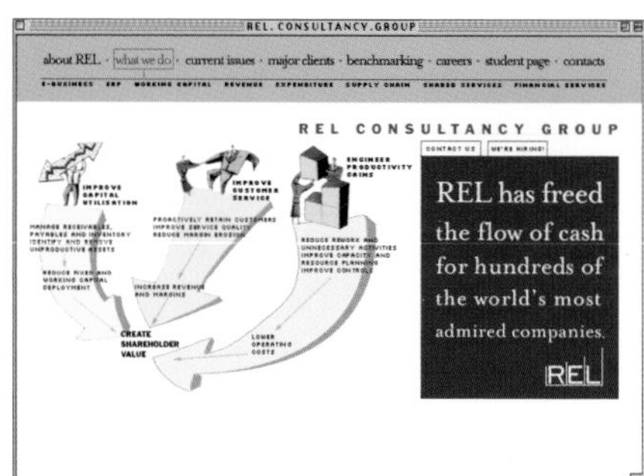

REL Consultancy Group needed a marketing communications system that was flexible enough to work for U.S. offices as well as their European and Asian locations. With printing occurring on three continents, everything from paper specifications to color matching systems required careful research and planning. The completed system includes a marketing communications package, identity and business papers system, new client reporting tools and a web site.

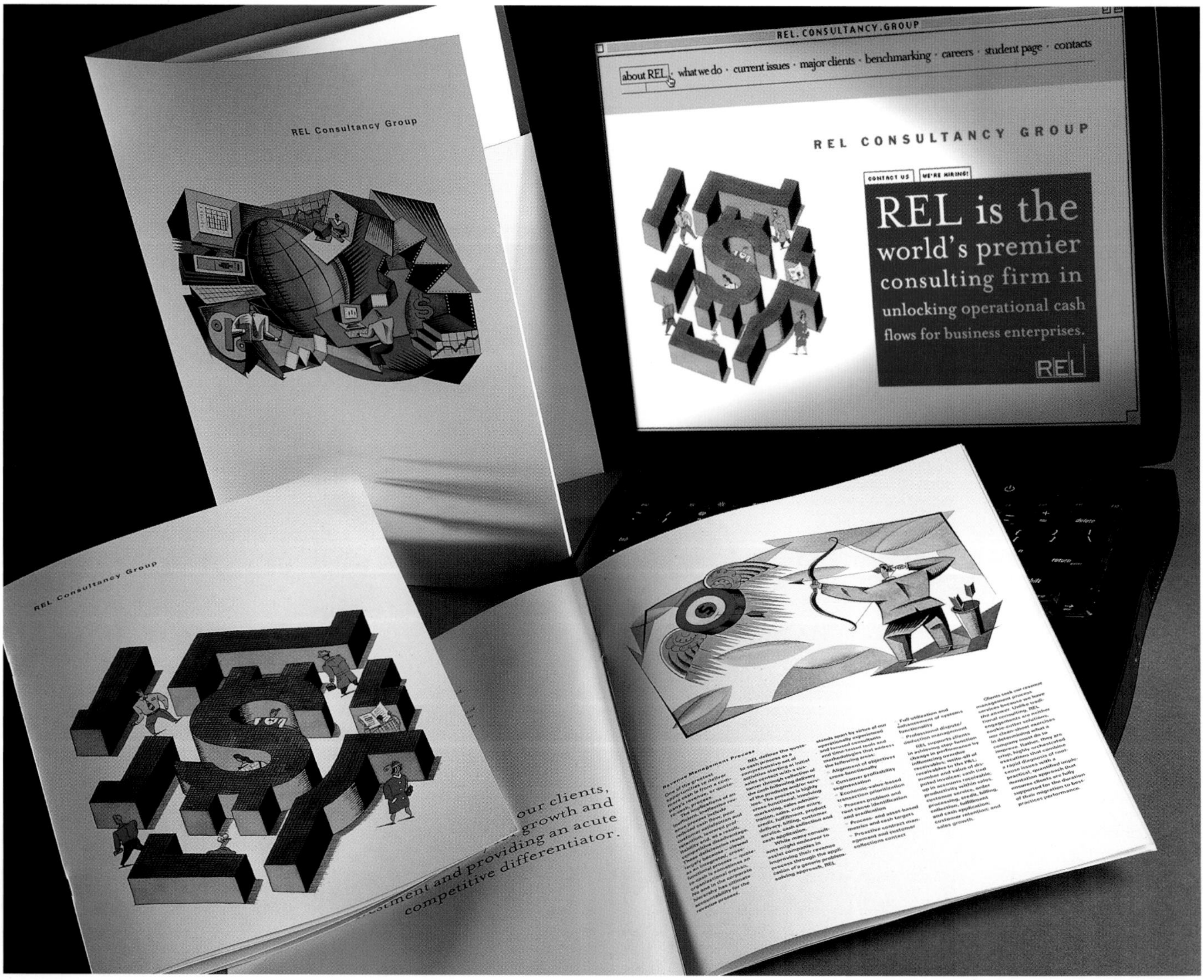

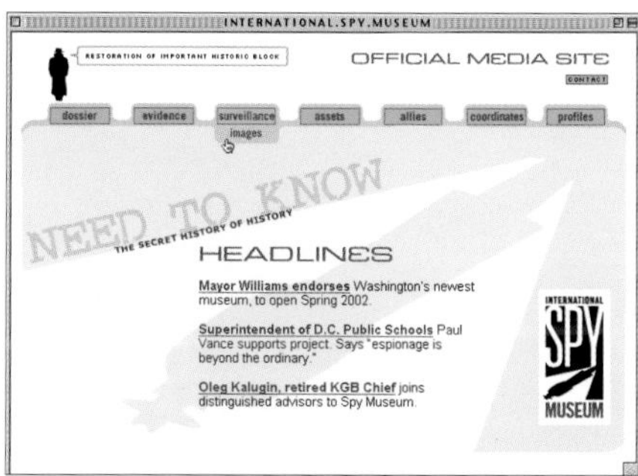

How do you create an identity for a soon to be opened museum when the exact needs are constantly evolving? Nesnadny + Schwartz's solution for the **International Spy Museum** was the development of a flexible identity that visually communicates — with and without words — the museum's purpose. This identity needed to be graphical enough to work on everything, including gift store merchandise — t-shirts, hats, tote bags and related items. The same visual attitude was used for every communications element including the web site, gift store packaging, business papers, signage and marketing communications materials.

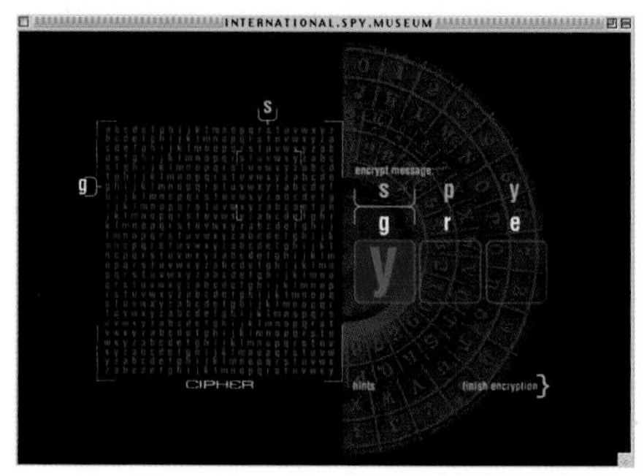

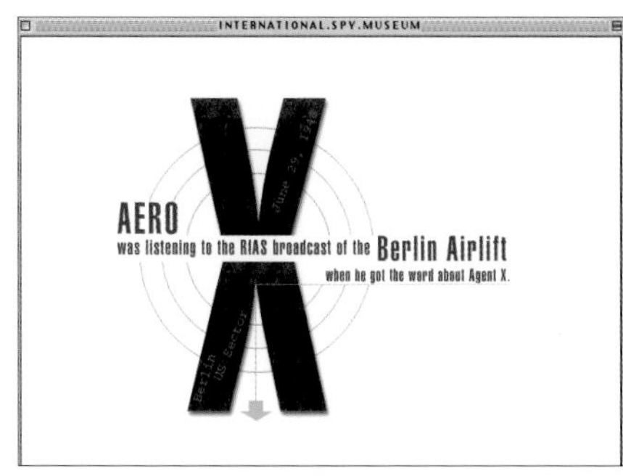

When Champion International Corporation and International Paper merged, one of the results was **SMART Papers** — a 106-year-old "new" company. In addition to inventing and visualizing the SMART name and brand, Nesnadny + Schwartz was responsible for virtually every aspect of the new corporate and product-related marketing communications initiatives. This included the identity system and related electronic manuals, trade shows, signage, merchandise, promotional packages, trade advertising, swatch books and all related materials.

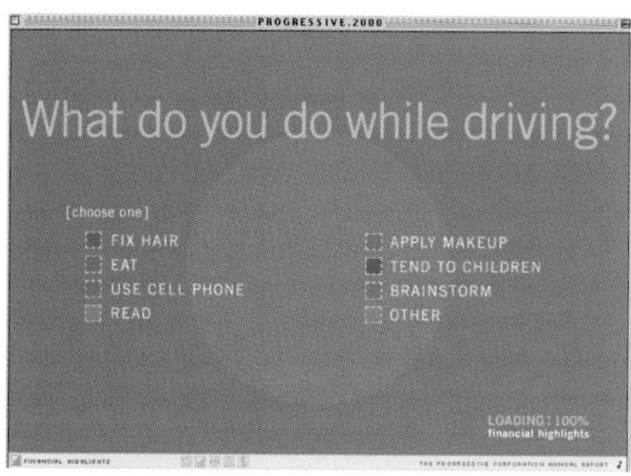

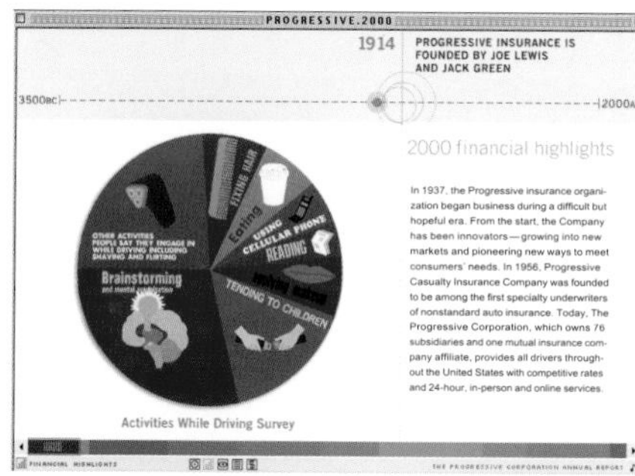

PROGRESSIVE

The Progressive Corporation has been a client of Nesnadny + Schwartz for 18 years. That's 18 annual reports, in nearly 1,152,000 total copies, 1,130 unique page designs, 18 design presentations and 18,000 chances for something in the working relationship to go awry. But it hasn't. The Nesnadny + Schwartz / Progressive collaboration has resulted in over 300 communications-related awards making these publications the most visible and praised works in the history of annual report design and production.

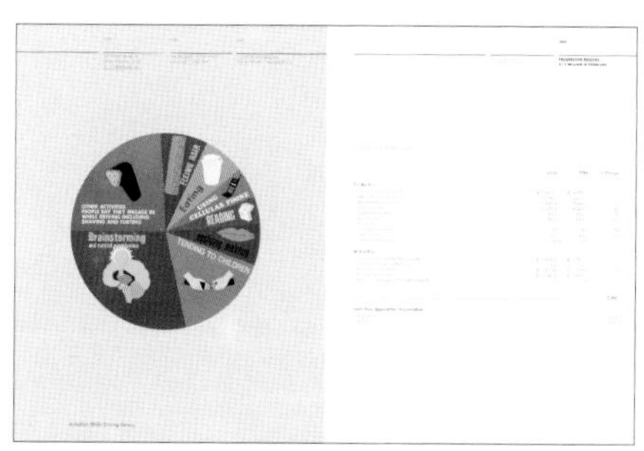

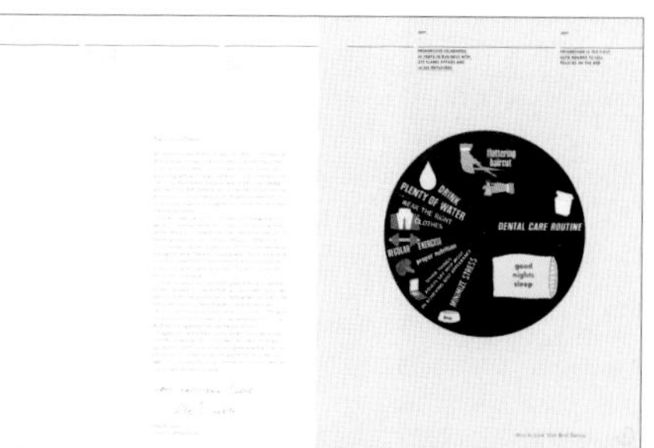

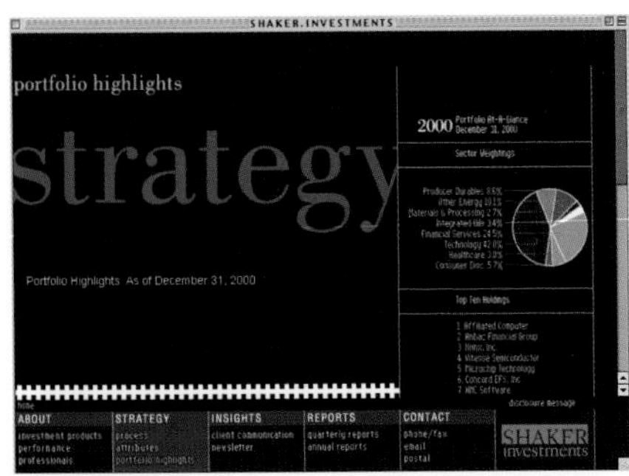

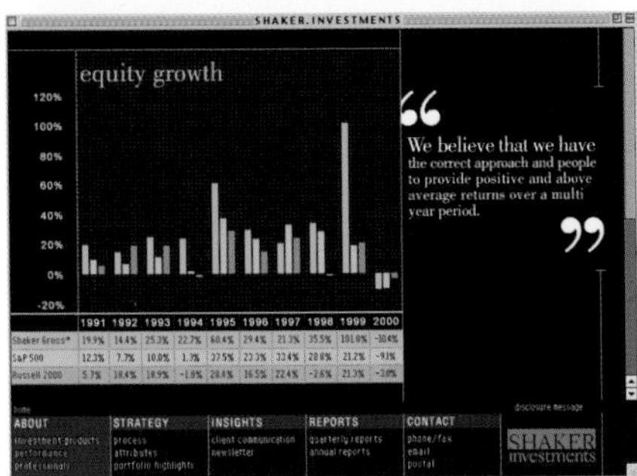

SHAKER
investments

When **Shaker Investments** approached Nesnadny + Schwartz they had little brand identity or visible recognition in the marketplace. While they were growing quickly and becoming increasingly successful, Shaker needed a strong, stable and fresh identity system and marketing communications program to help them further expand their business. Nesnadny + Schwartz invented a clean and flexible system of printed and web-based communications tools to help seamlessly underscore the client's key marketing communications initiatives.

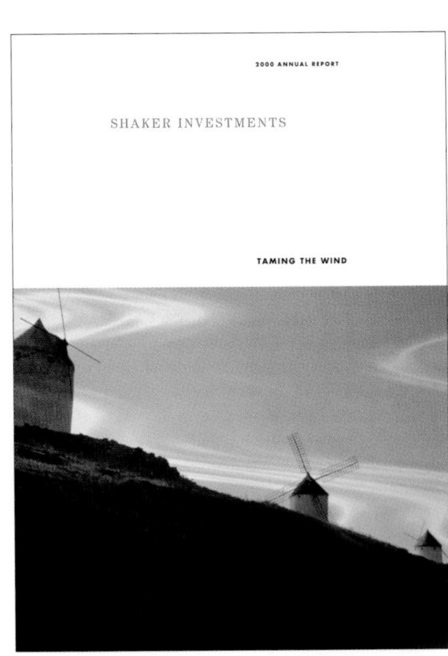

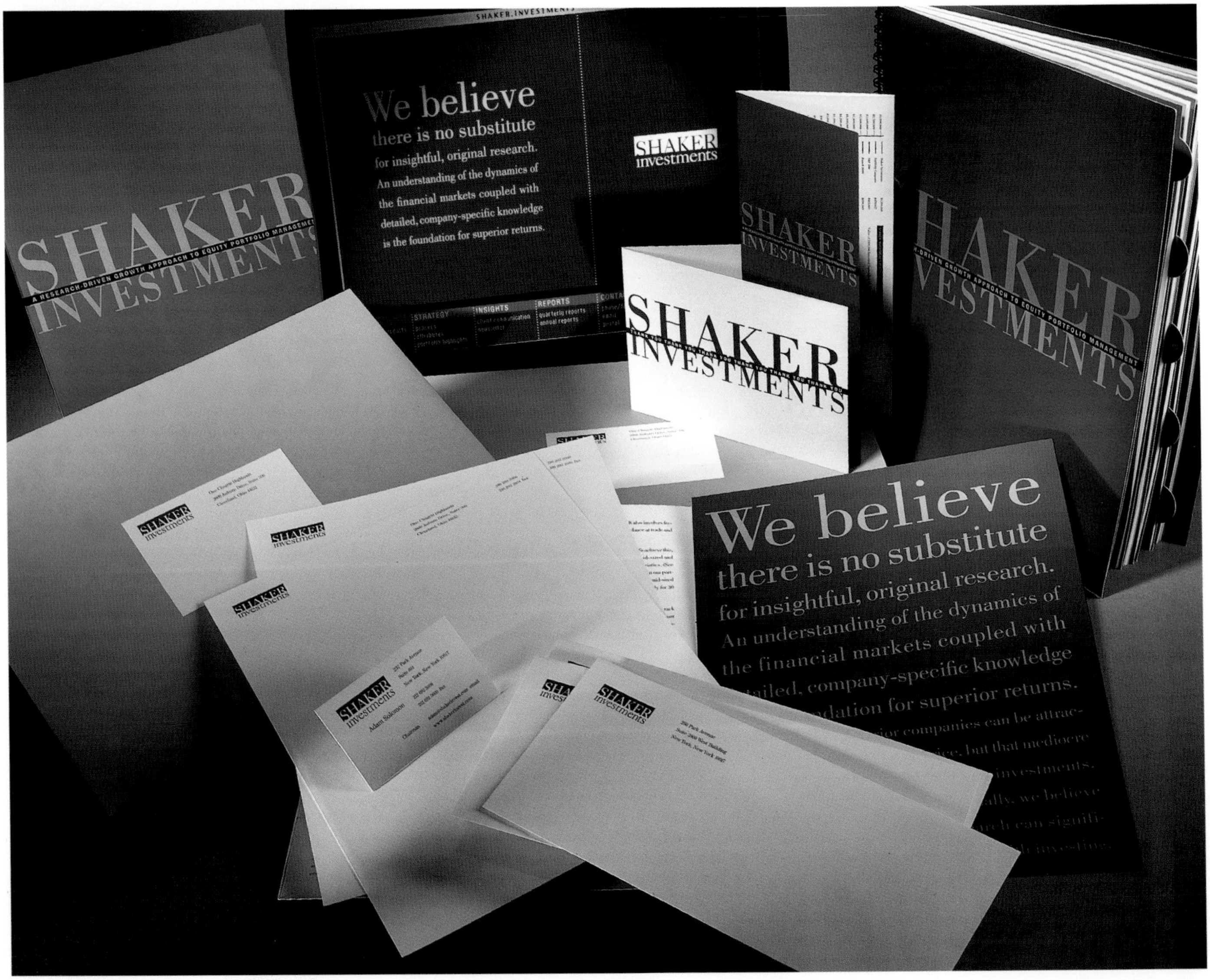

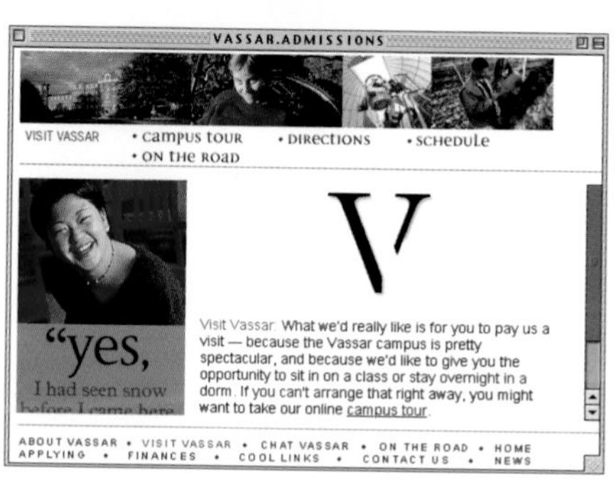

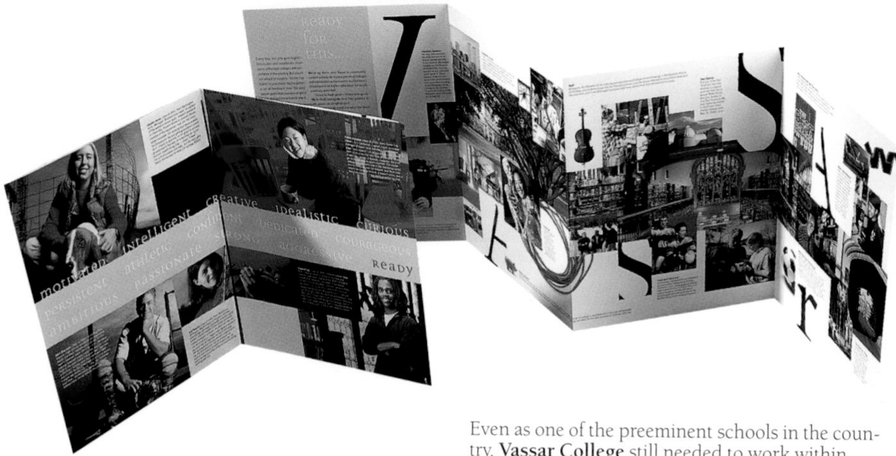

Vassar

Even as one of the preeminent schools in the country, **Vassar College** still needed to work within relatively tight budgets for their recruiting and admissions materials. Nesnadny + Schwartz developed a unique look that relied on strong typographical treatments which could be used in everything from letterhead to a new web site. The execution and management of the program led to a cost-effective solution with results that surpassed all previous admissions records — direct mail responses were up 12%, applications increased 17%, early decision applications rose 55% and selectivity increased.

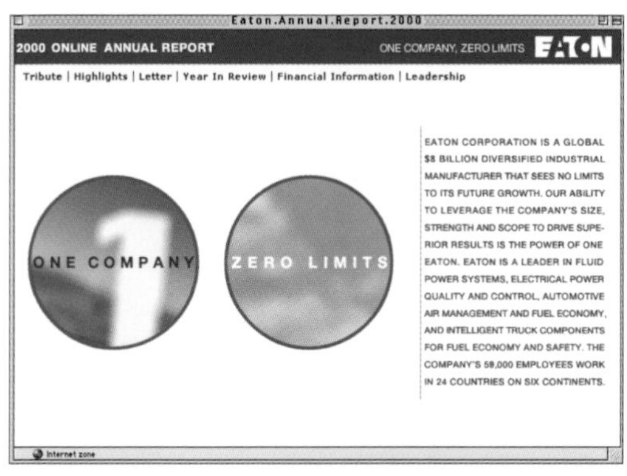

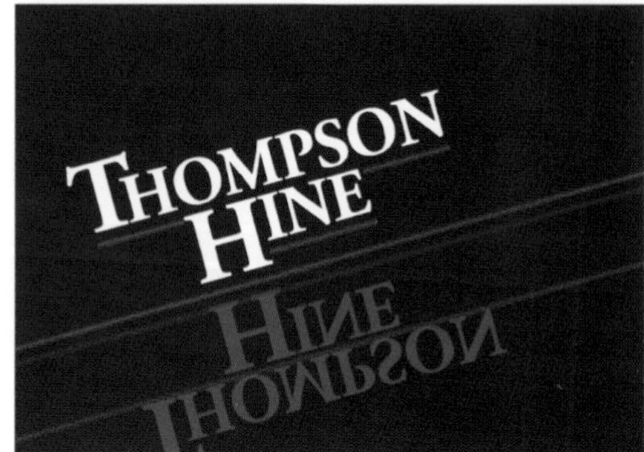

Crawford Museum of Transportation and Industry
Graphic Identity System

The George Gund Foundation 1999 Annual Report

Rock and Roll Hall of Fame and Museum
Fan Favorites Exhibition

Perkins School for the Blind Graphic Identity System

Cleveland Center for Contemporary Art
Signage and Wayfinding System

Eaton Corporation 2000 Online Annual Report

Lowenstein Durante Architects Graphic Identity System

Thompson Hine Computer Screen Saver
and Graphic Identity System

Parham Santana Inc
7 West 18th Street
New York, NY 10011
212 645 7501
jparham@parhamsantana.com
www.parhamsantana.com

PARHAM SANTANA INC.

Parham Santana is a brand strategy and design firm located in Manhattan, serving clients around the globe. We believe in great design. But we view design as a means to an end: success for clients in their marketing efforts.

It is our mission to provide strategy and design for two distinct niches:
1. Communications & Media Brands
2. Retail Brands

While we know many industries, we concentrate on Communications, Media and Retail because they're what we do best; and what we like to do most.

We have a distinct point of view.

We believe that branding is a human business. To position your brand or product indelibly in your customer's mind, you need to identify and connect with basic human needs and desires. We call it *brand the feeling*.

We have a defined, proven process.

We are distinguished by an approach where we discover the unique and compelling reason your brand exists. The core reason people buy your brand.

Through a three step process, Parham Santana identifies and maps a strategy to leverage your appeal.

We are easy to work with.

In every interchange, and every exchange of ideas and creativity, we strive to counsel, serve and collaborate, comfortably and cordially.

The work on the following pages is a result of our philosophy and approach. Please enjoy.

Re-Imaging Programs

Barbie
DAY AT THE MALL
DRESS UP!
BRAIDS ARE IN!
DENIM DOES IT!
FASHION AVENUE
Barbie
SCHOOL
FASHION AVENUE
FASHION AVENUE™
FASHION AVENUE™
FASHION AVENUE™
FASHION AVENUE™
Barbie
FASHION AVENUE™
Barbie
FASHION AVENUE™
PARHAM | SANTANA
brand the feeling™

Retail Programs and Brand Extensions

PARHAM | SANTANA
brand the feeling™

liz claiborne
www.lizclaiborne.com
liz claiborne
liz claiborne
liz claiborne

POLO RALPH LAUREN
KNIT BOXER
POLO RALPH LAUREN
POLO RALPH LAUREN POLO RALPH LAUREN

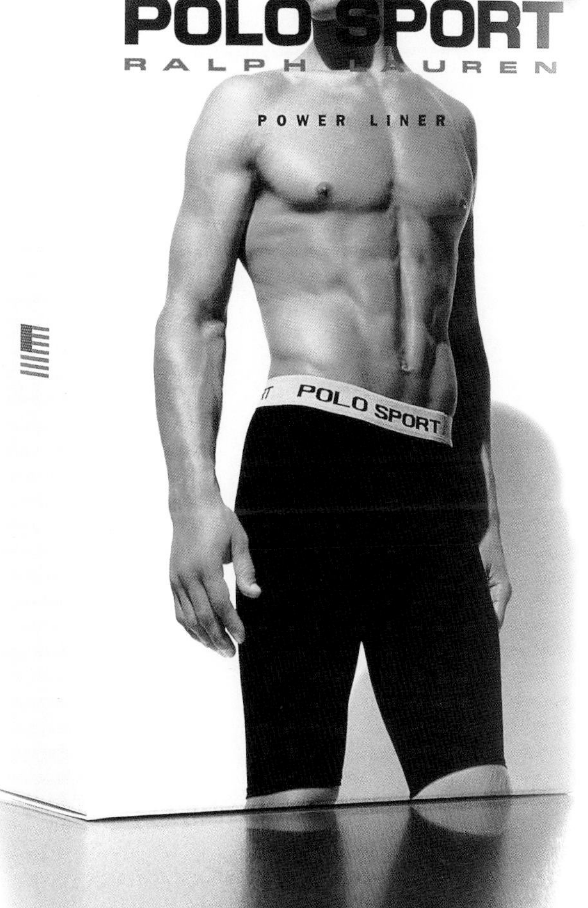
POLO SPORT
RALPH LAUREN
POWER LINER
POLO SPORT

PARHAM | SANTANA
brand the feeling™

Product Literature and Catalogs

Pinkhaus
2424 S. Dixie Highway
Miami, Florida 33133
305.854.1000
www.pinkhaus.com

Established April 1, 1985
Mission: to be a community of creative people whose passion and honesty combine to realize their full potential.

Bauhaus
Established April 1, 1919
Mission: to be a community of young people that builds a new man in a new environment and to liberate creative spontaneity in everybody.

Coincidence? Reincarnation? Updated version.

Abracadabra see what's brand
brand spanking new...

Hot off the press. Fresh. Pink. Juicy. Smells like new. State-of-the art. Glow in the dark.

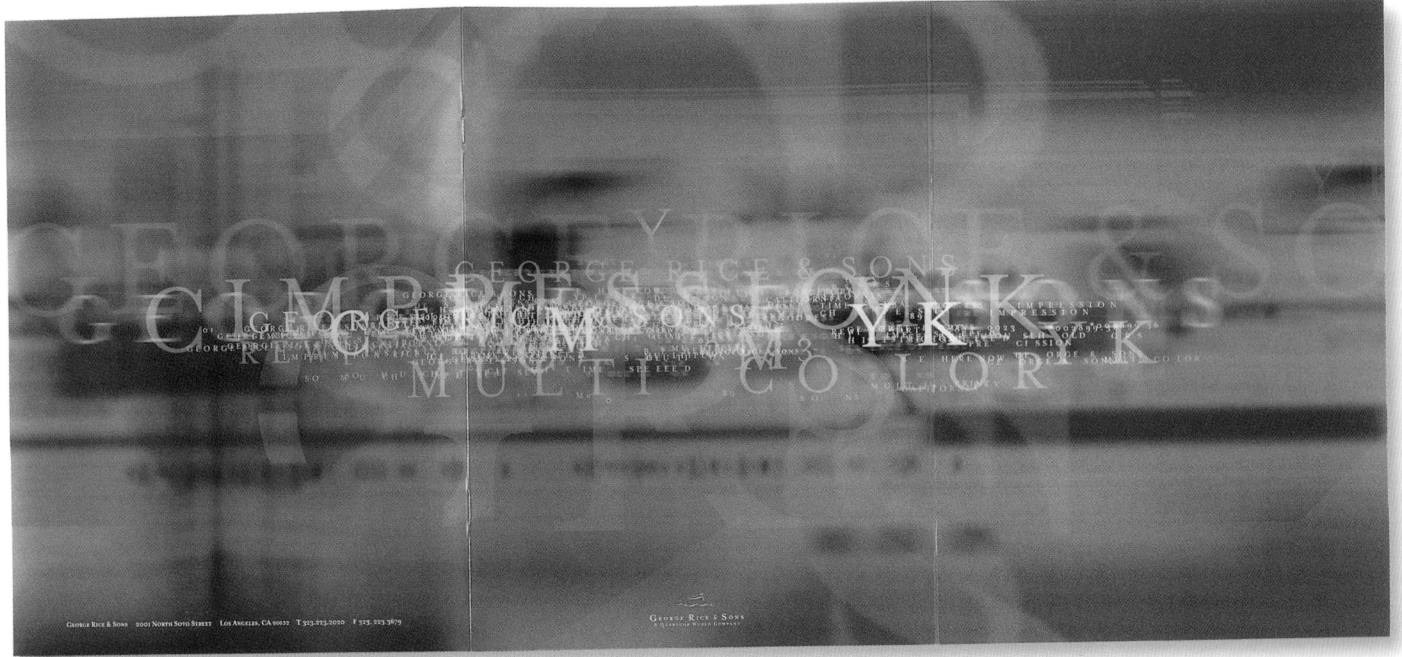

1

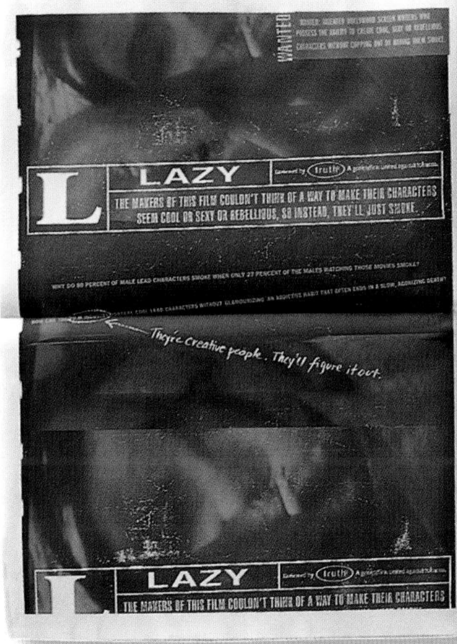

2

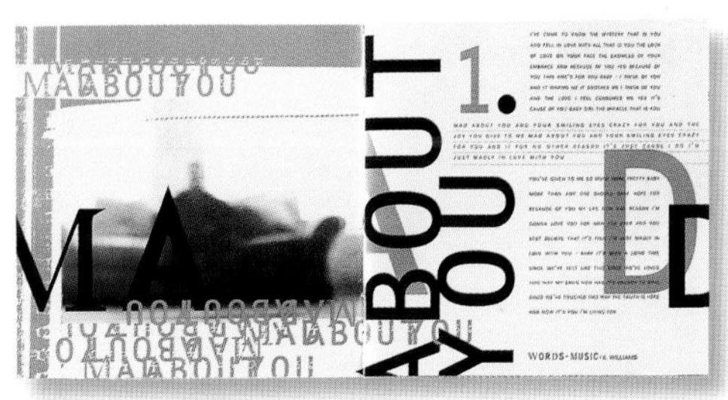

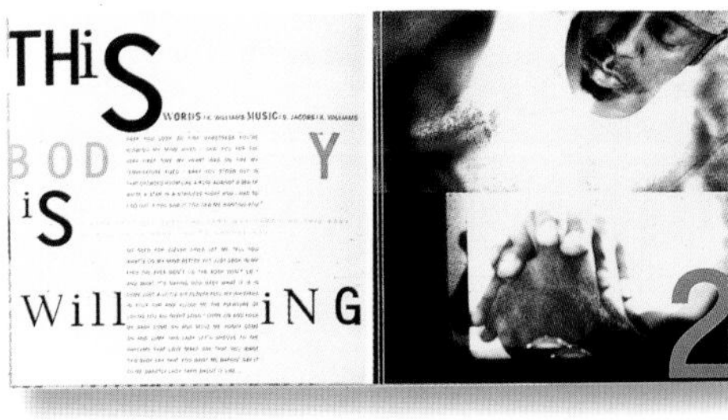

3

1. George Rice & Sons promotional brochure for a new 8-color web printing press.

2. Truth Newsletter: part of a national anti-smoking campaign targeted to youths.

3. Kirby Williams CD cover, booklet and interactive.

Mint condition. 0-120 3 seconds flat. Crank up the A/C. Radioactive. Straight off the showroom floor.

1

2

3

4

1. Sterling Commerce Employee Brand Awareness Video 1.
2. Sterling Commerce Employee Brand Awareness Video 2.
3. Lighthouse Grenada / FastForward On-Air Segments: music video program.
4. Mercedes Benz S-Class Launch video.

Smart not stiff. Strong as a nail. Saucy. Pull down the shades. Stay for a while. Customer satisfaction guaranteed.

1

2

3

4

5

6

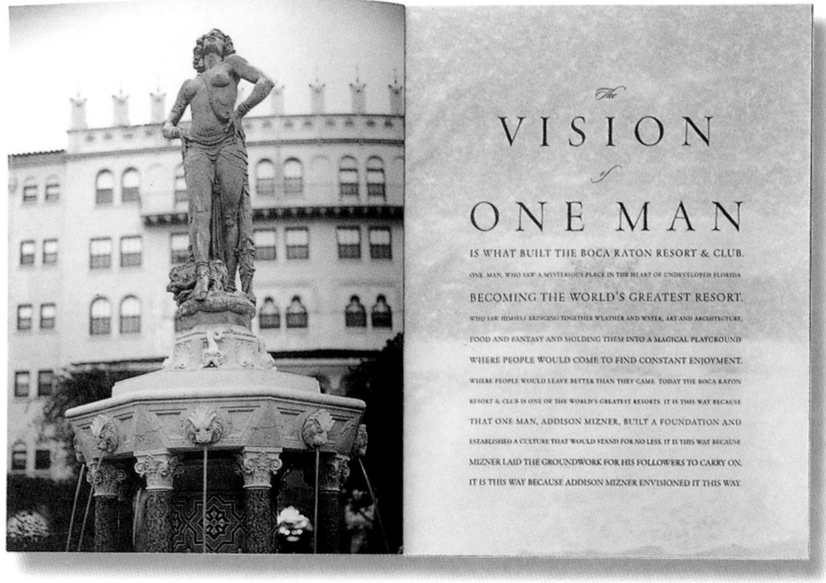

1. Mercury restaurant print advertisement.
2. Mercury restaurant stationery set.
3. Mercury restaurant menus.
4. Sun International Hotels annual report.
5. Sterling Commerce corporate brochure.
6. Boca Raton Resort and Club meetings and convention planner, rack brochure and new facilities announcement.

Experience. Experience. Experience. Hablamos español.

1

2

1. Blasius Erlinger photography promotional poster and postcards.

2. Political propaganda posters commissioned by Congreso Nacional Hostosiano, Puerto Rico.

212 West 10th Street
Studio D445
Indianapolis, IN 46202 USA

317.636.7838
www.ideaincubation.com

PLANET 10

Idea Incubation.

An environment where ideas are born, fostered and developed is Planet 10's approach to problem solving. Instead of distinguishing between the different disciplines, Planet 10 has dissolved them. The areas where advertising, design, marketing, PR, web presence, direct marketing, and sales promotion reside have been blurred. What this leaves you with is a company who can seamlessly build a brand and put into action a communication plan. We call this process *Brand Personality Profiling* and put it in terms even mere humans can understand.

When engaging into a relationship with a client Planet 10 looks to identify the trigger benefit in the brand. By identifying this benefit we can sharpen the message and communicate more effectively to the target audience. Planet 10 builds a stronger brand for our clients. Success hinges on information, Planet 10 doing its job thoroughly, a commitment to marketing by the client, and an honest assessment of perception vs. reality. We use a variety of ways to ensure that consumer and product insights are the foundation of our plan. We also never loose sight of the fact that researched, targeted and educated creative solutions will produce results.

Building a brand requires a plan. The next step is the implementation of a process we call *Brand Relationship Marketing*. The strength of our *Brand Personality Profiling* process is *Brand Relationship Marketing*. This is where a relationship is developed between the client and the target audience. It's designed not only to satisfy a functional need, but connect with the target audience and become a symbol or icon for the way someone chooses to make decisions in his or her life. Through touchpoints we generate brand loyalty and regardless if it's technology, tennis shoes or food the more brand loyal consumers we can create the more valuable we become to our clients.

1

4

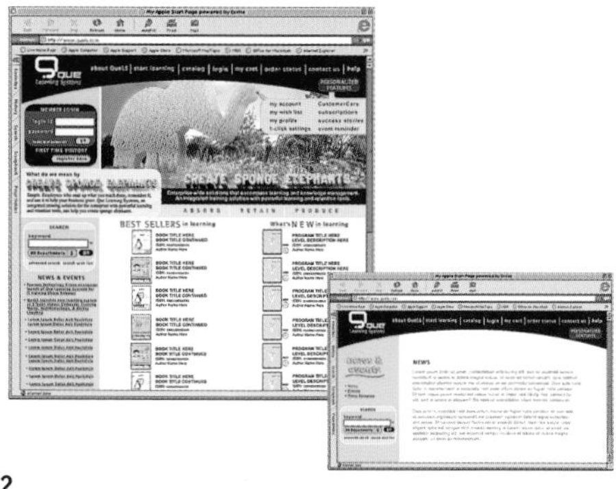

2

3

5

1. Que Learning Systems ad campaign.
2. Que Learning Systems web site.
3. Que Learning Systems demo show booth.
4. Que Learning Systems brand logo.
5. Que Learning Systems demo cd and packaging.

1

2

3

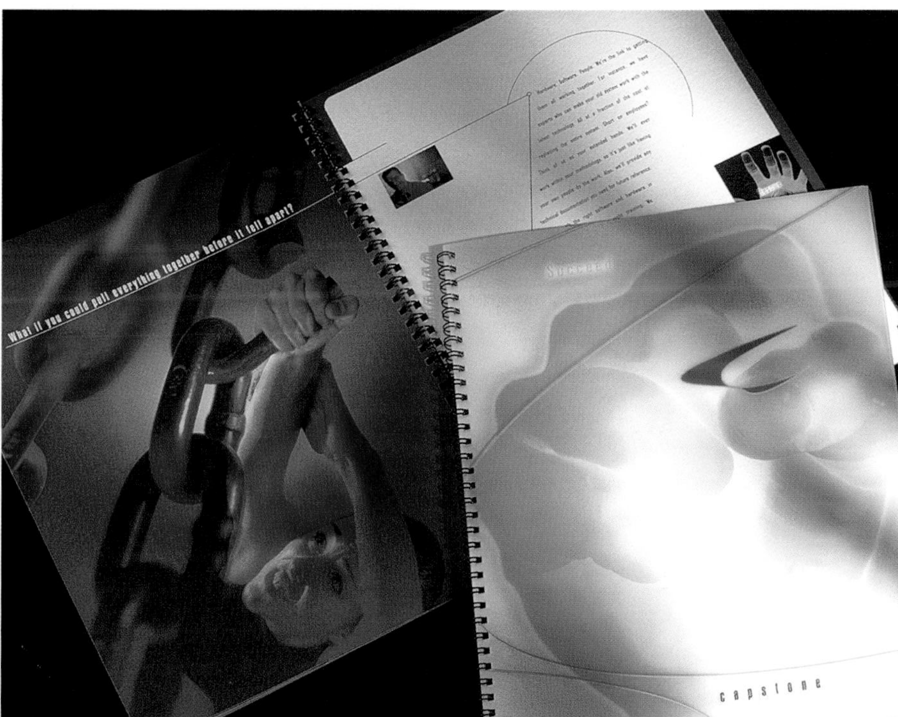

4

1-3. stēl Objekt brand identity, brochure and hang tag.

4. Capstone corporate brochure.

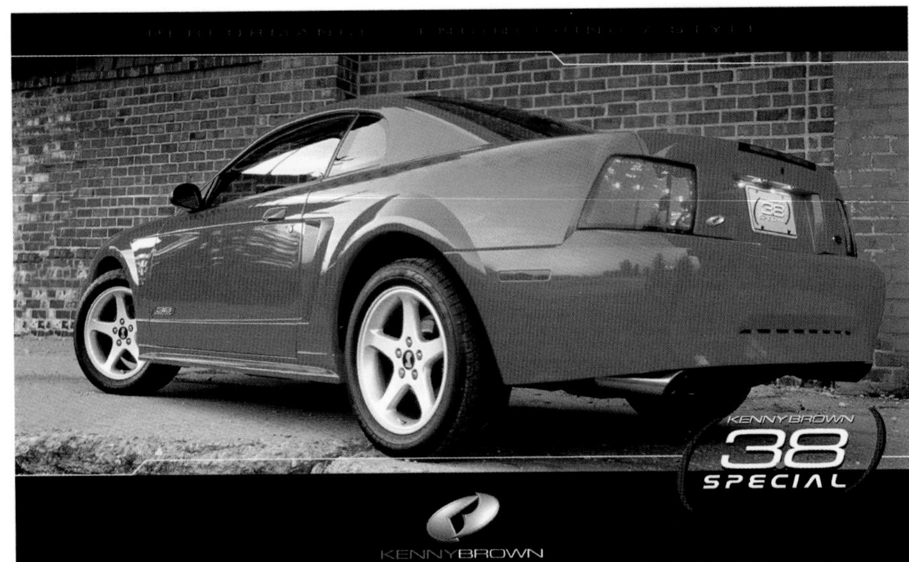
KENNY BROWN
38
SPECIAL
KENNYBROWN

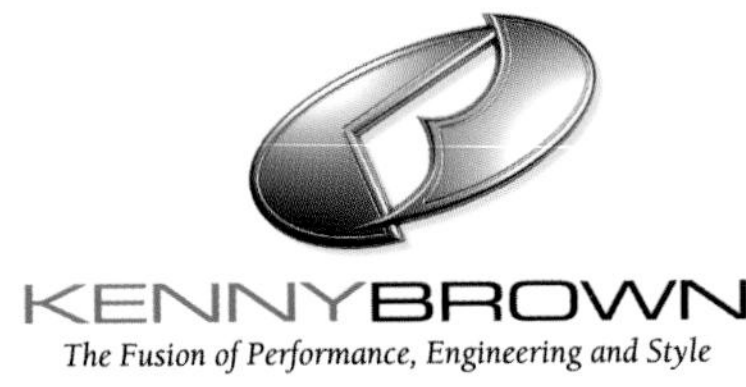
KENNYBROWN
The Fusion of Performance, Engineering and Style

4

some extra cash in your pocket
38 SPECIAL

The right product at the right time.

38 SPECIAL

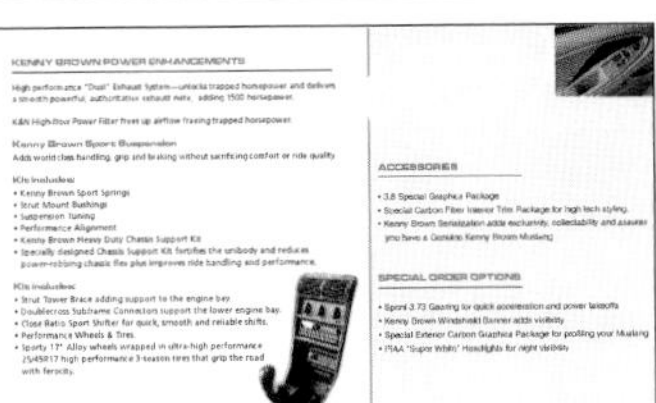

KENNYBROWN
38 SPECIAL
PERFORMANCE

5

1

MILLION
DOLLAR
AWARDS

2

NVIOUS
Thou shall party with a devilish grin

3

CAUSES OF PVD
PREVALENCE AND RISK FACTORS
UNDERSTANDING PERIPHERAL VASCULAR DISEASE
PERIPHERAL VASCULAR DISEASE (PVD)
WHAT NEXT?
Clarian Health

6

7

8

9

1. Kenny Brown product brochure.
2. Million Dollar Awards event mark.
3. Nvious upscale nightclub brand mark.
4. Kenny Brown Performance brand mark.
5. Kenny Brown Performance web site.
6. Clarian Health Peripherial Vascular Disease brochure.

7. Pop Weaver/NFL popcorn tin campaign.
8-9. Pop Weaver/NFL in-stadium signage.
10. Clarian Health Peripheral Vascular Disease ad campaign.

10

S IN I ONE X
GAME CHEST
NOT INTENDED FOR CHILDREN | 2+ PLAYERS

1

Phase 10
skip
Phase 10

2

SECURE YOUR VALUABLES
LIGHTWEIGHT | OVER-THE-SHOULDER DESIGN | FASHIONABLE COLORS
It's important to choose the right accessories. So wear your seat belt and improve your chances of surviving an auto crash by 80%.
SEAT BELTS. WEAR THEM EVERYWHERE.
DANGEROUS DRIVING
NETS

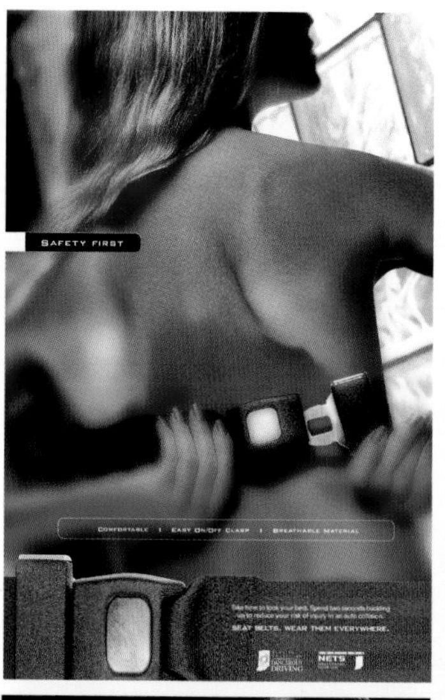
SAFETY FIRST

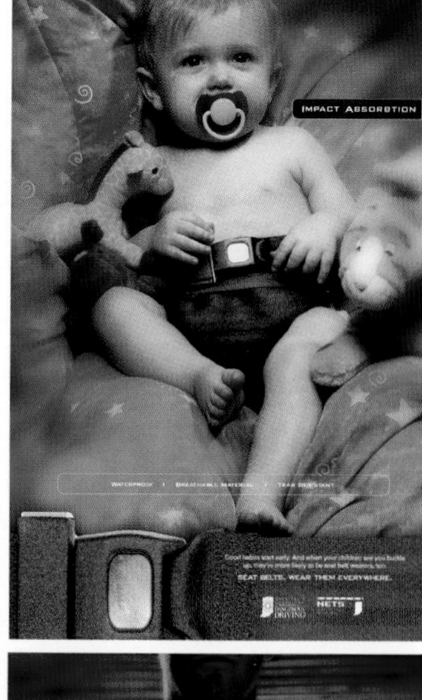
IMPACT ABSORBTION

SAVE YOUR NECK

THE ULTIMATE SELF DEFENSE

3

4

5

6

1. Fundex Games Six-in-One Game Chest packaging.
2. Fundex Games Phase 10, 20th Anniversary tin.
3. Seat Belt Safety Awareness poster campaign.
4. Playing Mantis, Fundex Games and Jada Toys brand packaging.
5. Humane Society of Indianapolis event invitation.
6. Fundex Games 2001 merchandising catalog.

1

6

7

8

2

3

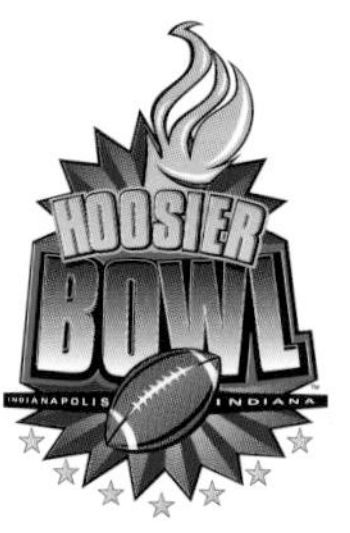

9

10

4

5

11

1. Total Sports Marketing corporate brochure.
2. New Riders sales kit.
3. Radius identity package.
4. Netisun identity package.
5. Netisun employee introduction kit.
6. Freedom Festival event mark.
7. Indiana State Museum logo.
8. Volunteers in Medicine logo.
6. Hoosier Bowl event mark.
10. Netisun logo.
11. Radius logo.

Peterson & Company
2200 N. Lamar Street
Suite 310
Dallas, Texas 75202
214.954.0522
www.petersonandco.com

PETERSON & COMPANY

Peterson & Company, a nationally respected corporate communication and college publication design firm, was founded in 1985 by Bryan L. Peterson. Located in a renovated turn-of-the-century warehouse, this Dallas studio is the perfect setting for Peterson & Company's relaxed but professional style.

The diversity of experience and talent within the Peterson & Company organization allows a broad range of project specialties including annual reports, corporate identities, web sites, marketing and capabilities brochures, business-to-business trade advertising, publications, posters, and sales collateral.

Scott Ray, a principal and senior designer at Peterson & Company since 1986, believes in "focusing on making our clients' jobs as easy and stress free as possible, at the same time creating the highest caliber of print and web design."

Success, after all, is a direct result of responsiveness to the clients' needs. Clients want results. Return on investment. Keeping results as the goal, Peterson & Company has built a client base that includes industries such as computer technology, education, retail, telecommunications, construction, food service, energy, transportation, and the performing arts.

Bryan L. Peterson's talents extend beyond exceptional design. He is the author of "Using Design Basics To Get Creative Results" by North Light Books, which is in college classrooms and on bookstore shelves across the United States.

Bryan's finesse in the area of client relations, along with his ability to attract and retain some of the best designers in the industry, has resulted in the creation of a successful, innovative, client sensitive, communication design firm.

1

2

3

1. Blockbuster Annual Report
2. Centex Corporation Annual Report
3. @ Track Annual Report
4. Micrografx Annual Report
5. Child Guidance Center Logo
6. EFG Companies Logo, Auto Sales Industry
7. Centex Construction Annual Report
8. Meeting Professionals International Membership Benefits Brochure
9. Dallas Society of Visual Communications "Rough Magazine"
10. Dallas Arts District Friends Brochure

4

5

6

7

MEMBERSHIP
BENEFITS
MPI

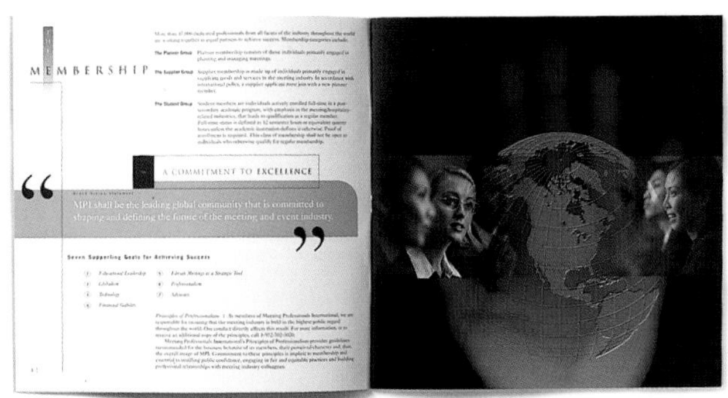
MEMBERSHIP
A COMMITMENT TO EXCELLENCE

8

DSVC
OCT 00
R
OUGH

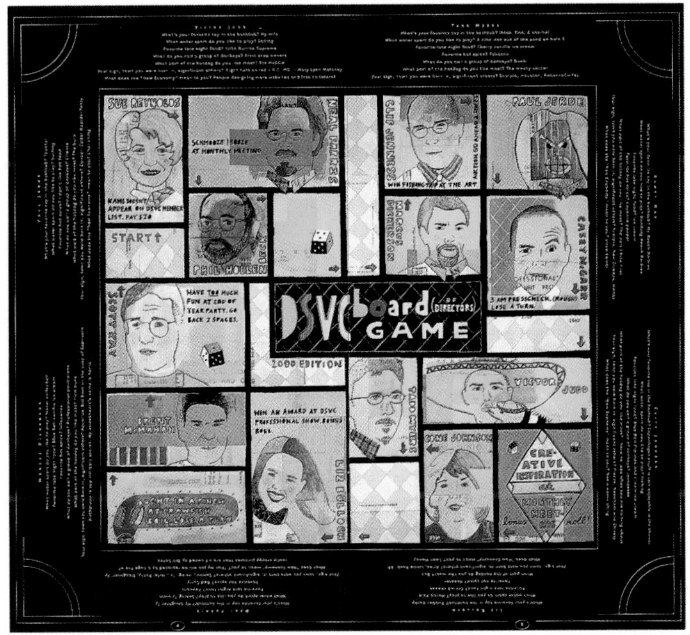
DSVC board (OF DIRECTORS) GAME
2000 EDITION
START

9

ARTS
neo-
classic
colossal

10

1

THE GOOD DEATH

Americans have become experts at striving for – and often achieving – the "good life," complete with good friends, good incomes, and good material trappings. Is it surprising, therefore, that they now also seek the "good death"? And can medical science, technology, and the law help them achieve it?

2

3

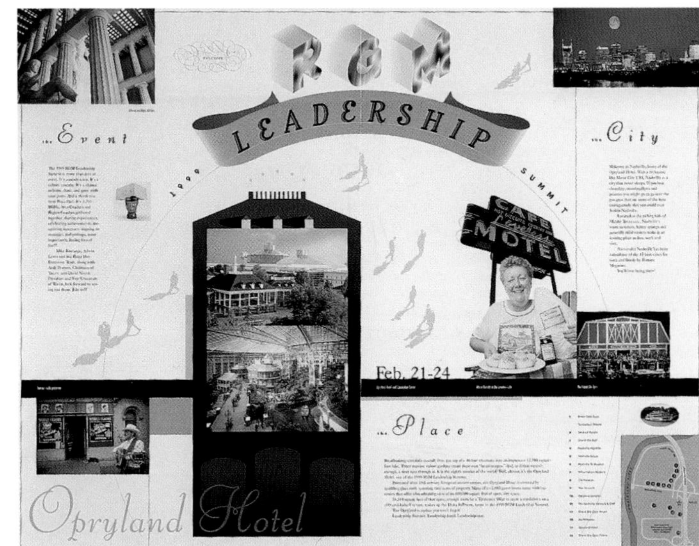

4

1. Kinexus Logo, a Museum of Moving Art
2. Santa Clara University Magazine
3. Portland State University Viewbook
4. Pizza Hut Newsletter "Slice of Reality"
5. Bucknell University Viewbook and Web Page
6. Meeting Professionals International Graphic Standards Brochure

5

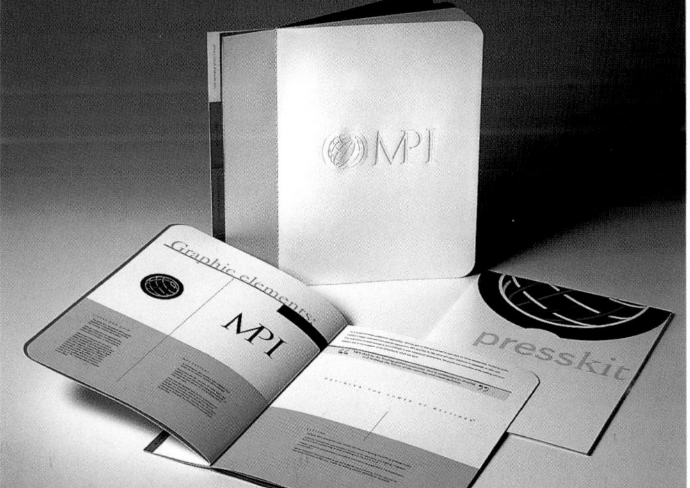

6

1. Data Race Capabilities Brochure
2. Dallas Society of Visual Communications Annual Crawfish Boil Poster
3. Poster for Musician Jimmy LaFave
4. "The Book of BE" Multimedia Presentation
5. Texas Instruments Ethics Brochure
6. YMCA Indian Guide Logo
7. Innovative Media Research Logo
8. See Pictures Logo, Artist Representatives
9. Editorial Spread for "Rough Magazine"
10. CD by Musician/Designer Bryan Peterson

1

2

3

4

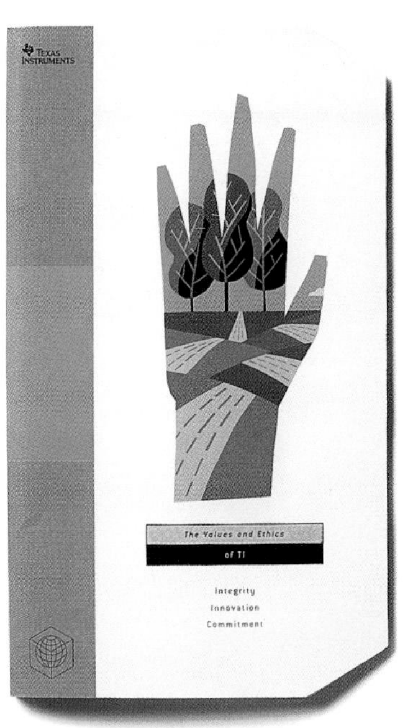
Texas Instruments
The Values and Ethics of TI
Integrity
Innovation
Commitment

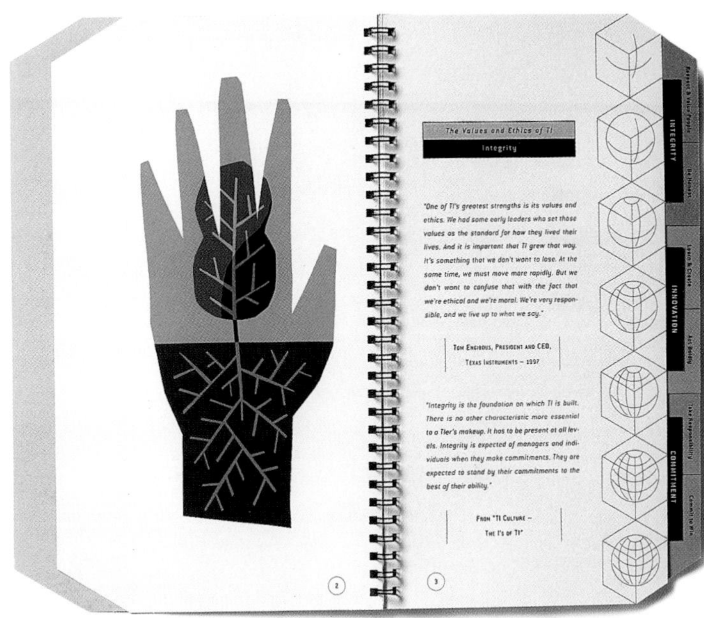
The Values and Ethics of TI
Integrity
"One of TI's greatest strengths is its values and ethics. We had some early leaders who set those values as the standard for how they lived their lives. And it is important that TI grew that way. It's something that we don't want to lose. At the same time, we must move more rapidly. But we don't want to confuse that with the fact that we're ethical and we're moral. We're very responsible, and we live up to what we say."
Tom Engibous, President and CEO, Texas Instruments – 1997
"Integrity is the foundation on which TI is built. There is no other characteristic more essential to a TIer's makeup. It has to be present at all levels. Integrity is expected of managers and individuals when they make commitments. They are expected to stand by their commitments to the best of their ability."
From "TI Culture – The I's of TI"
INTEGRITY
INNOVATION
COMMITMENT

5

6

7

8

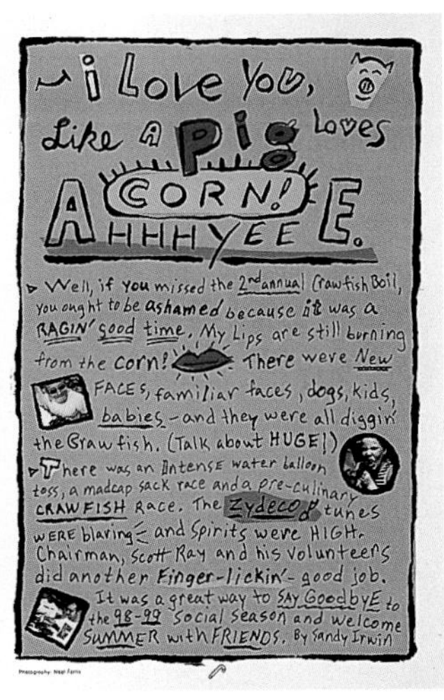
~ i Love You, Like a Pig Loves CORN! AHHHYEE E.
Well, if you missed the 2nd annual Crawfish Boil, you ought to be ashamed because it was a RAGIN' good time. My lips are still burning from the corn! There were New FACES, familiar faces, dogs, kids, babies – and they were all diggin' the Crawfish. (Talk about HUGE!)
There was an Intense water balloon toss, a madcap sack race and a pre-culinary CRAWFISH Race. The Zydeco tunes were blaring and spirits were HIGH. Chairman, Scott Ray and his volunteers did another Finger-lickin'-good job.
It was a great way to SAY GoodbyE to the 98-99 Social Season and welcome SUMMER with FRIENDS. By Sandy Irwin

9

back when i was simple
Bryan Peterson

10

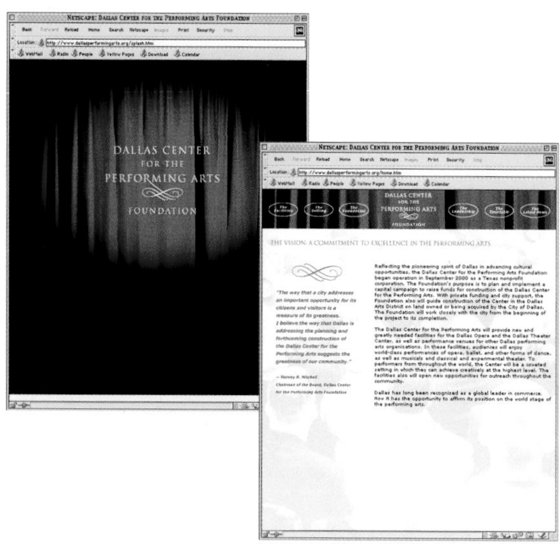

1

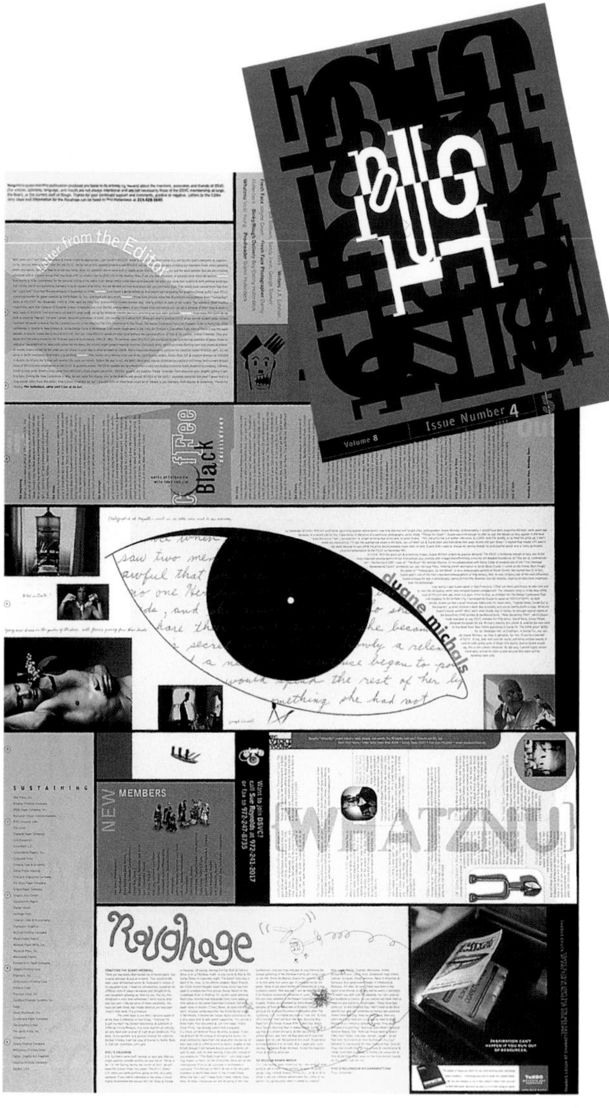

2

3

4

1. Dallas Center for the Performing Arts Web Site
2. Dallas Society of Visual Communications "Rough Magazine" in Poster Form
3. Dallas Society of Visual Communications Speaker Announcement for Art Director Max Malcorp from Holland
4. CD for Texas Musician Jimmy LaFave

Sayles Graphic Design
3701 Beaver Avenue
Des Moines, Iowa 50310
515-279-2922 • fax 515-279-0212
sayles@saylesdesign.com
www.saylesdesign.com

SAYLES GRAPHIC DESIGN

Sayles Graphic Design has a pretty simple philosophy: Let Creativity, Consistency, and Honesty guide whatever you do. And their business structure is just as unassuming: the concept they call "Art / Smart" means two things. Design and strategy go hand-in-hand in every project, and each staff member does what they do best, whether it's design or marketing or client service. When John Sayles and Sheree Clark founded Sayles Graphic Design in 1985, those simple missions were a firm foundation for their partnership, and they knew the ideals would serve them well as their company grew.

From the beginning, John's focus on, and his commitment to, traditional design methodology and tools gave him an edge -- an authenticity to his style that made his work stand out. As much fine artist as graphic designer, John still hand-renders the detailed illustrations and creates original typefaces found in his projects. He became known for his creative use of dimensional direct mail, his innovations with non-traditional materials, his bold design style. Awards piled up, and museums like the Smithsonian Institution and the United States Library of Congress added Sayles' work to their permanent collections.

The list of projects Sayles Graphic Design has produced is impressive, and the studio's client roster is just as long. Corporate identity and logos, company literature, direct mail, custom gifts, packaging, and other work including posters, t-shirts, trade show displays, print ads, billboards, publication and editorial design, menus, calendars, signage, catalogs, and vehicles have all received the Sayles touch.

As Sayles Graphic Design's reputation grew, so did the group's credibility. When Rockport Publishers was looking for an author for a new book about direct mail, John and Sheree were a natural choice. John designed and Sheree authored *Creative Direct Mail Design*, which was followed by two North Light books: *Great Design Using Non-Traditional Materials* and *Get Noticed: Self Promotion for Creative Professionals*. No visual communication or promotion has proved too big a challenge for this dynamic duo.

So when a friend who owned a restaurant approached John and Sheree about a logo for a new eatery he was planning, the partners jumped at the chance to expand their abilities in yet another area of design. Starting with logos and menus, matchbooks and tabletents, Sayles Graphic Design quickly added environmental expertise to their list of accomplishments. And now the studio has taken their restaurant work to another level, adding services like furniture design and retail product packaging.

Today, just as in 1985, Sayles Graphic Design is a full-service design studio, reinforcing the message that "graphic" doesn't just describe their design style, it defines it.

1. Building signage at Mezzodi's restaurant.
2. Mezzodi's features booth dividers made from plexiglas and wrought iron.
3. Curved wood creates an elegant wine cabinet at Mezzodi's.
4. Colorful posters decorate Mezzodi's walls.
5. Mezzodi's guests wait on a custom-built lobby settee.
6. Men's and Women's rooms at Mezzodi's are identified with metal monograms.
7. Frosted pendant lights hover above Mezzodi's curved bar.
8. An olive is found in the textured glass mirror above the bar at Mezzodi's.

1

2

3

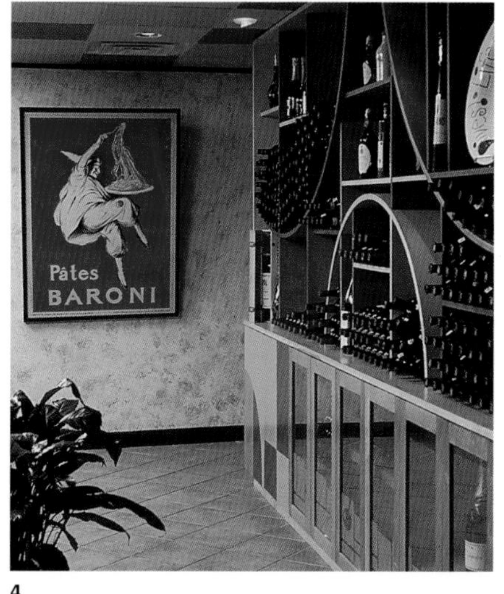

4

5

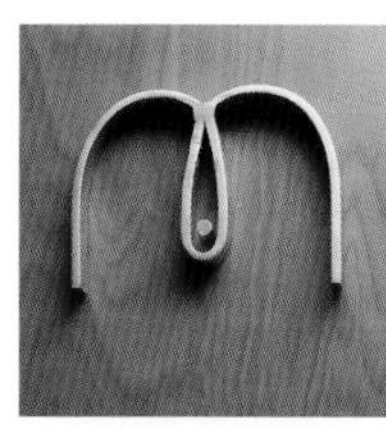

6

7

8

1. 801 Steak & Chop House is located in Des Moines' tallest building.
2. Take-out bags from 801 Steak & Chop House include vintage livestock photos.
3. Diners enter 801 Steak & Chop House through double-paned sand-blasted doors.
4. Etched glass and stained wood are found in the 801 Steak & Chop House lounge.
5. 801 Steak & Chop House menu selections are presented on an embossed board.
6. Spoons and coffee cups are found in the logo for Timbuktuu Coffee Café.
7. Timbuktuu Coffee Café uses traditional and monarch stationery.
8. A tall table at Timbuktuu Coffee Café is custom-made from steel and wood.
9. Wooden tabletops are painted with Timbuktuu's signature coffee bean graphics.
10. Inside Timbuktuu, individually-framed posters are printed on giant coffee bags.

1

2

3

4

5

6

7

8

9

10

1. Sbemco International's safety floor matting features are highlighted in a series of icons.

2. A portable presentation kit for Sbemco is printed on translucent corrugated plastic.

3. Boxes and bottles clearly identify Sbemco's floor mat care products.

4. Samples of Sbemco floor matting are sent in small boxes.

5. Sbemco product benefits are visible on a glassine handled bag.

1

2

3

4

5

1. Phil Goode Grocery's product signage are fabricated from neon, aluminum, signboard, and other materials.

2. A friendly character is found on Phil Goode coffee cups.

1

2

1. A charming beachcomber greets those attending the 2001 Miami Modernism show.
2. 1960s artifacts and a groovy couple promote the 1999 Miami Modernism show.
3. A silvery palm tree shades the heroine of the 1998 Miami Modernism show poster.
4. A 1940s couple are united in the poster for the 1997 Miami Modernism show.
5. The 1996 Miami Modernism show poster features mid-century objects of art.
6. A hand-rendered poster for the Miami Modernism show in 1995 has a deco style.

1

2

3

4

5

6

1

2

3

4

5

6

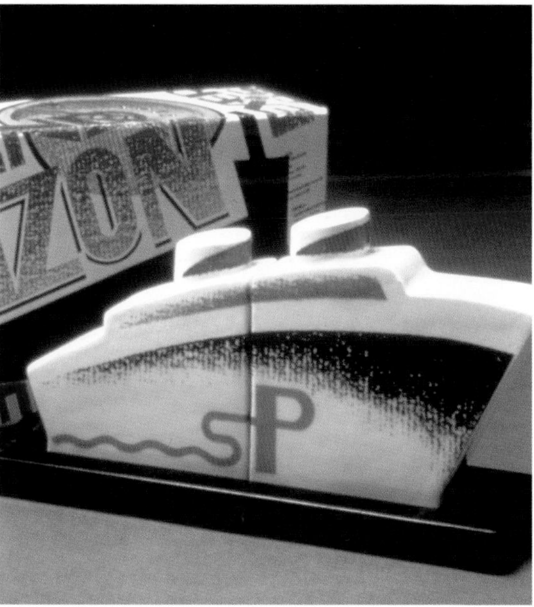

7

1. A special book commemorates a time capsule installed at the Hotel Pattee in Perry, Iowa.
2. Hotel Pattee menus include special touches inspired by the town's railroad history.
3. The guest services directory at the Hotel Pattee is highlighted with hammered copper.
4. Tiny embossed tins hold Gypsy Balm, a perfume from Gianna Rose.
5. Gianna Rose shaving products tell men to "Take Care Of Your Face."
6. A limited edition, hand-signed poster announces an incentive cruise.
7. Custom salt-and-pepper shakers are an appropriate gift for cruise guests.

Custom Designed Type Fonts

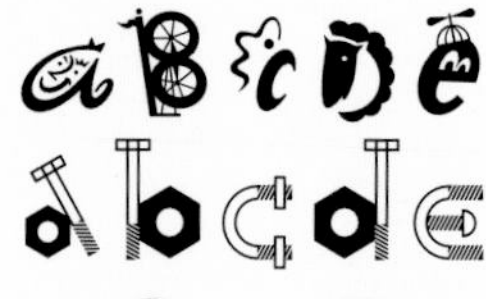
FAIR FONT REGULAR

NUTS & BOLTS LIGHT

OAK LEAF BOLD

SHARP EDGE BOLD

MARTINI BOOK

NEW MACHINE AGE BOLD

HOOK•LINE•SINKER LIGHT

DOG BONE BOLD

BENT NAIL BOLD

Selbert Perkins Design
1916 Main Street
Santa Monica, California 90405
310.664.9100
www.selbertperkins.com

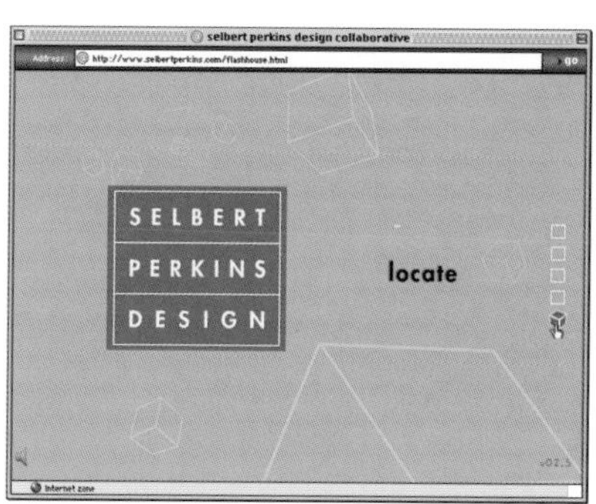

SELBERT PERKINS DESIGN COLLABORATIVE

Selbert Perkins Design Collaborative (SPD) is **a multi-disciplinary design firm** offering a broad range of services including brand identity design, environmental design, print and electronic communications, as well as landscape architecture, public art and sculpture. SPD combines a **strategic, market-driven process** with strong creative resources to develop powerful, position-based communications programs that achieve measurable success for their clients. With offices in California and Massachusetts, SPD collaborates on a daily basis with architects, developers, municipalities and corporations – nationally and internationally.

Selbert Perkins Design has a strong presence in the local Los Angeles community. The firm's work can be seen virtually everywhere; at the University of Southern California, along Santa Monica Boulevard, at Universal Studios, while arriving and departing from Union Station, and at Los Angeles International Airport where SPD designed the dramatic landmark gateway that greets millions of visitors each year. Selbert Perkins is also heavily involved internationally with numerous projects in Japan, China, Taiwan and Singapore.

The mission of Selbert Perkins Design is to create design that will **inform, educate, and entertain people around the world through the power of art, communications and environments.**

1

1. Los Angeles International Airport and Gateway

1. Effervé Sparkling Lemonade brand identity system: name, logo, and packaging
2. Universal Studios: site-wide vehicular and pedestrian wayfinding system, Hollywood, California and Orlando, Florida

1

2

1. USC Annenberg School for Communication: environmental communications
2. USC Annenberg: recruitment system and graphic standards
3. USC Marshall School of Business: recruitment system and graphic standards
4. Sega Gameworks: brand identity system, store front design, Seattle, Washington
5. Mills College: graduate and undergraduate recruitment system
6. 2001 Tournament of Roses: game and parade collateral system
7. 2002 Tournament of Roses: game and parade collateral system

1

2

3

4

5

6

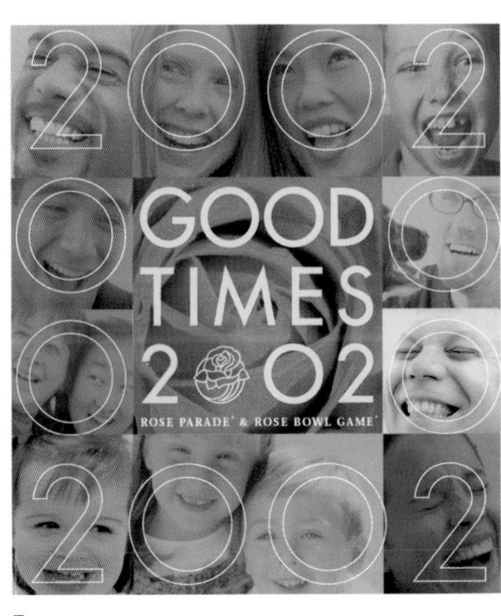

7

1. Fire, Electricity, Light and Water towers, Taichung, Taiwan
2. Avenues of Art and Design: logo, environmental communications, West Hollywood, California
3. The Boulevard: logo, environmental communications, West Hollywood, California
4. Walt Disney animated films: packaging and licensing guides
5. Union Station: entrance gateways and interior/exterior wayfinding, Los Angeles, California

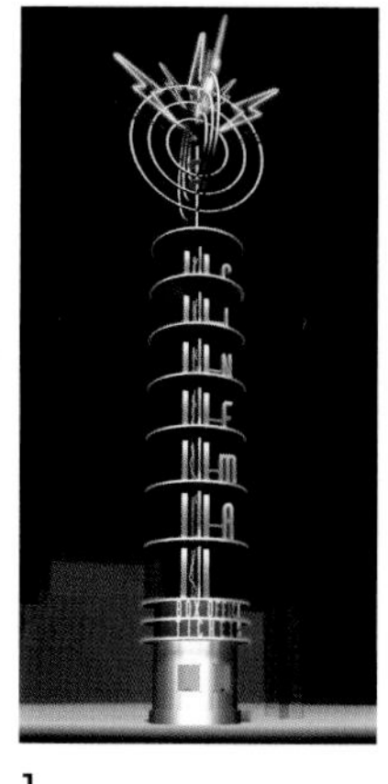

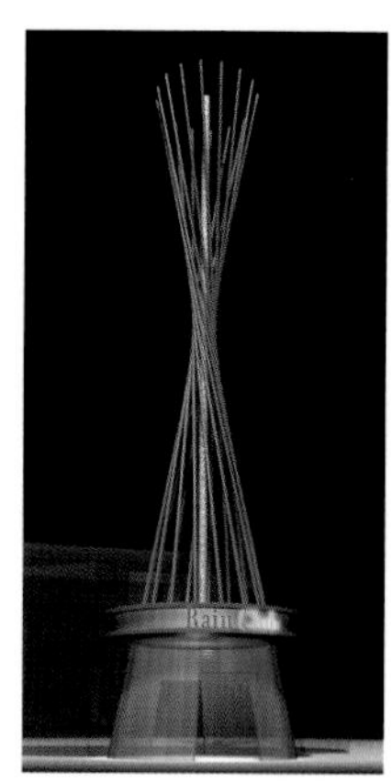

1

2

3

4

5

1

2

1. Canal City Hakata: brand identity system, logo, interior/exterior wayfinding, sculpture and merchandise line, Fukuoka, Japan
2. Millenia Walk: gateway and tenant sign criteria, Singapore

1

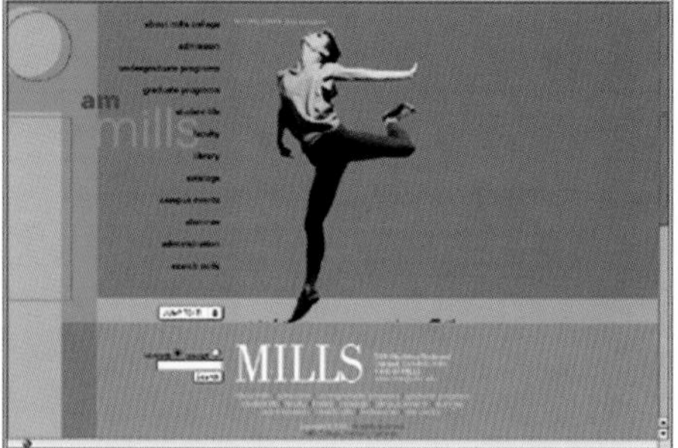

2

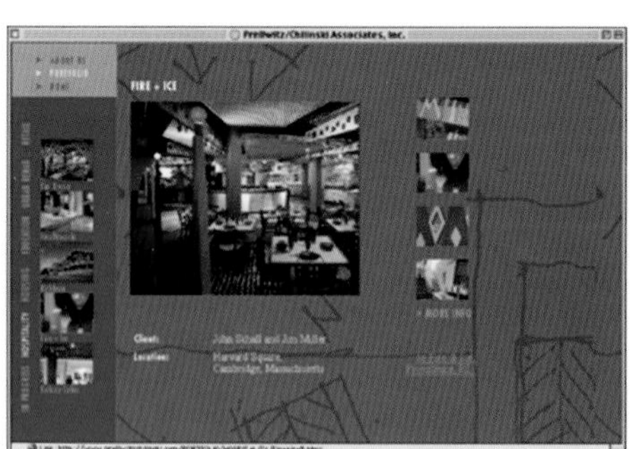

3

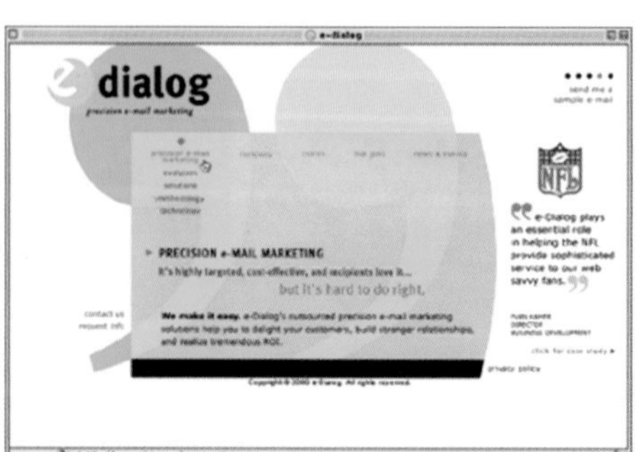

4

1. Fitlifestyles.com web site
2. Mills College web site
3. Prellwitz Chilinski Architects web site
4. e-dialog web site

p. 2 site photography by Anton Grassl, p. 3 site photography by Anton Grassl (lower left) and Andrew Davey (lower right), p. 4 product photography by Andrew Davey, site photography by Anton Grassl, p. 5 product photography by Andrew Davey, site photography by Anton Grassl (upper left) and Selbert Perkins Design (lower left), p. 6 product and site photography by Andrew Davey, p. 7 product and site photography by Selbert Perkins Design (upper), site photography by Alice Lu (lower)

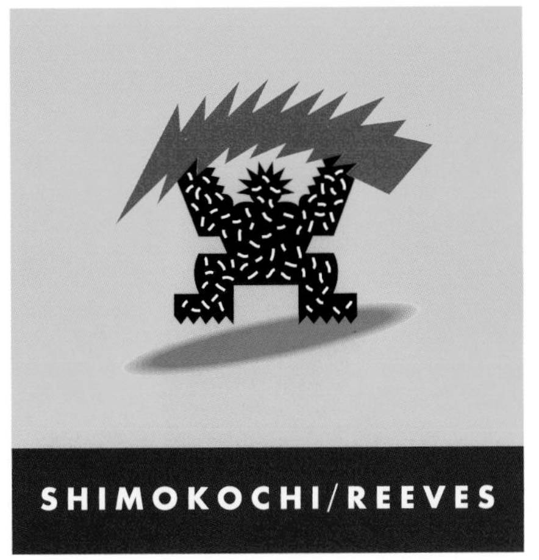

STRATEGIC VISUAL BRANDING

SHIMOKOCHI/REEVES
4465 Wilshire Blvd. Suite 305
Los Angeles, CA 90010-3704
P: 323.937.3414
F: 323.937.3417
E: info@shimokochi-reeves.com
www.shimokochi-reeves.com

SHIMOKOCHI/REEVES

Persuasive branding solutions that foster instant recall set Shimokochi/Reeves apart from other branding design firms. Brands have just seconds to break through the visual clutter with a clear and consistent message. Shimokochi/Reeves meets the challenge head-on with fresh and compelling designs that stand out in the global marketplace.

Mamoru Shimokochi's keen understanding of what it takes to create a strong brand presence is a thirty year evolution of identity work. Beginning his career at Saul Bass & Associates, Mamoru created identities such as United Airlines, United Way and the California Cheese brand symbol. Partner Anne Reeves, with twenty-five years design and marketing expertise in both the US and UK, adds a strong business focus to help clients realize their goals.

Nationally recognized for design excellence, Shimokochi/Reeves attributes the firm's longevity and success to the strategic partnership they form with their clients. The personal commitment of the principals, Mamoru Shimokochi and Anne Reeves, ensures their clients a clear channel of communication throughout each phase of the design process, and solutions that achieve results!

1. Smucker Quality Beverages, Inc.
Brand restage and 60-SKU packaging system for the After The Fall juice line

2. Line extension for aseptic juices

1. Packaging system for After The Fall's extensive Spritzer line

2. Umbrella branding program for promotional materials

1. TAG Toys, Inc.
Identity and branding program
for a diverse range of educational toys

2. Branded TAG Toys' t-shirts

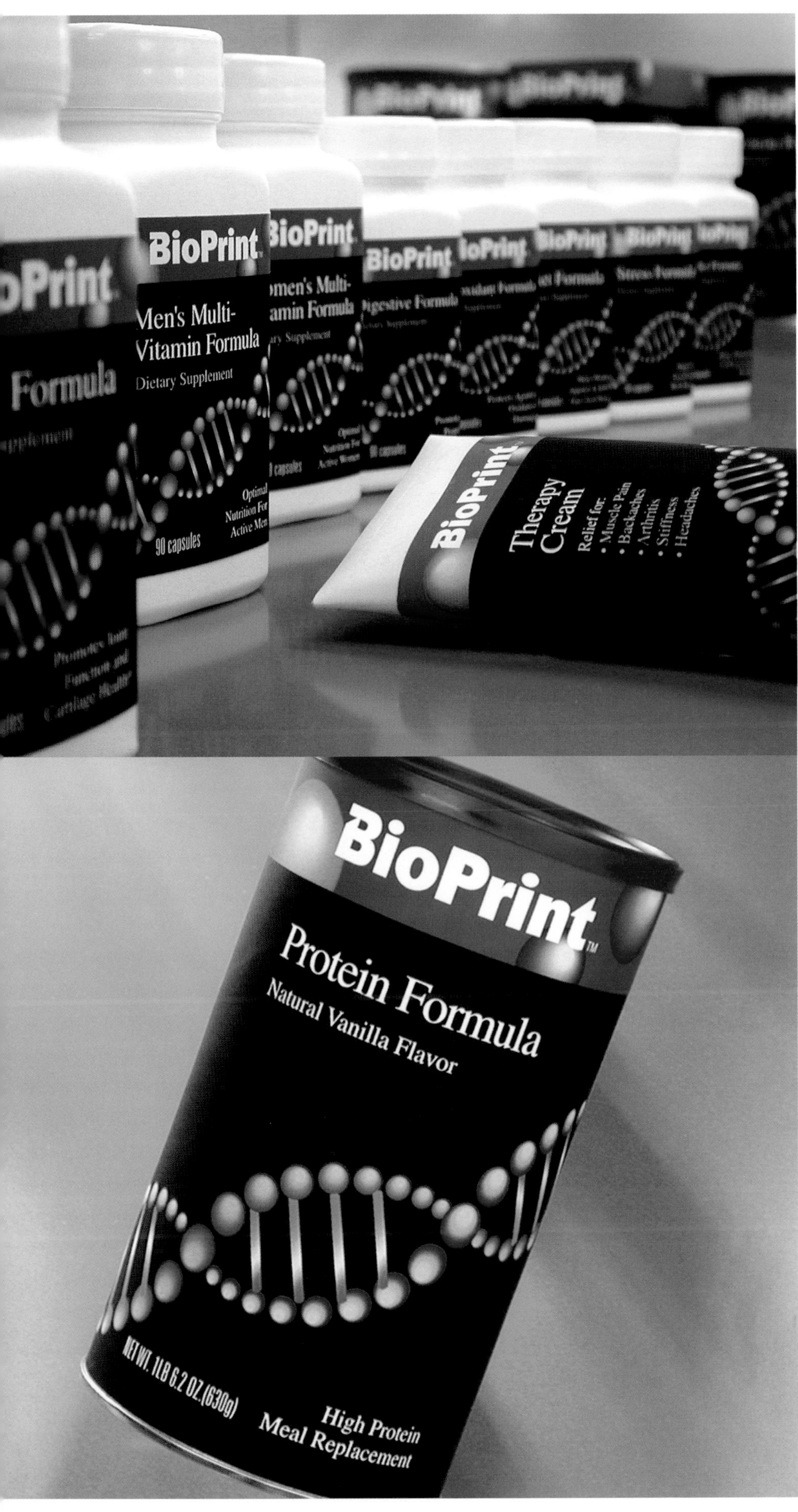

1. Fitness Today Corporation
BioPrint brand identity and package design for a new line of supplement and fitness products

2. BioPrint protein powder line

1. Richmoor Corporation
Natural High brand identity and packaging of healthy freeze-dried foods for camping and back-packing

2. Camino Real Foods, Inc.
Stuffovers brand name, brand identity and package design for a new frozen food line

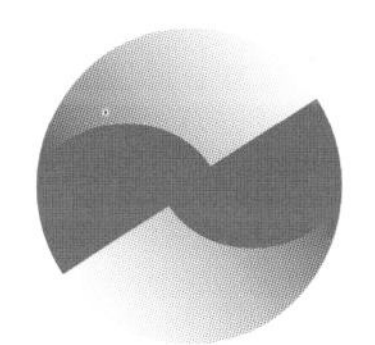

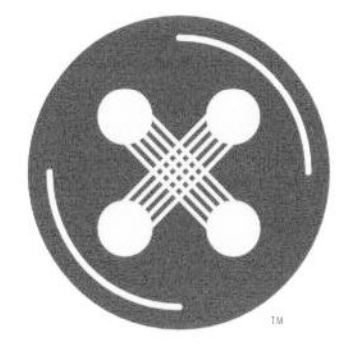

1. Camino Real Foods, Inc. - Tina's
2. Smucker Quality Beverages, Inc. After The Fall
3. X-Century Studios, Japan
4. Mingtai Insurance Company, Taiwan
5. Fitness Today Corporation - BioPrint
6. TAG Toys, Inc.
7. World Children's Baseball Foundation
8. JamboTECH, Inc.
9. Zig Ziglar Network, Inc. - Zinera
10. Beverly Sassoon International, LLC.
11. UCLA, School of Theater, Film and Television
12. Clothes The Deal
13. Warp Music, Inc., Japan
14. Tokyo Broadcasting System, Japan
15. Rainmaker Digital Pictures ROR Production Studio, Inc.

1. Warp Music Inc., Japan
Warp identity and package design for a series of CDs

2. Madison Square Press
Hot Graphics USA book cover design

AUSTIN

Sibley/Peteet Design
2905 San Gabriel
Suite 300
Austin, Texas, 78705
512.473.2333
www.spdaustin.com

DALLAS

Sibley/Peteet Design
3232 McKinney
Suite 1200
Dallas, Texas, 75204
214.969.1050
www.spddallas.com

SIBLEY/PETEET DESIGN

Two partners, two offices and two cities comprise our company, Sibley/Peteet Design. We started the studio in 1982 as a two person shop, consulting with large advertising agencies on identity and packaging and providing creative and illustration services to our small, but national, client base.

Since that time, we have grown to a staff of twenty between the offices and have developed an expertise in a spectrum of disciplines, from annual reports and packaging, to environmental graphics and web design. Our mission and passion is to become partners with our clients to develop consistent, comprehensive identities, tell their individual stories creatively, and help establish their unique personalities, in all of their medias of delivery.

After almost two decades of creating great work for folks such as Coca-Cola, Dell, Southwest Airlines, Mary Kay Cosmetics, Nokia, and the US Olympic Committee, our studios have created quite a diverse and impressive portfolio. The complexion of the works' personalities ranges from the quiet elegance of a world-famous luxury resort hotel, to the fun and frivolity of a national family restaurant group.

The pages that follow are a snapshot of recent work, as well as a few of our favorites. If you would like a closer look at SPD, stop by our virtual studios (spddallas.com or spdaustin.com). For a live visit, call Rex Peteet in Austin (512.473.2333) or Don Sibley in Dallas (214.969.1050).

Meanwhile, enjoy the printed tour.

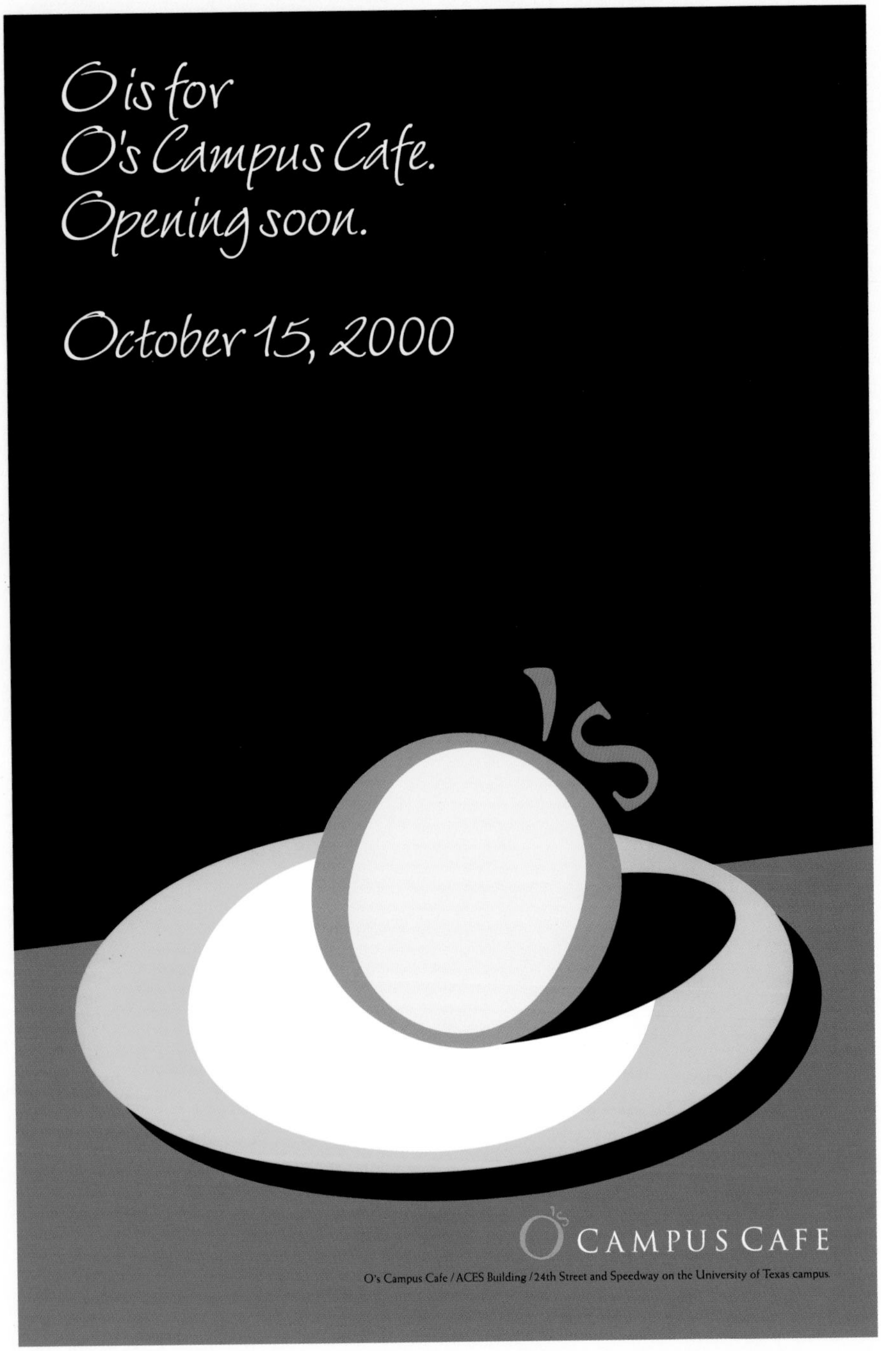

O is for
O's Campus Cafe.
Opening soon.

October 15, 2000

O's CAMPUS CAFE

O's Campus Cafe / ACES Building / 24th Street and Speedway on the University of Texas campus.

1

2

3

1. O's Campus Cafe grand opening poster
2. Logo series for O's Campus Cafe
3. Identity system for O's Campus Cafe

1-9 *(Top-Bottom, Left-Right)*

1. Bares Capital Management
2. Tips Iron & Steel
3. Scotland Yards, a designer fabric boutique

6. Hyde Park Gym, a hardcore lifters gym
7. Texas Commission for the Arts
8. 180°, Savane's 'all terrain' clothing line

7. Lone Star Donuts
8. American Heart Association
9. Paramount Theatre, a performing arts venue

Sibley/Peteet Design, Austin

1

2

3

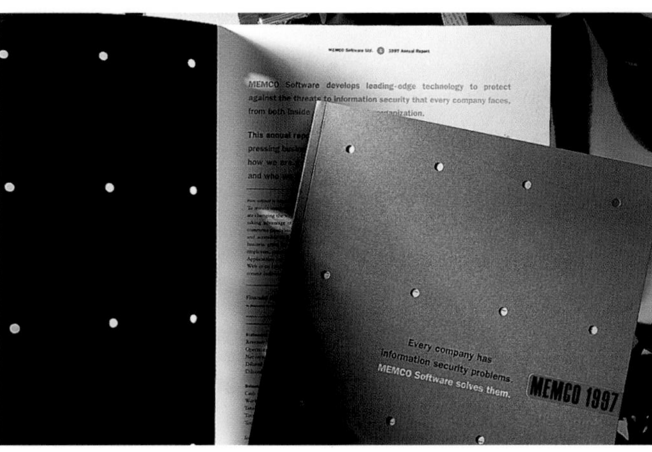

4

5

6

1. Training Process icons from the Temple-Inland 2000 Annual Report
2. Temple-Inland 2000 Annual Report
3. Coca-Cola environmental brochure
4. MEMCO 1997 Annual Report
5. The 401(k) Company marketing brochure
6. The 401(k) Company sower icon

1

WatersMark

2

1. Brochure for Watersmark, a golf course and residential community resort
2. Watersmark logotype

1

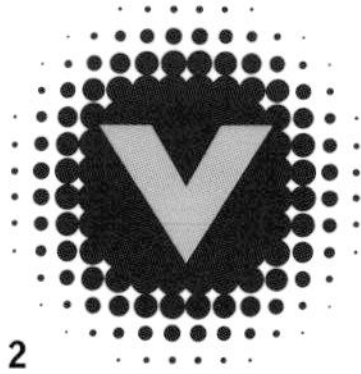

2

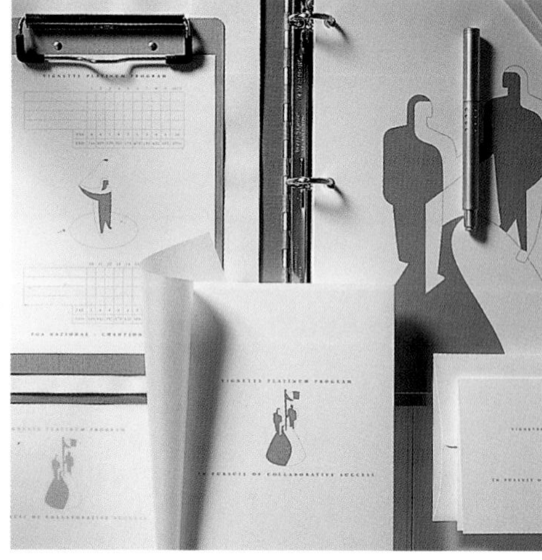

3

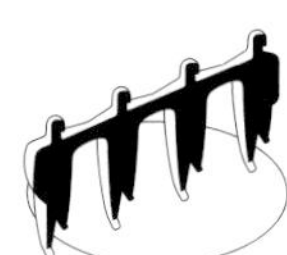

4

1. Vignette packaging system
2. Logo for Vignette, a web content management software developer
3. Vignette Platinum Program brochure/system
4. Collaborative Success icons from the Vignette Platinum brochure

1

2

1. Gattitown graphics, interiors & apparel, a destination that serves food, fun and festivities for the entire family
2. G-force logo, Gattitown's pizza delivery service

1

spa at home
magnets+heat
feel good. lift your spirit of wellness.
SOLUNA.

3

2

1. Hydrade sports drink packaging and icons
2. Soluna packaging, a product line that combines heat with magnetic therapy
3. Soluna spa at home poster

1-20 *(Top-Bottom, Left-Right)*

1. King Photography
2. Mindgames.tv
3. AvenueOne Properties
4. Zilliant
5. Austin Film Festival
6. Mary Kay Cosmetics
7. Texas Assoc. for Stolen Children
8. Graduate School of Business, UT
9. GSD&M Advertising
10. rx.com
11. BocaVision
12. Mother Hen Software
13. Shiner Beer
14. Wardrobe Clothing
15. Waters Edge
16. HandTech.com
17. Critical Communications
18. Vectris Communications
19. Haggar Apparel
20. FamilyForward

1

2

1. Logo for Haggar Clothing Co. Spring Collection
2. Series of promotional brochures for Weyerhaeuser Paper: Form, Fashion, and Food
3. Promotional brochure for Weyerhaeuser Paper: Pozos, The Lost Legend of Mexico

3

1

1. Branding and retail packaging for the Bellagio, Las Vegas

1

2

3

4

1. Illustrations for Shiner Beer packaging
2. Packaging for Veratrim, a line of nutritional weight management products
3. Logo and packaging for Mary Kay
4. Packaging for Shiner Beer

1

2

3

4

1. Packaging from Scattergories from Milton Bradley
2. Packaging for Taboo from Milton Bradley
3. Packaging for Ruffles Slammers, canned potato chips
4. Packaging for Pete's Wicked Sampler

1

2

3

1. Icon and cookbook for Nuevo TexMex from Chronicle Books
2. Sales promotional literature for Avesta, a managed 401(k) plan from Chase Bank
3. Promotional brochures for The Image Bank

1. Indresco Annual Report
2. Pillowtex Annual Report
3. Zale Corporation Annual Report

4. TXU 1999 Annual Report
5. ACS Annual Report
6. TXU 2000 Annual Report

7. Global Industrial Technologies Annual Report
8. Belo Annual Report
9. RadioShack Annual Report

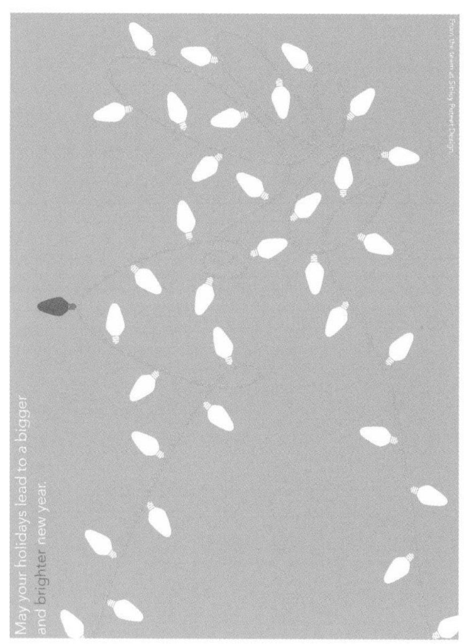

1

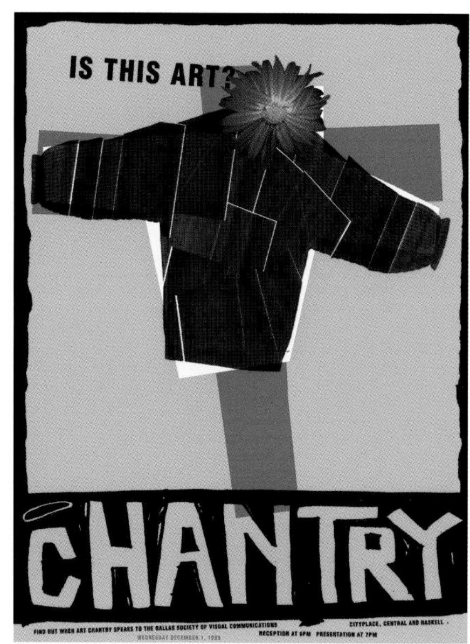

2

3

1. Holiday greeting poster for Sibley Peteet Design
2. Poster for the Dallas Society of Visual Communications (DSVC) announcing a talk by Art Chantry
3. Web sites for Belo, TXU, Zale Corporation, and Shiner Beer

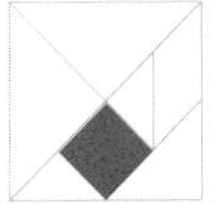

1424 Marcelina Avenue
Torrance, CA 90501
Phone: 310. 381. 0170
Fax: 310. 381. 0169
www.soohoodesign.com

SOOHOO DESIGNERS

At SooHoo Designers, we treat the creative process itself creatively to develop solutions to the varied challenges our clients present. Our approach is to explore thoroughly to find the best solution possible. Yet, while reaching for the distinctive, we never lose sight of what is strategically sound.

SooHoo Designers consistently produces award-winning, challenging, yet tactically solid solutions for companies in a broad range of industries. This ability to wield traditional tools in nonconventional ways exemplifies our global design approach. Our clients, serving regional, national and international markets, also benefit from our experience and multi-lingual capabilities.

There is no single "SooHoo Look." Each of our solutions is unique and is intended not just to meet, but to surpass, our clients' needs and expectations.

1. Epson Stylus Pro Series product brochure.
2. Epson brand packaging.
3. Packaging style guide.

::STRATEGIC BRANDING::

1

2

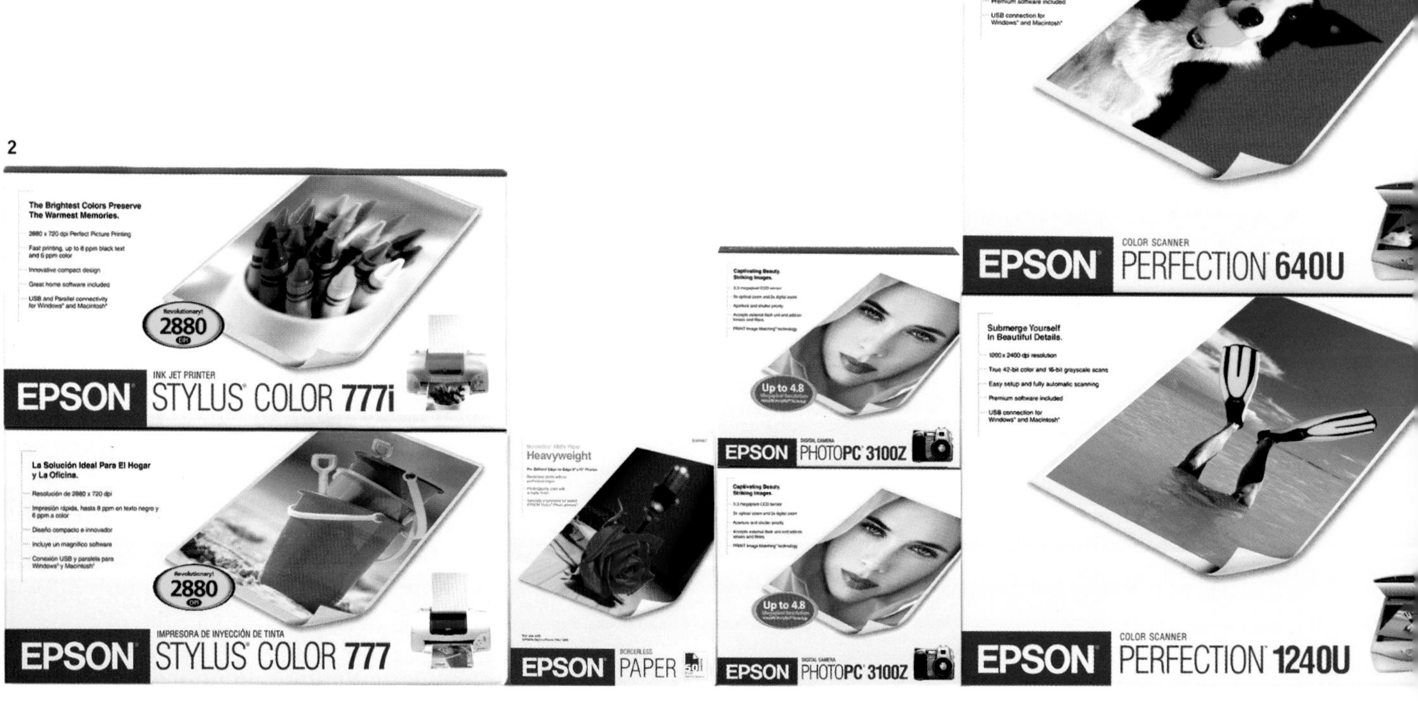

PACKAGING
NOMENCLATURE CALLOUTS
LAYOUT TYPOGRAPHY SPECIFICATIONS
EPSON Retail Packaging Guidelines
PRINTERS
EPSON PRINTERS
Premium Performance
That's Right On Target.
Revolutionary!
2880
DPI
INK JET PRINTER
STYLUS COLOR 000

3

Premium Performance
That's Right On Target.
2880 x 720 dpi Perfect Picture Printing
Ultra fast, Photo Quality color and up to 13 ppm laser sharp black text printing
Professional options – Postscript and networking
Heavy duty 5000 page per month capability
USB and Parallel connectivity for Windows and Macintosh
Revolutionary!
2880
DPI
EPSON
INK JET PRINTER
STYLUS COLOR 980
STYLUS COLOR 880i
STYLUS COLOR 880
Photo Paper 4"x6"
Premium Glossy Photo Paper
EPSON PAPER
EPSON INK

SooHoo Designers

1. Elar Partners promotion.

2. Sales incentive program premiums.

3. Stationery, forms, and luggage tags for sales incentive program.

4. Promotional trip itinerary booklet.

1

2

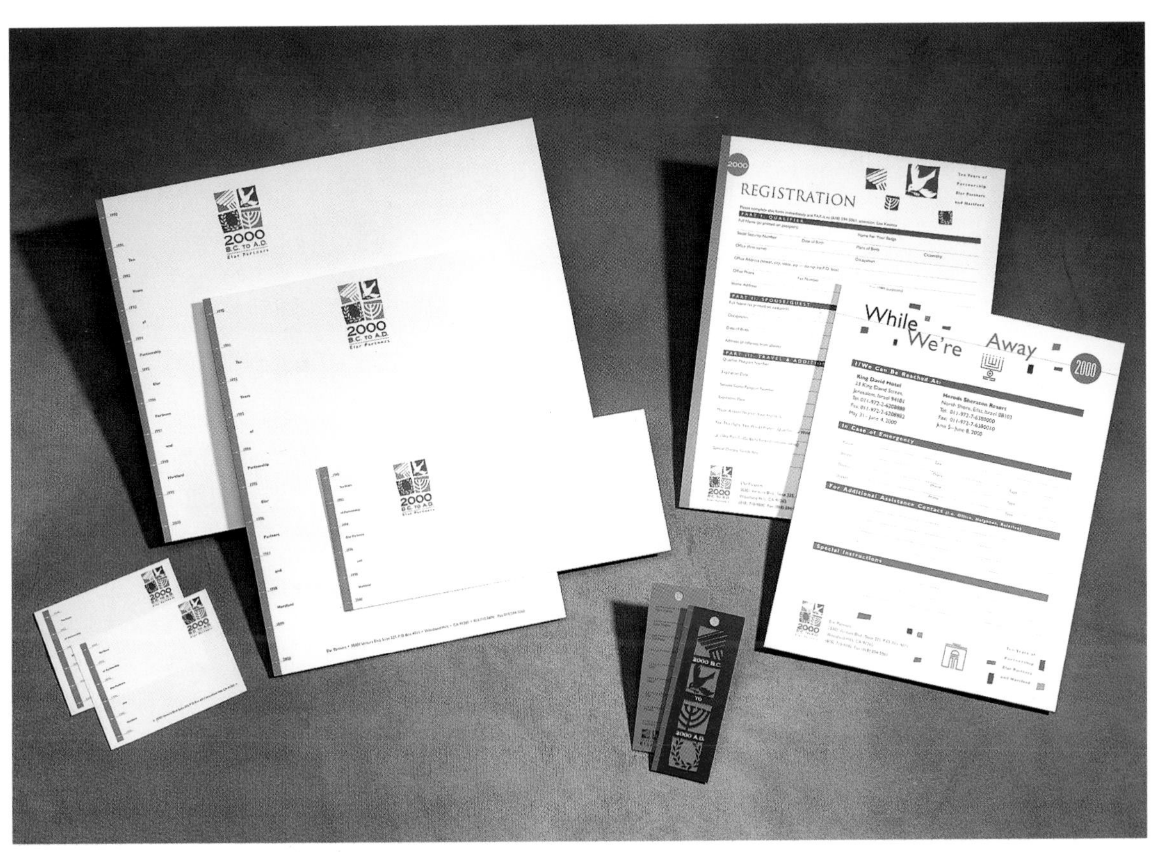
REGISTRATION
While We're Away
2000
2000 B.C. to A.D.

3

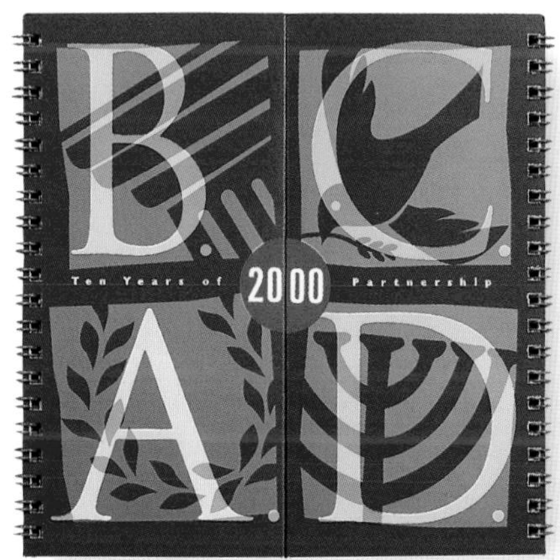
B.C.
Ten Years of 2000 Partnership
A.D.

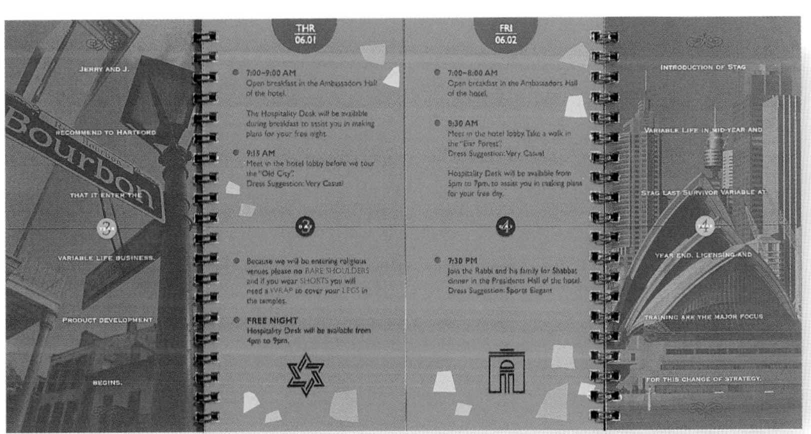
THR 06.01
FRI 06.02
Bourbon
FREE NIGHT

4

1. Identity and stationery program for Union Transport Corporation.
2. Corporate identity guide.
3. UTi corporate capabilities brochure.
4. Logo for Iida Transport.
5. Identity for CDC teen health awareness campaign.
6. Identity for UTi Corporation.
7. Identity for GSC.
8. Identity for CDC teen health awareness campaign.
9. Program identity for Elar Partners.
10. Identity for Wings Messenger Service.
11. Program identity for Elar Partners.
12. Proposed logo for Ontario Visitors & Convention Bureau.

1

2

3

4

5

6

GSC

ORGANIZATION
STRATEGY
DESIGN & DEVELOPMENT

7

keep-it-movin'

8

9

10

11

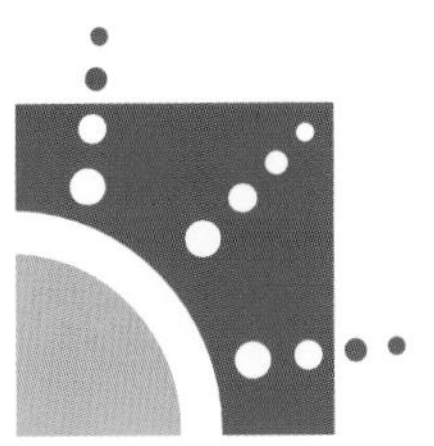

12

1. Web site design for Shimoda Design Group.
2. Proposed web site development for Cocuyé Jazz Club and Restaurant.
3. Web site design for Top Flight Golf Club.

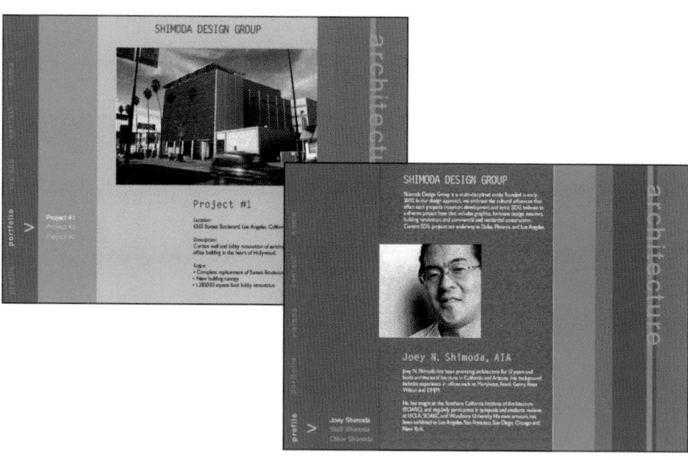

1

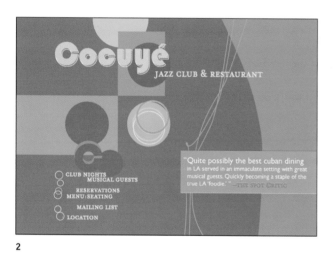

2

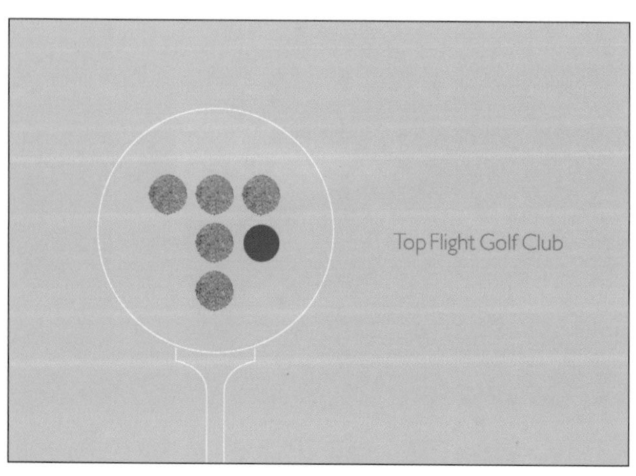

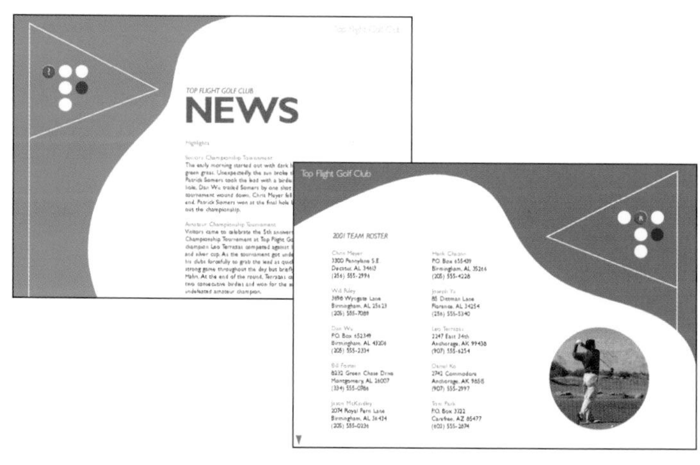

3

Stoltze Design, Inc.
49 Melcher Street, 4th floor
Boston, Massachusetts 02210
617.350.7109
clif@stoltzedesign.com
www.stoltzedesign.com

STOLTZE DESIGN, INC.

The creative process is driven by
ideas that begin
to
form and take shape
by
emerging from,
evolving from,
growing larger than,
and
gaining momentum with
the ideas you had
just a short moment before.

Working through the creative process is an organic, unpredictable way to spend your day–but for those who work at Stoltze Design, it is the only way to get work done–and done well. As a collaborative of designers, project managers and technologists who share ideas and lead exploration that goes beyond the expected, the studio is committed to a thorough understanding of the nuances and details of every project it takes on. In fact, the depth of creative curiosity is most evident in the studio's diverse portfolio and eclectic client list. It's an approach that works well for Stoltze, and ultimately their clients, since keen insight initiates the creative process in the first place.

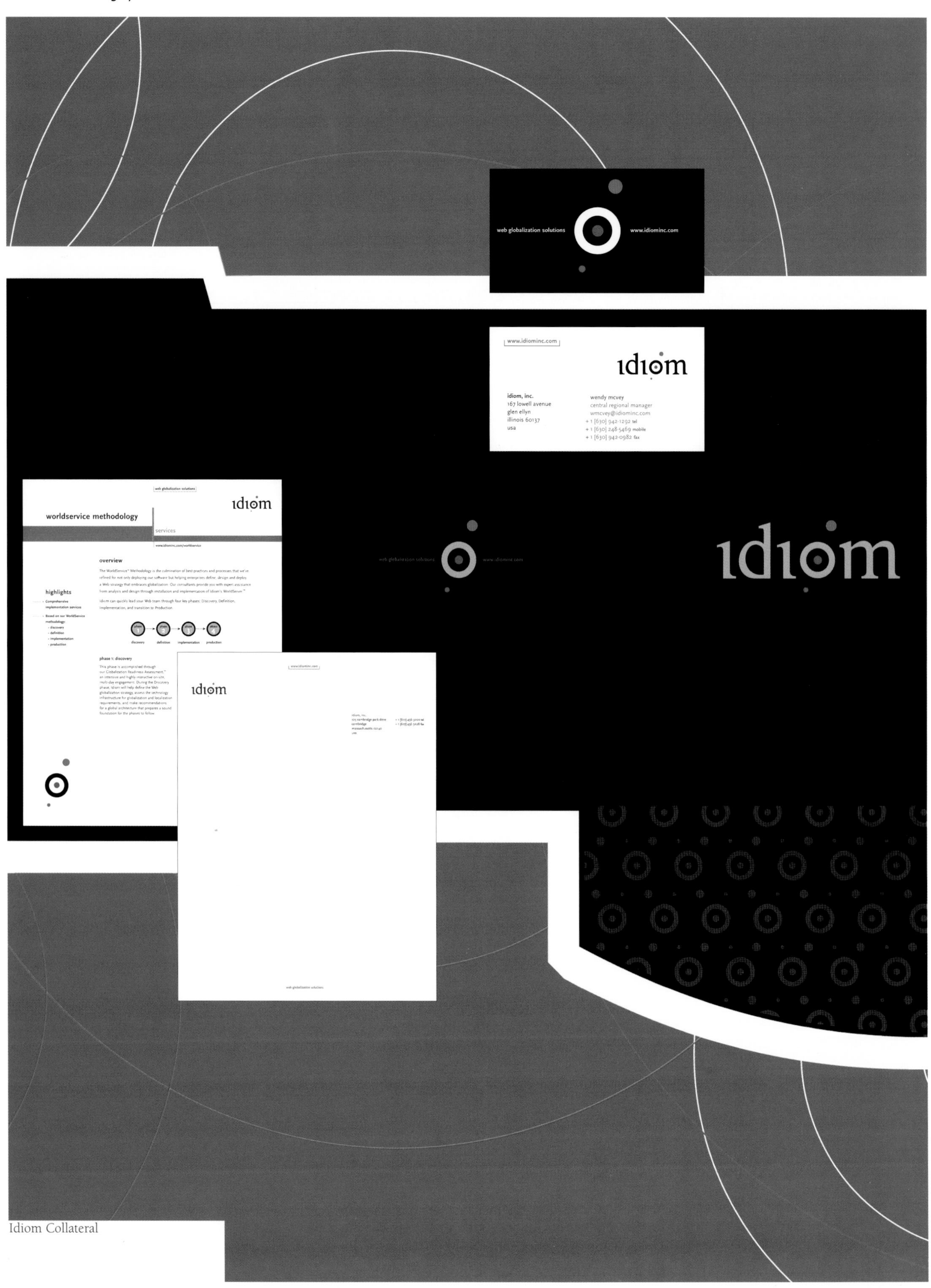

Idiom Collateral

01

02

03

04

05

06

07

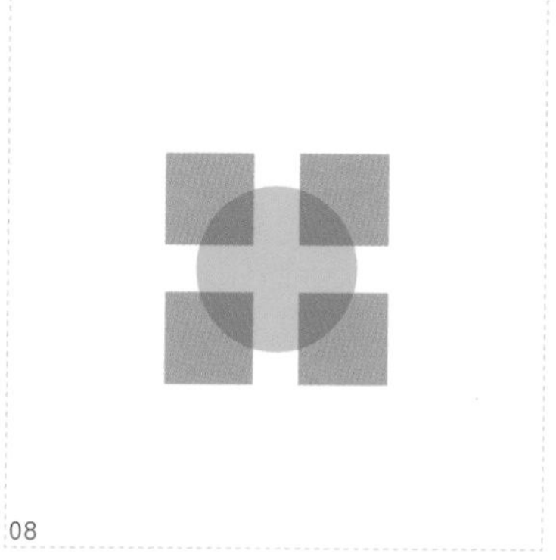

08

09

CORPORATE IDENTITY

THE PROVERBIAL CHANCE AT MAKING A STRONG FIRST IMPRESSION.

01 Lunch TV
02 Six Red Marbles
03 Empirix
04 Fact Monster <www.factmonster.com>
05 Opholio
06 September Productions
07 Cakewalk
08 Planet Interactive
09 Chelsea Pictures

INTEGRATED COMMUNICATION

TRANSCENDING MEDIUMS WITH ONE UNIFIED DESIGN APPROACH.

01 MassArt Website <www.massart.edu>

02 MassArt Graduate School Viewbook

03 MassArt Undergraduate Viewbook Cover and Interior Spreads

04 MassArt Postcard Series

01

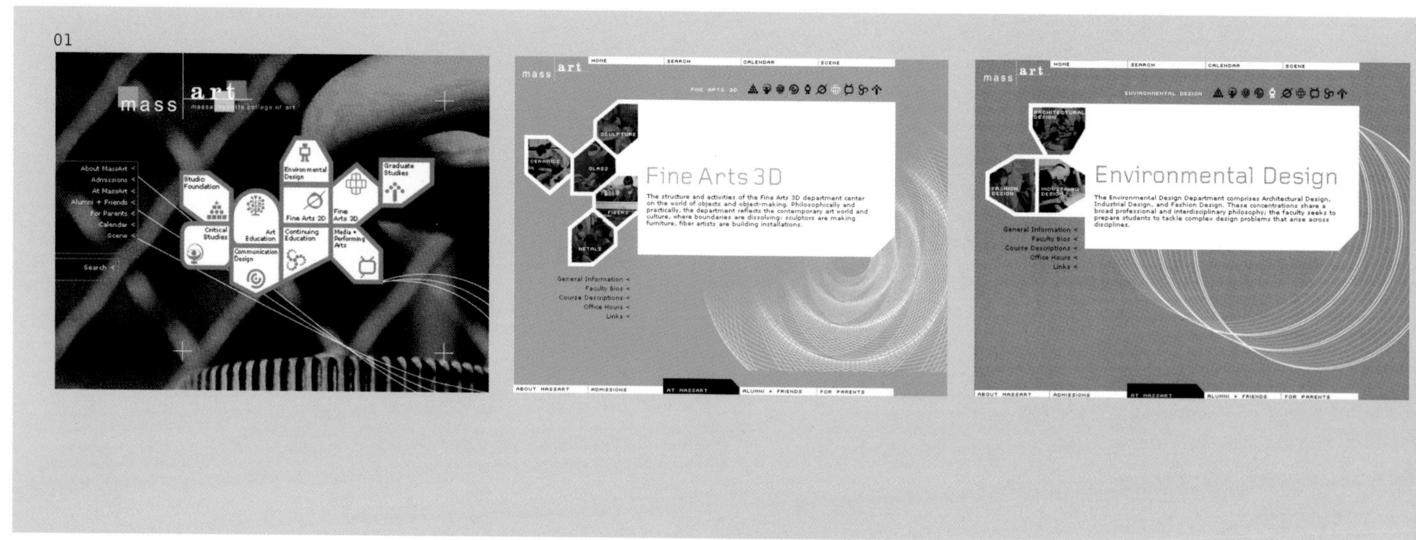

02

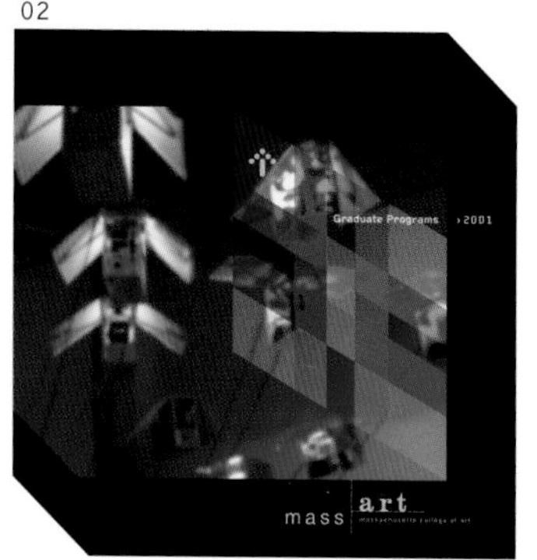

03A

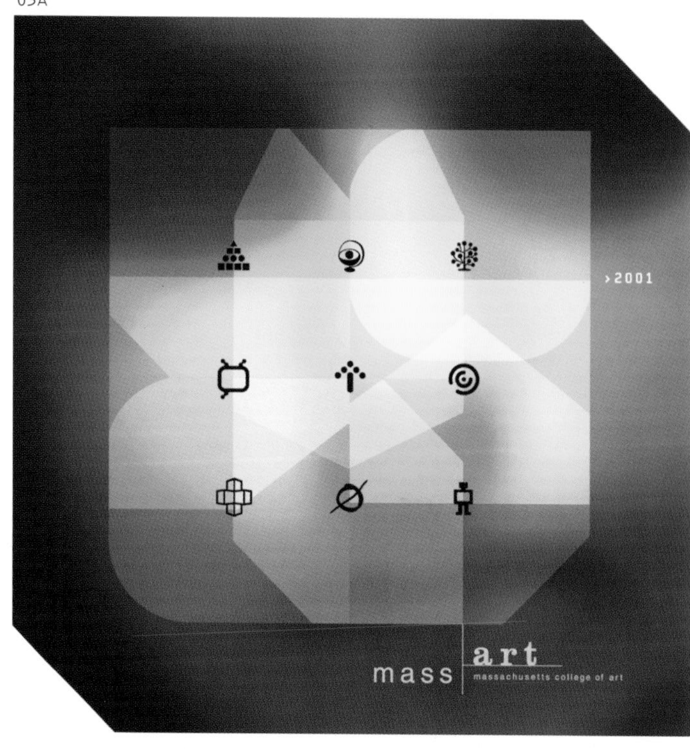

04

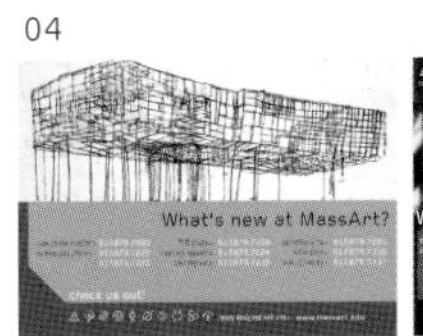
What's new at MassArt?
check us out!

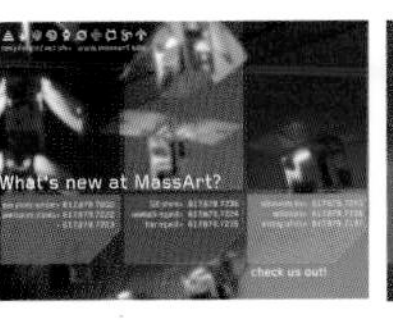
What's new at MassArt?
check us out!

What's new at MassArt?
check us out!

What's new at MassArt?

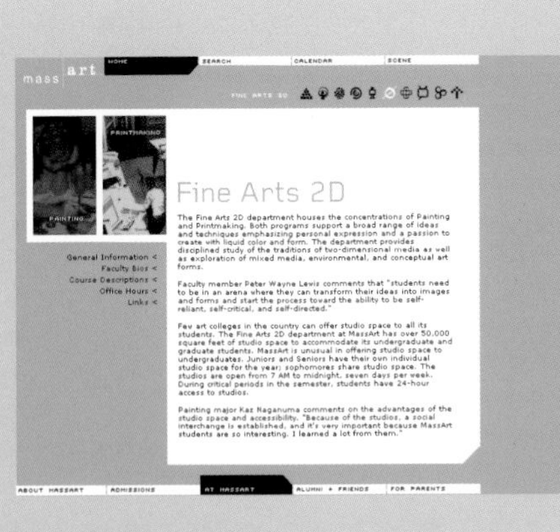
mass art
HOME
SEARCH
CALENDAR
SCENE
Fine Arts 2D
General Information <
Faculty Bios <
Course Descriptions <
Office Hours <
Links <
ABOUT MASSART
ADMISSIONS
AT MASSART
ALUMNI + FRIENDS
FOR PARENTS

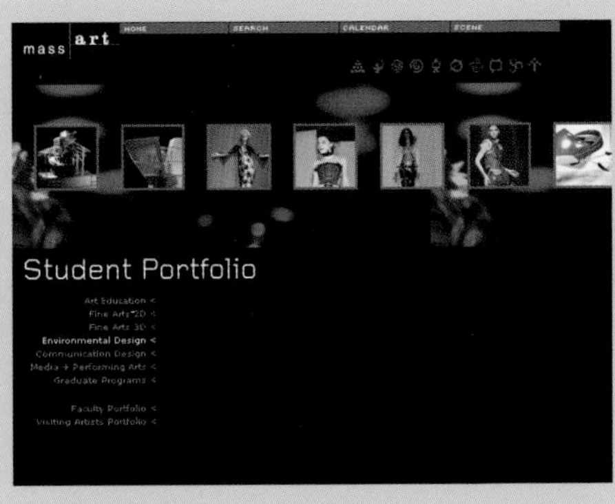
mass art
HOME
SEARCH
CALENDAR
SCENE
Student Portfolio
Art Education <
Fine Arts 2D <
Fine Arts 3D <
Environmental Design <
Communication Design <
Media + Performing Arts <
Graduate Programs <
Faculty Portfolio <
Visiting Artists Portfolio <

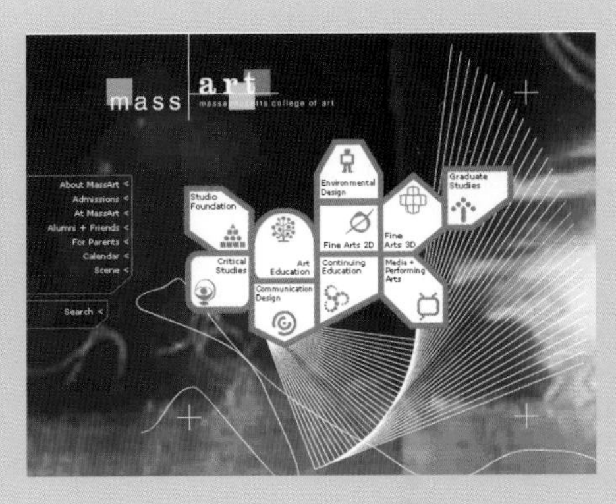
mass art
About MassArt <
Admissions <
At MassArt <
Alumni + Friends <
For Parents <
Calendar <
Scene <
Search <
Studio Foundation
Environmental Design
Graduate Studies
Critical Studies
Art Education
Fine Arts 2D
Fine Arts 3D
Continuing Education
Communication Design
Media + Performing Arts

03B

table OF contents
06 President's Statement
10 Exhibitions
11 Visiting Artists
14 Studio Foundation
18 Critical Studies
24 Art Education
28 Communication Design
34 Environmental Design
40 Fine Arts 2D
46 Fine Arts 3D
52 Media + Performing Arts
62 Art Education Graduate Programs
66 Master of Fine Arts

Fine Arts 3D

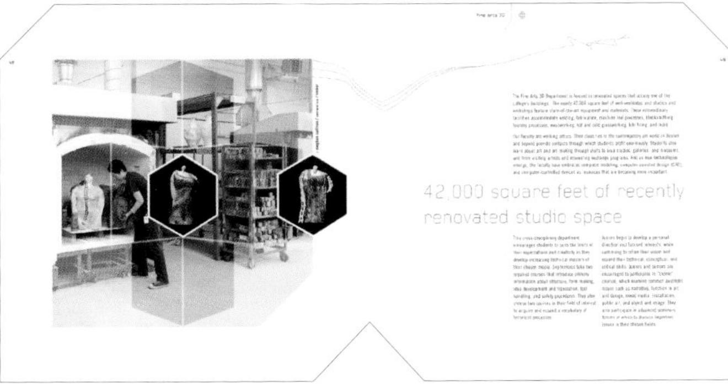
42,000 square feet of recently renovated studio space

AUDIO VISUALS

CREATING A STRONG CONNECTION BETWEEN SIGHT AND SOUND.

01 Splashdown CD
02 Pell Mell LP Front and Back
03 Charlene Single
04 Annette Farrington CD
05 Trance 3-CD Box Set

Ohm 3-CD Box Set

01

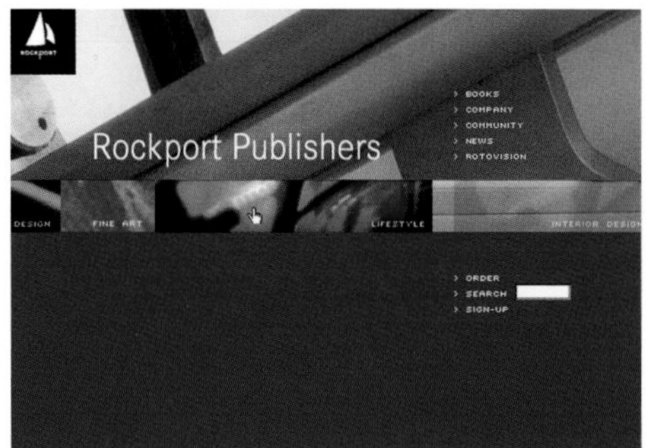

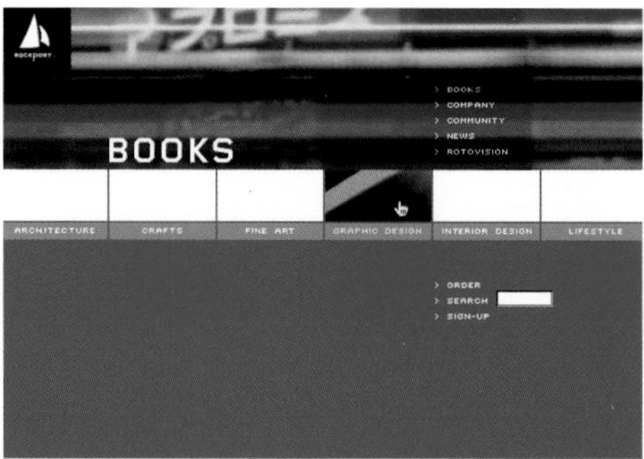

02

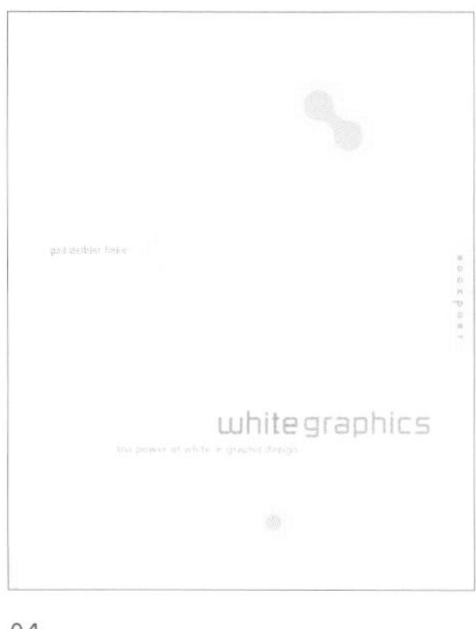

03 04 05

BOOK SMARTS

TYPOGRAPHY AND STYLE THAT WELCOMES A BOOK BE JUDGED BY ITS COVER.

01 Rockport Website <www.rockpub.com>
02 Minimal Graphics Book
03 Packaging Graphics Book
04 White Graphics Book
04 New Design Book Series

Studio 2055
2055 Westwood Drive
Carlsbad, California 92008
760.729.8205
www.studio2055.com

STUDIO 2055

Beginning as a small coastal design studio with big ideas, Studio 2055 remains true to its founding principles by creating design, advertising and marketing campaigns that resonate with consumers and clients alike.

"Our long-term goal was to attract a group of respected clients without simultaneously building an enormous staff and overhead," recalls Creative Director Nanette Newbry. "We wanted to live near the beach and pursue our artistic careers while working with clients who appreciate intelligent design and advertising as well as effective branding programs. We've succeeded far beyond our anticipated goals."

Richard Dowdy, Nanette's partner in Studio 2055, is a long-time surfer and resident of San Diego's North County. His extensive knowledge of popular culture, coupled with his talent for writing, bring a depth to the studio that balances Nanette's creative strengths, forming an in-demand design and marketing team.

Studio 2055 in Carlsbad has assembled a dedicated creative staff that has helped attract a stellar list of clients. The firm's success-based regimen consists of an intense company and product analysis prior to beginning each project, focusing on creating an effective partnership with each client. This process has enabled Studio 2055 to build a strong reputation for results-driven programs. The emphasis on marketing communications, advertising, corporate identity, product branding, creative writing and website design has kept Studio 2055 humming at a constant pace for the past 19 years.

The principles as espoused by the partners of Studio 2055 are best exemplified by the company's tagline: "Smart Thinking, Creative Solutions."

IPMOBILENET

2

1

3

1. Corporate identity and collateral: IP MobileNet
2. Icons for book: Hot Springs Portable Spas
3. Corporate capabilities brochure: HM Electronics
2. Environmental fleet graphics: Taylor Made/ adidas Golf

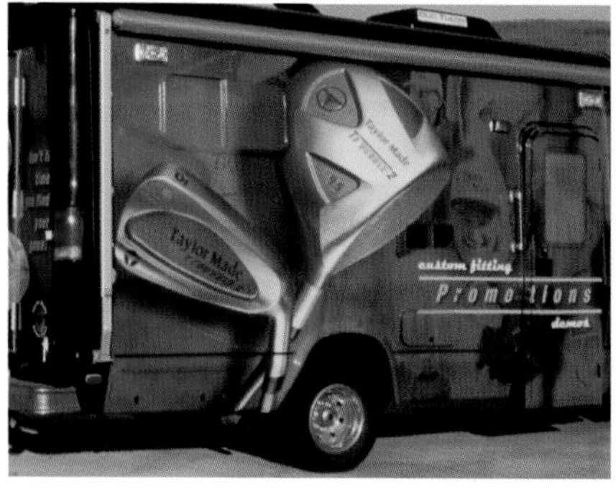

4

1

1. Program identity and collateral in English and Spanish: CalWORKs

2. Publication design and illustration: Taylor Made/adidas Golf

3. Investment relations: Collateral Therapeutics

2

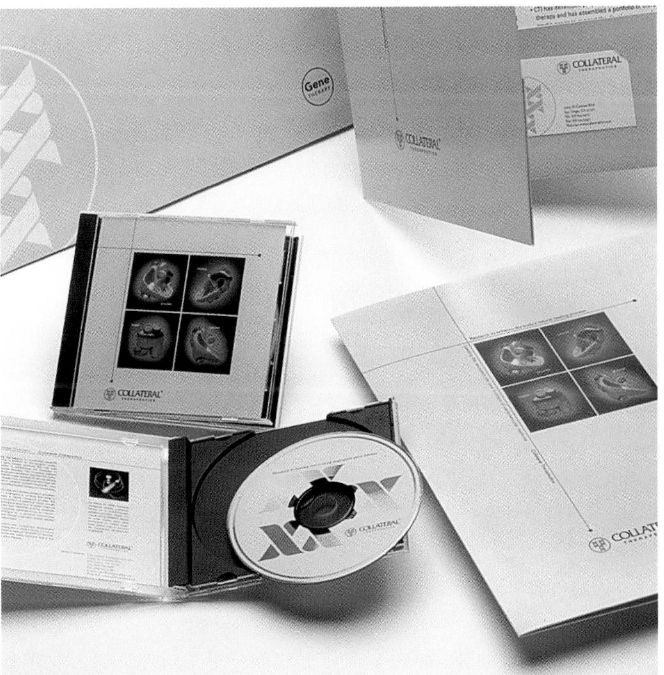

3

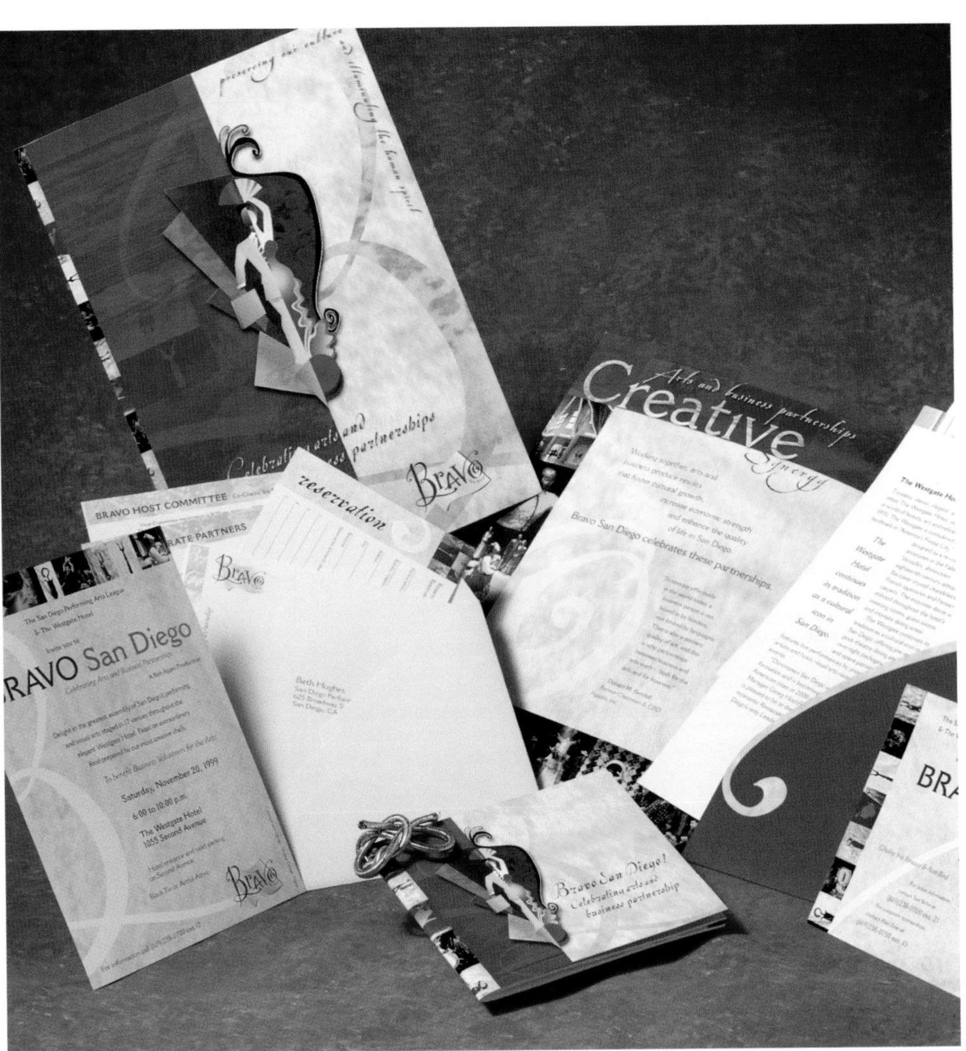

1

MAINLY MOZART

2

3

4

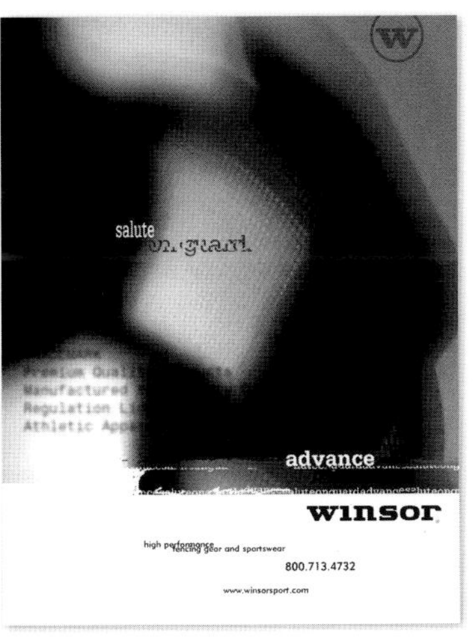

5

1. Event identity, collateral and advertising campaign: San Diego Performing Arts League
2. Corporate identity and brochure: Mainly Mozart
3. Real estate development package: Villa La Estancia
4. Apparel design, product branding: Winsor Sport Fencing
5. Advertising campaign: Winsor Sport Fencing

1. Special edition packaging: Stolichnaya Gold Vodka
2. Product design and holiday packaging: Cutty Sark
3. Book design and packaging promotion: Westwood Writers Group

1

2

3

1. Education catalogs: Gemological Institute of America
2. Website design: Rotary Club International
3. Website design and development: Photron
4. Website design and development: Gemological Institute of America

1

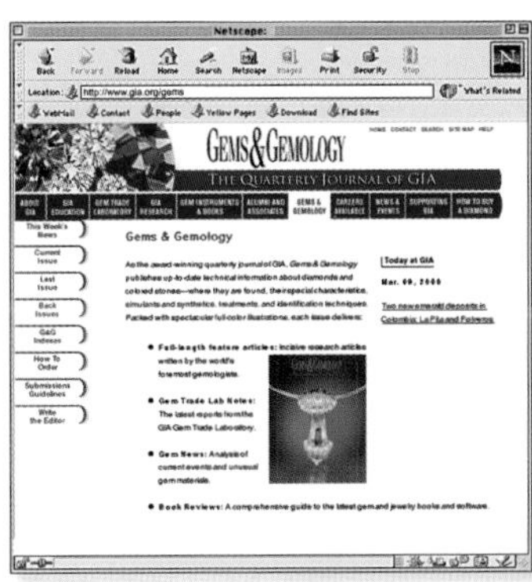

2

3

4

1	2	3	4
5	6	7	8
9	10	11	12

1. Hewlett-Packard
2. Reebok
3. American Cancer Society
4. Upper Deck
5. Hybritech
6. Voit Sports
7. Hot Springs Portable Spas
8. Self-promotion
9. Broadbandbid.com
10. Winsor Sport Fencing
11. Rachel Grosvenor Home for Women & Children
12. International Engine Works

2055 Westwood Drive Carlsbad, California 92008 P. 760.729.8205 F. 760.729.2557 www.studio2055.com info@studio2055.com

Suissa Design
12000 Biscayne Boulevard
Suite 510
Miami, FL 33181
t- 305.899.9991
f- 305.899.1110
www.suissadesign.com

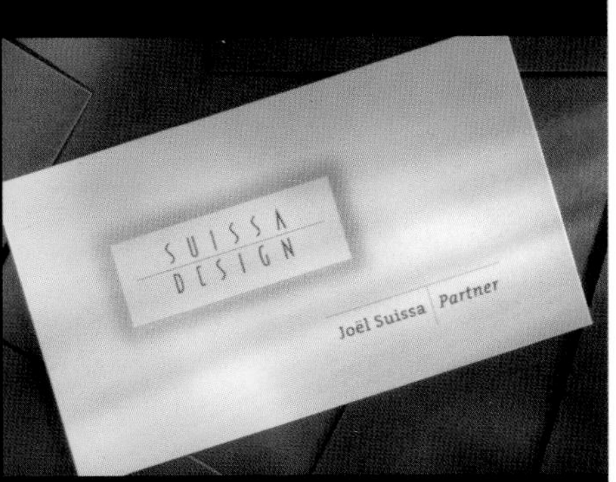

SUISSA DESIGN

Understand.

Interpret.

Communicate.

☺

1. Ad congratulating Steven Soderbergh on his double Oscar nomination
2. New products media kit
3. Annual report
4. Product labels
5. Hurricane preparedness brochure

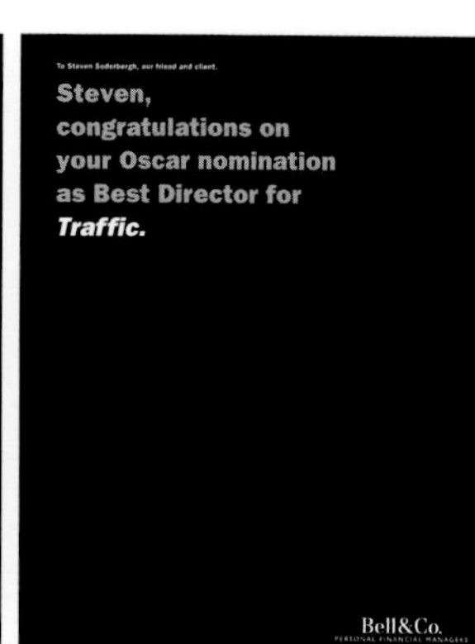

1

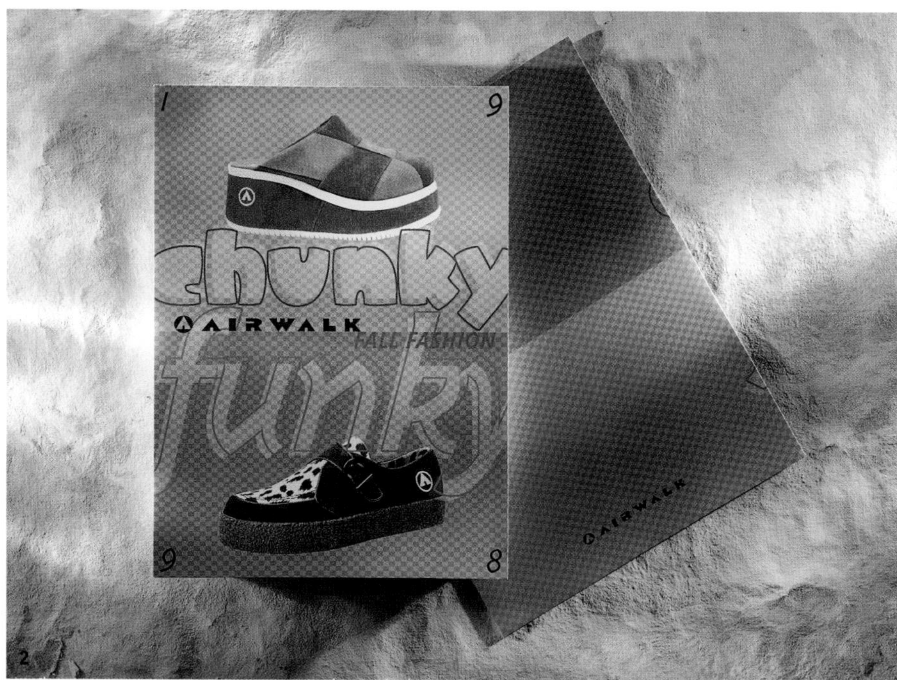

2

3

4

5

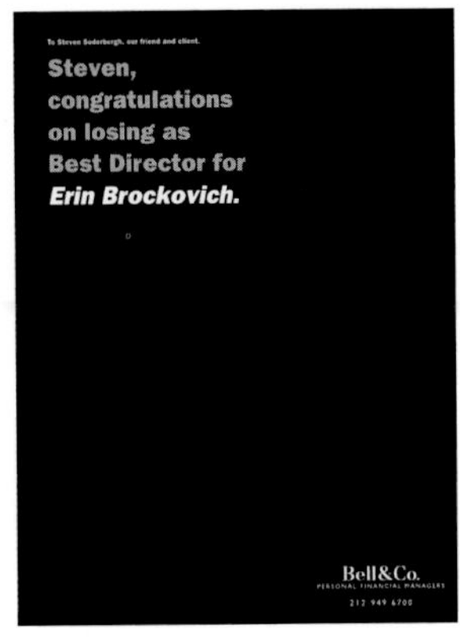

1. Ad congratulating Steven Soderbergh on his Oscar award
2. Hospital brochure series
3. Travel promotional brochure
4. Exhibit display banners
5. Promotional products catalog
6. Restaurant gift certificate package
7. Product labels

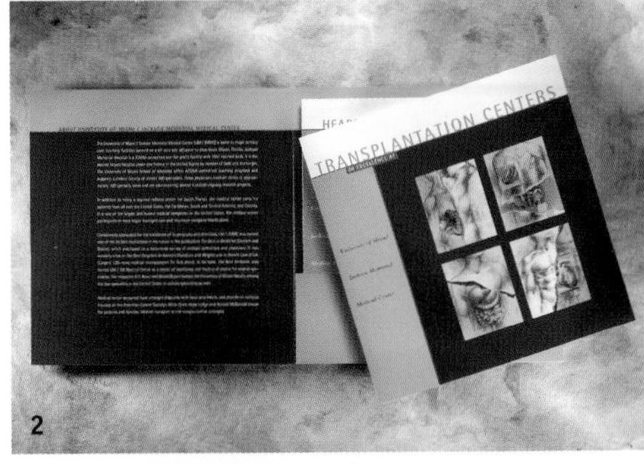

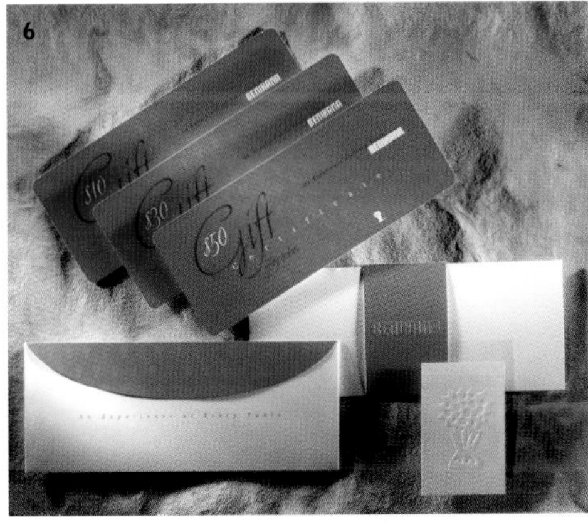

1

2

4

3

5

1. Ad congratulating Peter MacNicol on his Screen Actors Guild nomination
2. Annual report
3. Annual report
4. Label and bottle design
5. Corporate identity and stationery

1

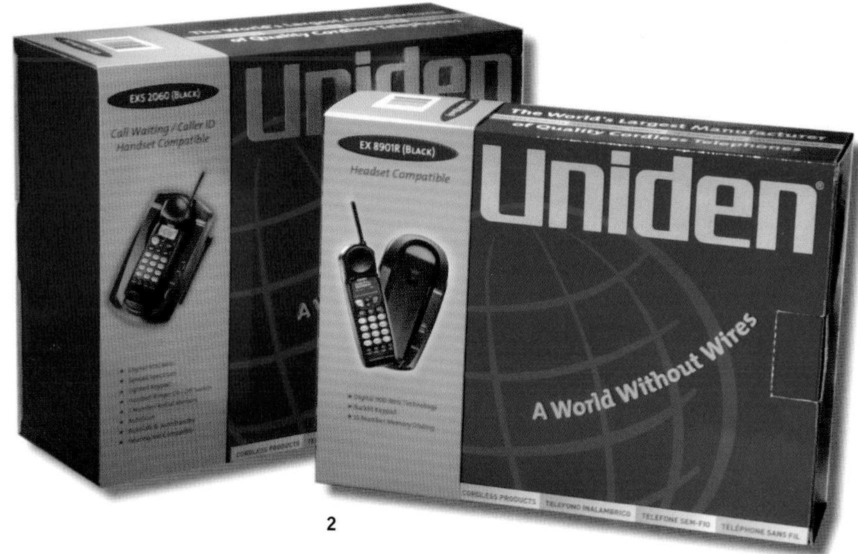

2

1. Ad congratulating *Sabrina, the Teenage Witch*, on its 100th episode
2. Packaging system
3. Package and wrapper design
4. Identity and package design for digital camera
5. Package design
6. Media sales kit

3

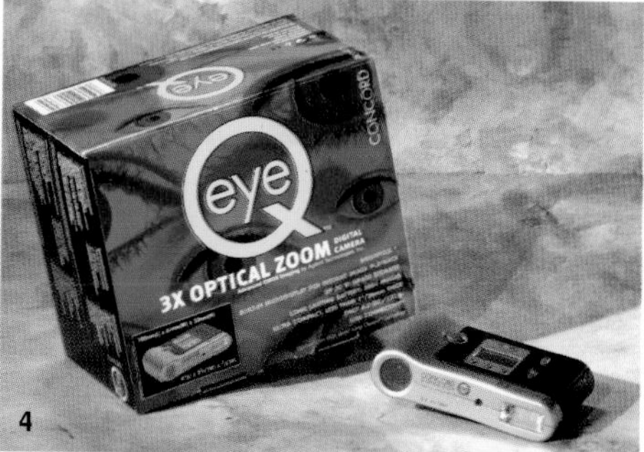

4

5

6

1

2

1. Ad congratulating Bill O'Reilly for reaching the *New York Times* Bestseller List
2. Identity and promotion design
3. Room service menu
4. Museum exhibit catalogs
5. Identity and stationery design
6. Media kit and product catalog

3

4

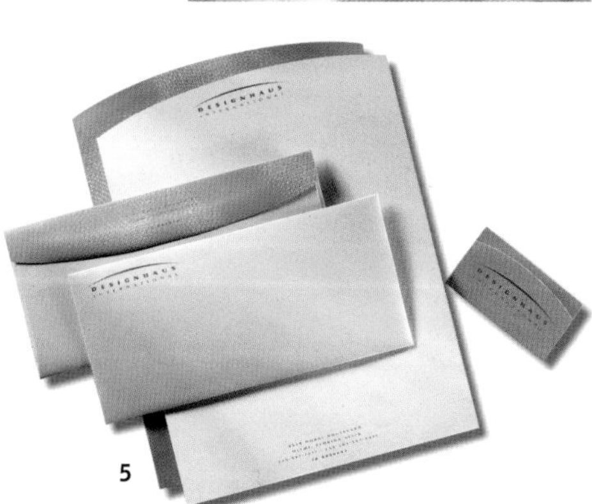

5

6

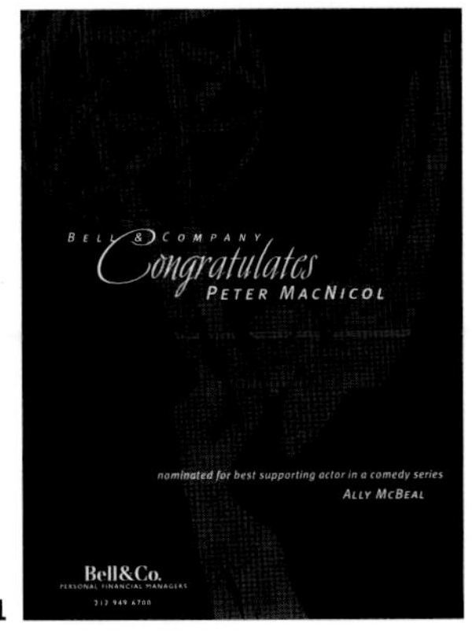

1. Ad congratulating Peter MacNicol on his Emmy nomination
2. Media kit for the Pat Metheny Group
3. Capabilities brochure
4. Museum inaugural invitation
5. Annual report

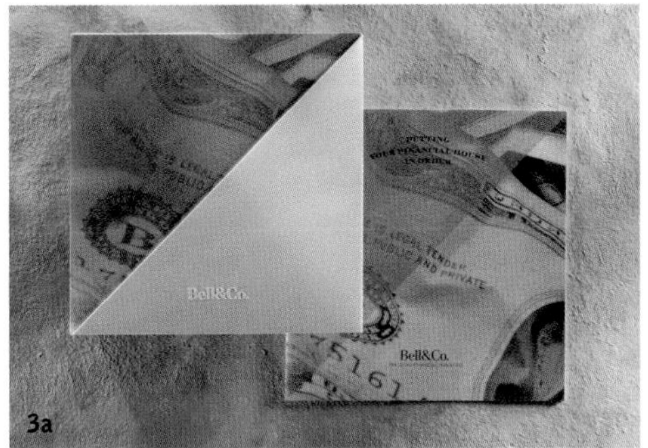

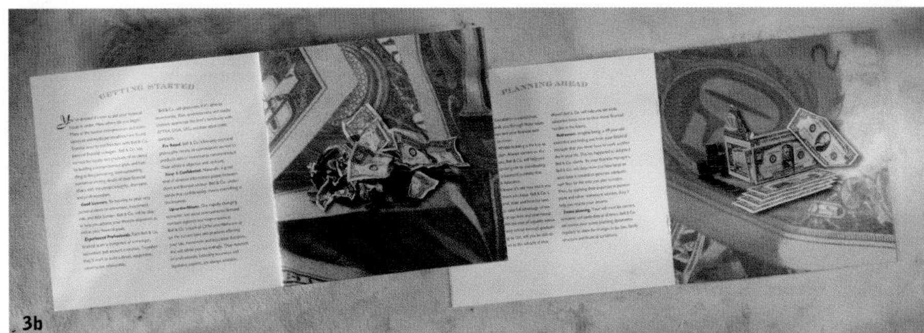

1. Birth announcement for Jonah Suissa
2. Birth announcement for Rebekah Suissa
3. Birth announcement for Hannah Suissa

SullivanPerkins
2811 McKinney Avenue, Suite 320
Dallas, Texas 75204
214.922.9080
mark.perkins@sullivanperkins.com
ron.sullivan@sullivanperkins.com
www.sullivanperkins.com

SULLIVANPERKINS

Extraordinary service, smart people, great work, good fun.

That's the corporate vision of SullivanPerkins. It's how they see themselves, and it's also what clients see when they look to SullivanPerkins for solutions and results.

Since 1984, SullivanPerkins has delighted in handling design and advertising challenges for corporate clients worldwide. And each solution, from a single logo to a mammoth publishing project that requires its own dedicated staff, begins with the smart strategic thinking that underlies SullivanPerkins' work.

1.

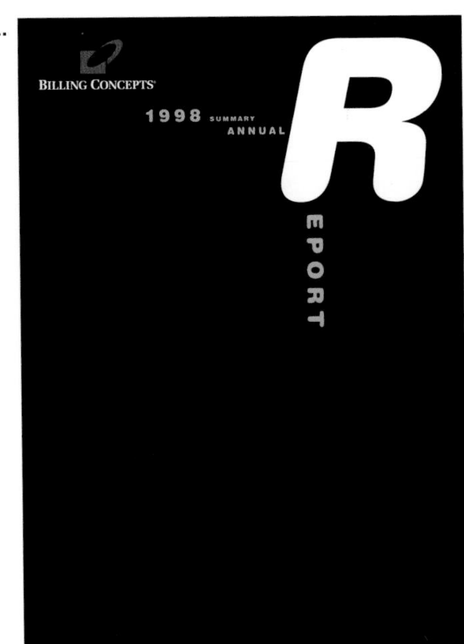

Billing Concepts is a company with a proven history of recognizing and skillfully responding to trends within the rapidly expanding telecommunications industry. We've had a front-row seat at the telecom revolution, and we've adapted to benefit from the new opportunities that have emerged.

In ten years, Billing Concepts has evolved from a third-party biller facilitating the efficient payment of long distance charges to a technology-driven company that provides complete billing solutions and back office support functions for a variety of telecom services for companies of all sizes.

The Company's remarkable ability to evolve in the face of new industry dynamics has resulted in several consecutive years of solid growth, industry-leading market share, an extremely favorable reputation and high customer retention.

Billing Concepts is part of one of today's most vibrant growth industries. We are focused on leveraging our strengths to expand our existing solution set as we penetrate broader segments of the billing marketplace. We are operating in revolutionary times, and we believe we have the expertise, the financial strength and the scale to turn these dynamic times into the best of times for our customers and for our Company.

2.

At Paymentech, the success we've enjoyed since our founding in 1985 is based, in part, on a truism we've discovered. If different can be better, it's better to be different. Developing products and services that make Paymentech the better choice for clients is a very smart way to compete. As such, our strategy has been to develop significant ways we can distinguish ourselves from our competitors.

Paymentech provides industry-leading payment processing solutions through our three major lines of business — transaction processing for merchants in a variety of industries; third-party processing services for financial institutions and independent sales organizations; and commercial card issuance. In everything we do we focus on identifying customer needs, and then we respond with the appropriate value-added solutions. Advanced technology resources and expert people that are solely dedicated to payment processing have been the keys to differentiating Paymentech from other companies in our industry.

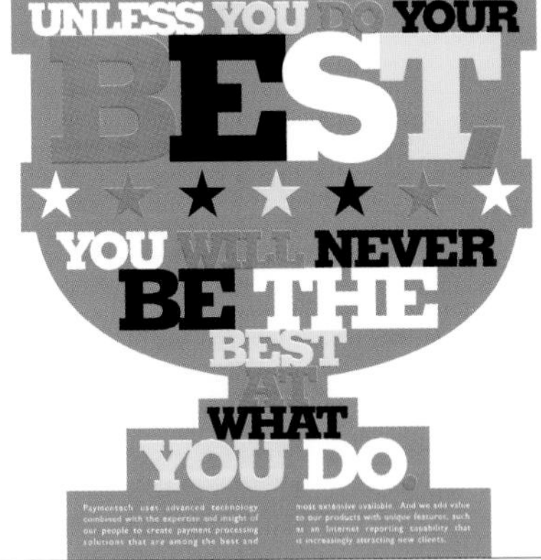

The majority of our business is providing transaction processing for retail merchants, either at the point of sale or in non-face-to-face transactions. In other words, we enable merchants to accept credit and debit cards and other electronic payments in exchange for their goods and services. In this recurring revenue business we've developed a wide variety of industry-specific applications for direct response, hotels, restaurants, petroleum outlets and specialty retailers. And we've developed relationships with many of the related industry associations, which endorse our service.

But to be a leader in our industry, and to differentiate yourself in a positive way, you need to do more than simply provide accurate and efficient payment processing services. You need to add value. Paymentech adds value to our processing solutions by giving our merchants added features to enhance their own business operations. As merchant size, sophistication and technological advancements continue to accelerate in our core markets, we increasingly need to flexibly support message formats and communication methods, and to add functionality to our host systems.

3.

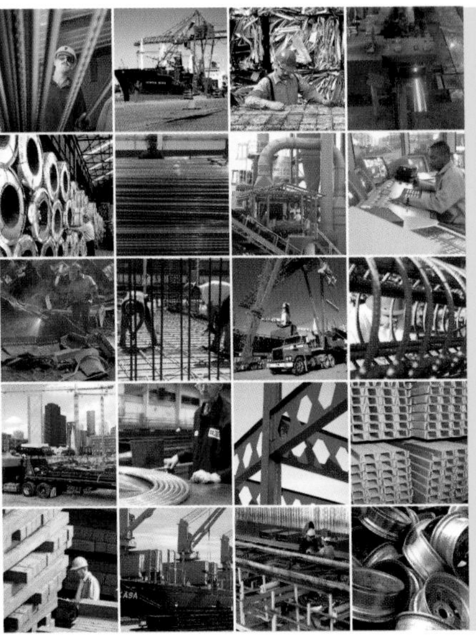

IF CONSISTENT EARNINGS AND STRONG GROWTH INTEREST YOU, READ ON.

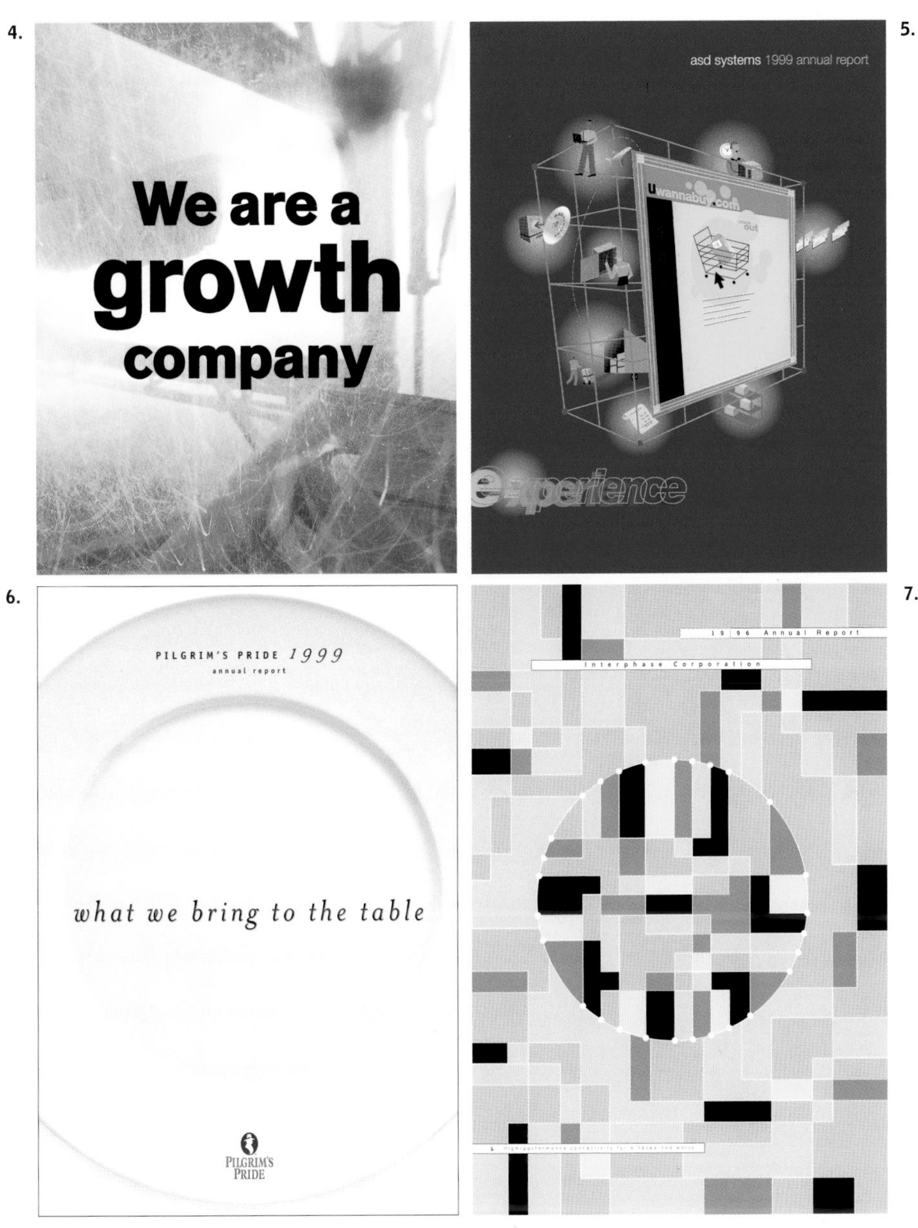

ANNUAL REPORTS

1. Billing Concepts: Provides complete billing solutions and back-office support functions for a variety of telecom services.

2. Paymentech: Offers industry-leading payment processing solutions.

3–4. Commercial Metals Company: Manufactures, recycles and markets steel and metal products and related materials.

5. ASD Systems: Provides a range of back-office solutions for e-commerce.

6. Pilgrim's Pride: A leading supplier of prepared and fresh chicken.

7. Interphase Corporation: Offers connectivity solutions for computer networking environments.

1.

2.

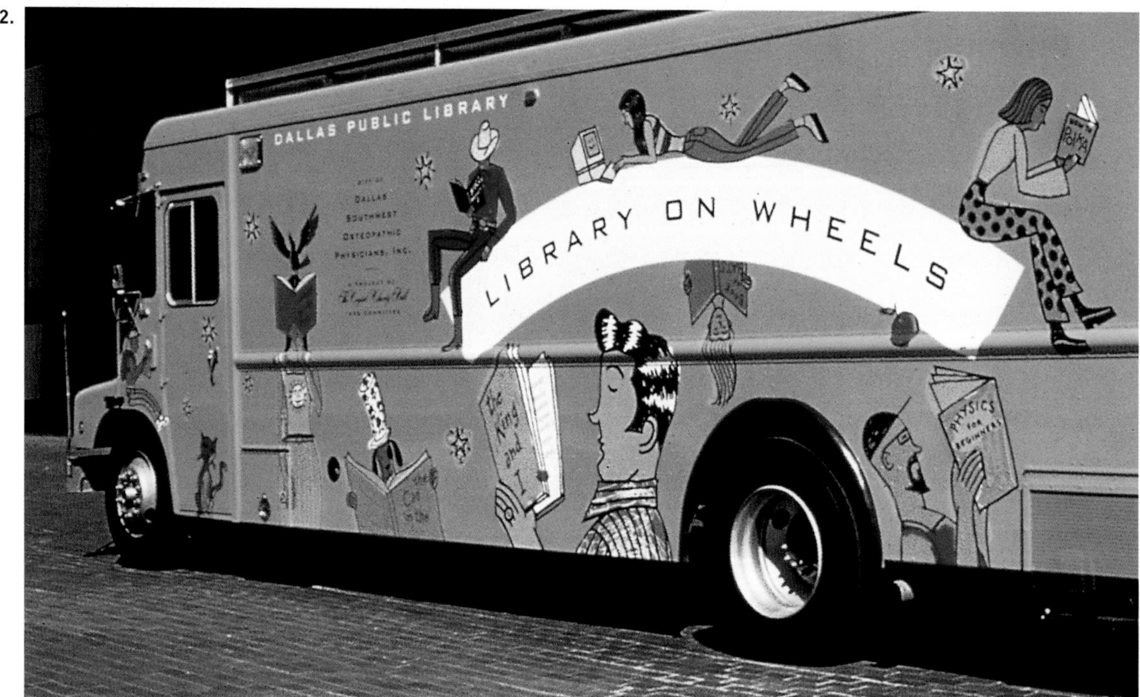

1. FYInetworks: Signage for a company that specializes in electronic research, editorial commentary and logistics print management for professional publishers.

2. The Library on Wheels: The Dallas Public Library's mobile ambassador to neighborhoods.

1.

2.

TI | navigator

3.

4.

5.

6.

impulsity

7.

8.

9.

10.

11.

12.

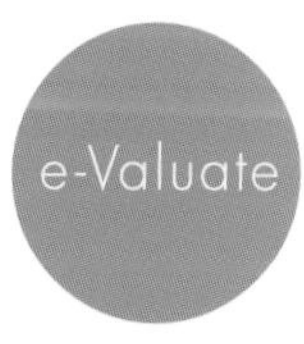

LOGOS

1. Best Press: A Dallas printing company.
2. TI-Navigator: A classroom learning system from Texas Instruments.
3. Longhorn Pipeline: A lengthy natural gas pipeline in Texas.
4. Performance Consulting International: A Dallas-based consulting group.
5. Dallas Public Library: Celebrating the library's 100th anniversary.
6. Impulsity: A mobile technology company.
7. Hotwire: A San Francisco-based online discount travel site.
8. Round Up at the Ranch: An identity for a private school fundraising event.
9. Kitchen Dog Theater: A Dallas theater troupe.
10. Landlock Seafood Company: A seafood distribution company turns 20.
11. American Museum of Miniature Arts: A museum in downtown Dallas.
12. e-Valuate: Services for the private equity marketplace.

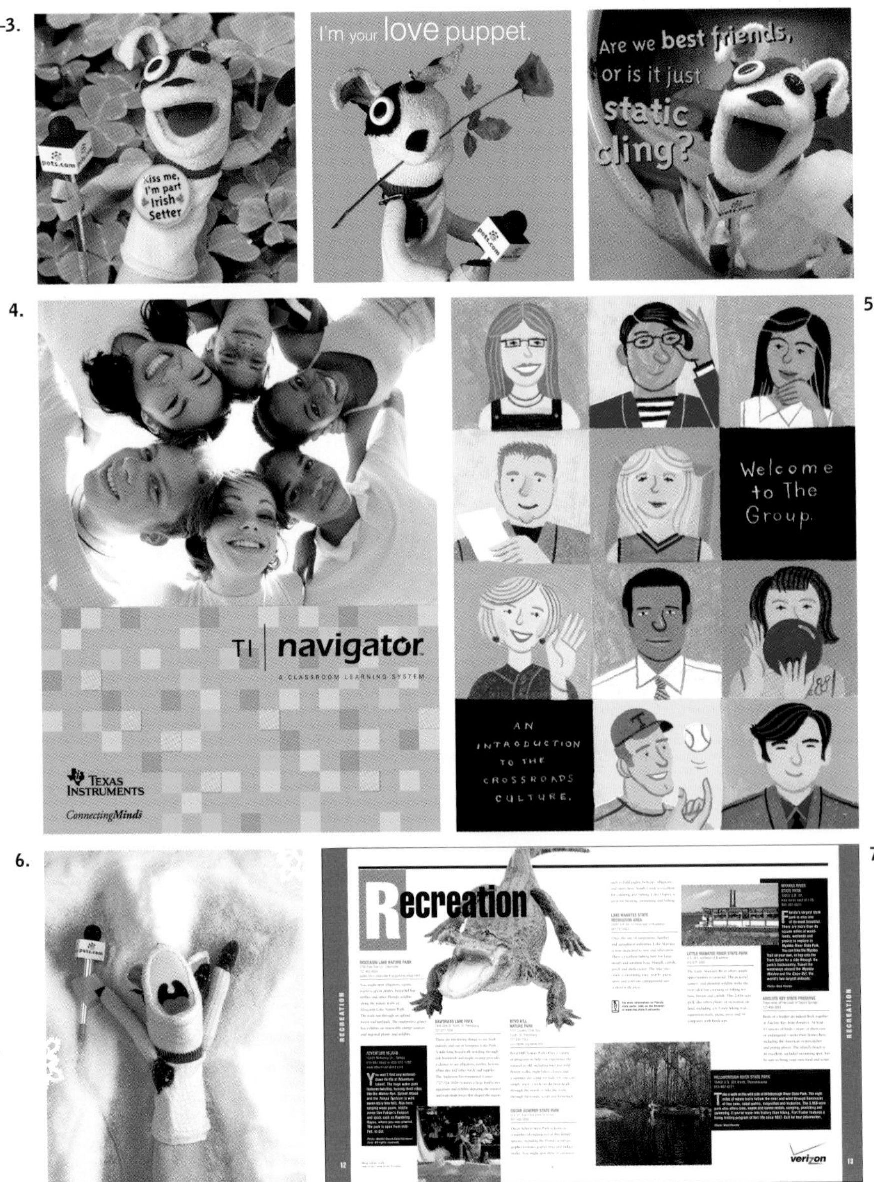

1–3. Pets.com: e-cards for St. Patrick's day, Valentine's Day and Friendship.

4. TI-Navigator: An introductory brochure for Texas Instruments' new classroom learning system.

5. The Crossroads Group: An employee handbook for a venture capital and private equity investment organization.

6. Pets.com: Holiday card featuring the Pets.com Sock Puppet.

7. Verizon: A spread from *Inside Look*®, a magazine bound into phone books nationwide.

1.

2.

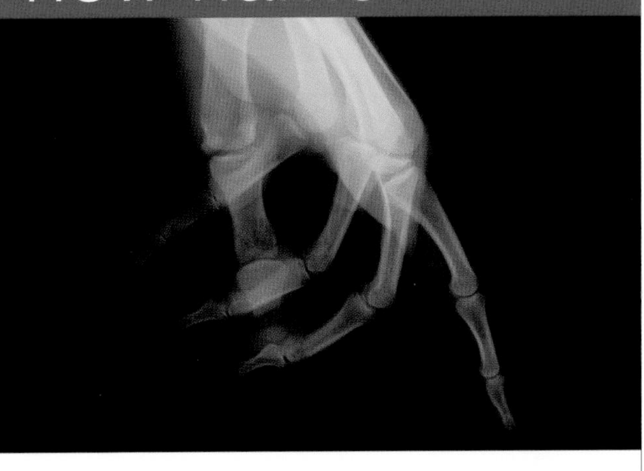

As of September 1, 1999, this PrimaCare location, owned and operated by Primary Health Inc., will become Med CareNow. The name is changing, but everything else will stay the same. Same great doctors. Same great staff. Of course, our commitment to giving you the best care in the most convenient way remains unbroken.

3.

Are you spending more time looking into your network than looking out for your business in the marketplace? Do pedestrian problems with your LAN or WAN bring you to a virtual standstill? What about help desk support? Or security? Don't worry. We're GTE Communications Corporation. We're part of one of the largest, most experienced communications companies in the world.
What do you worry about?
And we're here to help you. Because we have the products, the services, and the scalability to meet your varying needs in Data, IP, and Voice. For your broadest range of problems, GTE Communications has solutions. Solutions that can help your business be more productive, cost-efficient, and profitable. So you can stand out in even the most highly competitive market.
GTE
GTE COMMUNICATIONS CORPORATION
We focus on your network, so you can focus on your business.™
For more information, call toll-free at 877-88-GTECC.

1. The Crossroads Group: Marketing materials for a leading venture capital and private equity investment organization.
2. Med CareNow: Poster and direct mail announcing the name change for a group of primary care clinics.
3. GTE: A double-page ad for one of the world's premier communications companies.

1.

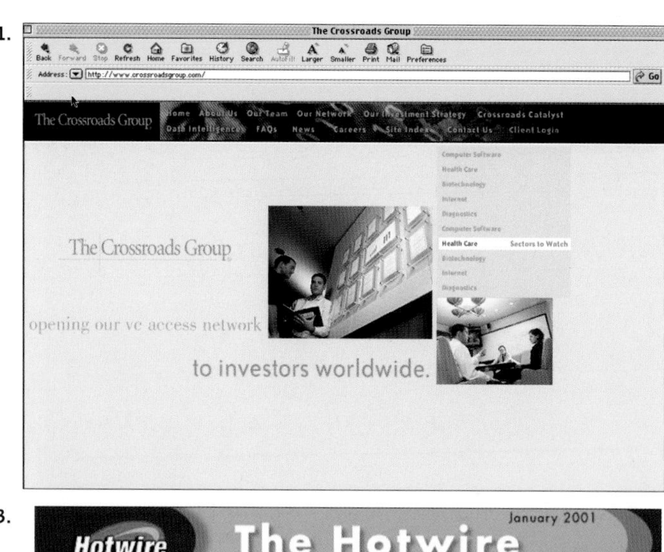

2.

3.

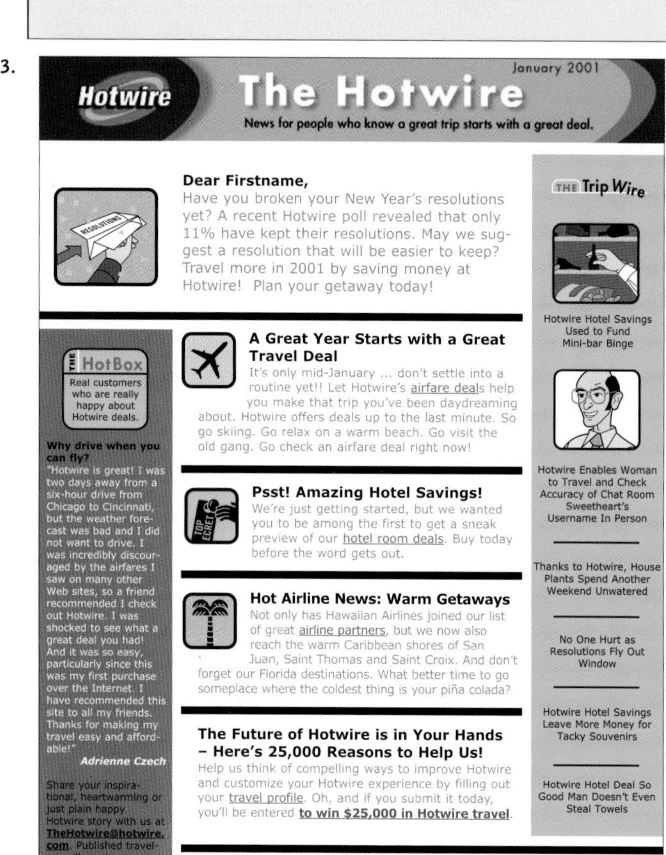

Hotwire

The Hotwire

January 2001

News for people who know a great trip starts with a great deal.

Dear Firstname,
Have you broken your New Year's resolutions yet? A recent Hotwire poll revealed that only 11% have kept their resolutions. May we suggest a resolution that will be easier to keep? Travel more in 2001 by saving money at Hotwire! Plan your getaway today!

A Great Year Starts with a Great Travel Deal
It's only mid-January ... don't settle into a routine yet!! Let Hotwire's airfare deals help you make that trip you've been daydreaming about. Hotwire offers deals up to the last minute. So go skiing. Go relax on a warm beach. Go visit the old gang. Go check an airfare deal right now!

Psst! Amazing Hotel Savings!
We're just getting started, but we wanted you to be among the first to get a sneak preview of our hotel room deals. Buy today before the word gets out.

Hot Airline News: Warm Getaways
Not only has Hawaiian Airlines joined our list of great airline partners, but we now also reach the warm Caribbean shores of San Juan, Saint Thomas and Saint Croix. And don't forget our Florida destinations. What better time to go someplace where the coldest thing is your piña colada?

The Future of Hotwire is in Your Hands – Here's 25,000 Reasons to Help Us!
Help us think of compelling ways to improve Hotwire and customize your Hotwire experience by filling out your travel profile. Oh, and if you submit it today, you'll be entered **to win $25,000 in Hotwire travel**.

To unsubscribe (sob!), click here: [URL]

Comments or suggestions for The Hotwire? Email TheHotwire@hotwire.com.
For password and other site issues, contact support@hotwire.com.

THE HotBox
Real customers who are really happy about Hotwire deals.

Why drive when you can fly?
"Hotwire is great! I was two days away from a six-hour drive from Chicago to Cincinnati, but the weather forecast was bad and I did not want to drive. I was incredibly discouraged by the airfares I saw on many other Web sites, so a friend recommended I check out Hotwire. I was shocked to see what a great deal you had! And it was so easy, particularly since this was my first purchase over the Internet. I have recommended this site to all my friends. Thanks for making my travel easy and affordable!"
Adrienne Czech

Share your inspirational, heartwarming or just plain happy Hotwire story with us at TheHotwire@hotwire.com. Published travelers will receive a moment of fame and glamorous Hotwire accessories.

THE Trip Wire

Hotwire Hotel Savings Used to Fund Mini-bar Binge

Hotwire Enables Woman to Travel and Check Accuracy of Chat Room Sweetheart's Username In Person

Thanks to Hotwire, House Plants Spend Another Weekend Unwatered

No One Hurt as Resolutions Fly Out Window

Hotwire Hotel Savings Leave More Money for Tacky Souvenirs

Hotwire Hotel Deal So Good Man Doesn't Even Steal Towels

4–5

1. The Crossroads Group: A website for a venture capital and private equity investment organization.

2. Kitchen Dog Theater: A poster for a Dallas theater troupe.

3. Hotwire: An animated monthly newsletter for an online discount travel site.

4–5. The Rouse Company: A series of holiday cards for one of the nation's premier publicly held real estate development and management companies.

Supon Design Group
1232 31st Street, NW
Washington, DC 20007
202.835.0177
202.775.5198
www.supon.com

SUPON DESIGN GROUP

In every minute at Supon Design Group, there is progress. Whether chatting with a client, brainstorming with a colleague or experimenting with a technique, ideas are communicated. Within this environment of progress is a dynamic landscape. Characterized by an international staff and a global clientele, relationships thrive on diversity and foster a rare creative spirit.

It is this same spirit that led to the creation of Supon Design Group in 1988. After leaving his native Thailand to finish school in the U.S., Supon Phornirunlit opened a design studio in his home. In the 13 years since then, his venture has grown into a team of 30 designers, illustrators and copywriters, housed in an expansive studio in the heart of Washington, D.C. In the process, Supon Design Group has earned more than 1,000 national and international awards, including best of show honors in print, new media, broadcast, advertising and packaging.

The studio offers clients a full range of design services, including identity campaigns, product packaging, marketing strategy, copywriting, websites, and even interior design. From the U.S. to Europe and Asia, and from non-profit organizations to multinational corporations, the studio has forged long-term creative partnerships with a vast and loyal clientele.

Supon Design Group's international book division has produced and written dozens of titles that have won various copywriting and design awards. The studio's profile has appeared in numerous international publications, and its work has been featured in art media worldwide. In May 1999, Supon Design Group merged with Multi-Media Holdings, Inc. (MHI), uniting the firm with 16 other creative and marketing-oriented companies.

From a one-person studio to an international enterprise, Supon Design Group is one of the most recognized and respected studios today. In thinking beyond design—to understanding clients' businesses and goals intimately—solutions transcend visual images to complement marketing objectives and strategies. It is through this process—this progress—that Supon Design Group provides comprehensive value for its clients.

1. Coquico: Identity and product development of toy chirping frogs representing the coquí, Puerto Rico's official animal.
2. Grand Palace Foods International, Thailand: Logo and packaging for Milk, aimed at encouraging children to drink more of the calcium-rich beverage.
3. Host Marriott: Promotional graphic identity for food and beverage vendors at Ronald Reagan Washington National Airport.
4. Apartment Zero: Identity for a hip, urban furniture and housewares retailer.
5. Central/Zen Department Stores, Thailand: Merchandising identity aimed at capturing the teen/20s retail market.
6. Wana Zoo: Wayfinding signage and identity for a zoological park in Laos.
7. Black Entertainment Television: Marketing kit promoting BET's multiple networks to cable operators.
8. IBM: Sponsorship identity for the 1996 Atlanta Olympic Games combining the corporation's ubiquitous blue bars with original illustrations.
9. Cow Parade: Logo for a promotional event whereby international artists decorate life-size, fiberglass cows for public display throughout various cities.
10. Arthur Ashe Kids' Day: Logo for an event sponsored by the United States Tennis Association to encourage children to appreciate and learn the game of tennis.
11. Space Adventures: Logo for a corporation promoting tourism in outer space.
12. International Gay and Lesbian Football Association: Logo for a gay and lesbian World Cup soccer tournament.
13. FIFA U-17: Logo for an international soccer championship for players under age 17.

1

3

2

4

5

6

9

10

7

11

12

8

13

1. United States Patent and Trademark Office: Logo utilizing an eagle and light bulb to represent American ingenuity.
2. Woodrow Wilson International Center for Scholars: Logo for this public policy organization chartered by the U.S. Congress.
3. United States Department of Agriculture: Logo suggestive of America's diverse and fertile landscapes.
4. United States Botanic Garden: Logo suggesting that our capital city's conservatory is abloom.
5. United States Postal Service: Logo for Celebrate the Century, a program highlighting the last 100 years of commemorative stamps.
6. Smithsonian Institution: Identity and exhibit design for America's Smithsonian, a traveling exhibition honoring the national museum's 150th anniversary.
7. United States Postal Service: Souvenir book promoting the first day of issue of the Bugs Bunny commemorative stamp.
8. Woodrow Wilson International Center for Scholars: Annual report featuring the people and diverse activities of this public policy organization.
9. National Mediation Board: Annual report for an organization which helps mediate the employment disputes of airline and railroad companies.
10. American Psychological Association: Media guide describing opportunities for advertising in APA's diverse publications.
11. Associated Press: Annual report for this news subscription service retells current events as it describes AP's own year in pictures and text.
12. The Points of Light Foundation: Annual report for an organization supporting and facilitating increased volunteer efforts.
13. National Center for Family Philanthropy: Publication encouraging charitable giving to promote the welfare of families.
14. Newspaper Association of America: Sales kit featuring information on and benefits of advertising in newspapers.

1

2

3

4

5

6

8

9

7

www.apa.org/ads/ratecard
MEDIA PLANNING GUIDE
AMERICAN
PSYCHOLOGICAL
ASSOCIATION
Discover the Power of Advertising

10

AP
The Associated Press

11

Annual Report 1998
WE BELIEVE THAT THE WORLD WILL BE A BETTER PLACE
IF MORE PEOPLE ARE ENGAGED AS VOLUNTEERS.
POINTS OF LIGHT FOUNDATION

12

NATIONAL CENTER JOURNAL VOLUME I
RESOURCES for FAMILY PHILANTHROPY
FINDING THE BEST PEOPLE, ADVICE, AND SUPPORT
NATIONAL CENTER FOR FAMILY PHILANTHROPY

13

OPPORTUNITY KNOCKS AGAIN!
NEWSPAPERS
CHARACTERISTICS OF CURRENT HOME
NEWSPAPERS:
The Foundation Of A Successful Home Search

14

1

2

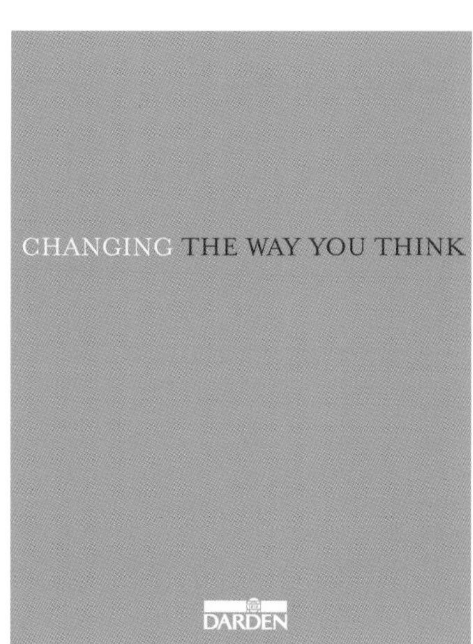

3

4

5

1. American Language Academy: Catalog promoting programs and schools at which international students can learn English and experience the breadth of life in the U.S.A.
2. Episcopal High School: Viewbook illustrating diverse student lifestyles and curricula available at this northern Virginia campus.
3. The Darden School: Viewbook promoting the unique MBA program offered at the University of Virginia's graduate business school.
4. The George Washington University: Viewbook illustrating the wide cross-section of experiences available to undergraduate GW students—in the classroom, on campus, and in the city.
5. The George Washington University: Product developement of a whimsical cookie jar depicting the University's trolley contrasts with the slick and techy viewbook.
6. Pace: Capabilities brochure for an energy services company featuring a die-cut version of the newly designed logo.
7. EMM: Self-promotional package for this marketing company utilizing playful copy and bold graphics.
8. Mannington: Promotional identity featuring a redesign of all materials aimed at commercial clients (architects and interior designers) of the company's floor coverings.
9. BrandHarvest: Logo for a marketing company specializing in brand launches.
10. HortiCare: Logo for a landscape design and installation company.
11. E-satisfy: Logo for a company which measures customer service and brand loyalty.
12. Clean & Polish: Logo for a building maintenance company specializing in commercial window-washing.

PACE | Global Energy Services
Setting the PACE in Energy

6

"I THINK, THEREFORE I EMM"
Great Minds Think Alike.

7

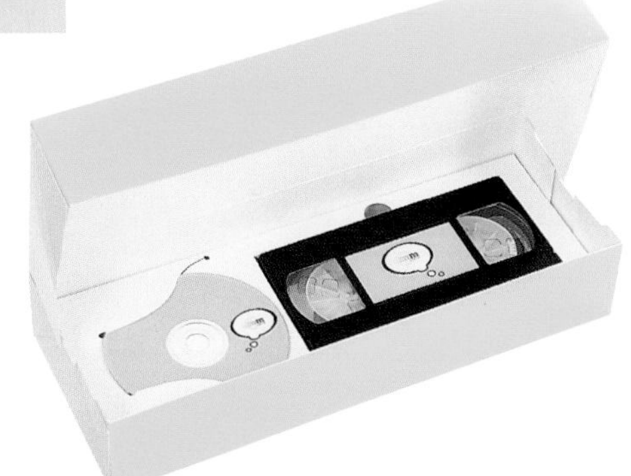

MANNINGTON COMMERCIAL | Gyro

8

BrandHarvest

9

horticare

10

-satisfy

11

CLEAN&
POLISH

12

1

TeleworX

2

3

4

5

winstar
ODYSSEY OF EXCELLENCE
2001

winstar

6

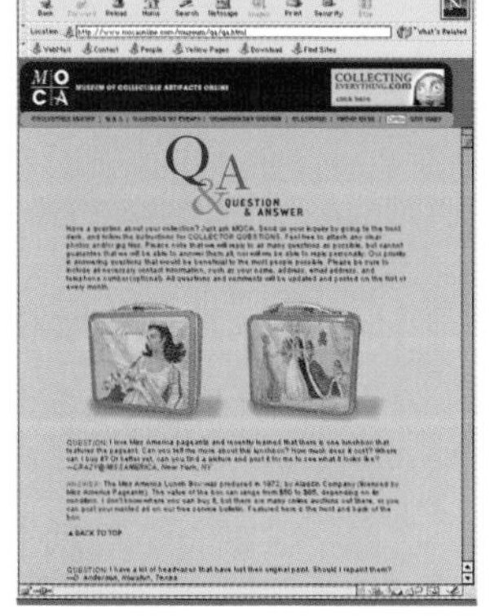

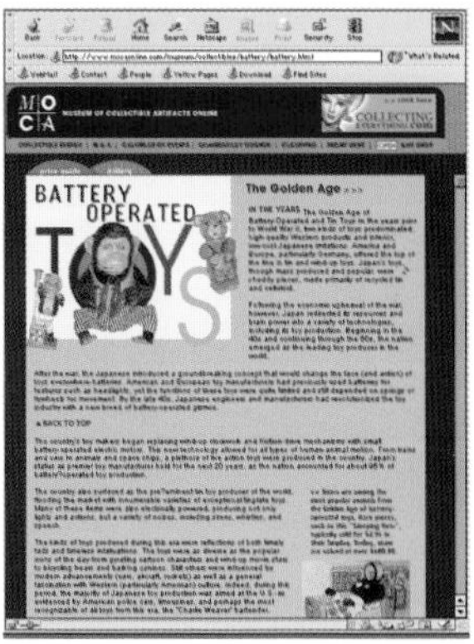

7

1. ThruPort Technologies: Logo for a developer, producer, and host of Internet portal applications for businesses.
2. Teleworx: Logo for a telecommunications consulting and software firm.
3. ServerVault: Logo for a company which develops online security systems for Internet companies.
4. Ad Juggler: Logo for a software product which manages online advertising.
5. Built2XL: Logo for a company advocating fitness for tall and large-bodied individuals.
6. Winstar: Poster promoting this telephone company's internal sales incentive program.
7. Museum of Collectible Artifacts: Identity and website for MOCA, an online source for information on a wide variety of collectibles.

Sussner Design Company
212 3rd Ave N, Suite 505
Minneapolis, Minnesota 55401
612.339.2886
inquire@sussner.com
www.sussner.com

SUSSNER DESIGN COMPANY

Ethical work and a work ethic. Blue-collar elevated and exalted. Design both human and humane. Sussner Design Company is about reality-based solutions that stand up to the "yeah-but-will-they-get-it?" scrutiny. SDCo. is a little blue around the collar. We're proud of our conceptually callused hands. The human hand carries the power to create, to caress, to crush. 27 bones per with miles of ligament, muscle and tendon allowing dexterity and flexibility beyond description. We say, "Use it all." Design-by-hand is about blending the technical and the tactile, the computer and the craftsmanship. At SDCo., we proudly smear our bluish fingerprints over everything we create (metaphorically speaking, of course). We're out to bring the pleasingly bugged-eyed to the otherwise bored. We're here to deliver the appropriate, yet unexpected slap across the everyday face of things. We want to make a dent, a difference.

We want to pinch the public on the cheek and leave a mark. We want our clients noticed (not us) for all the right reasons. SDCo. is a graphic design firm working in all manner of brand creation and support. SDCo. is lead by chief Sussner, Derek Sussner. The doors at Sussner Design Company were flung open in 1999 and haven't been locked since.

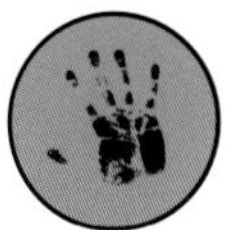

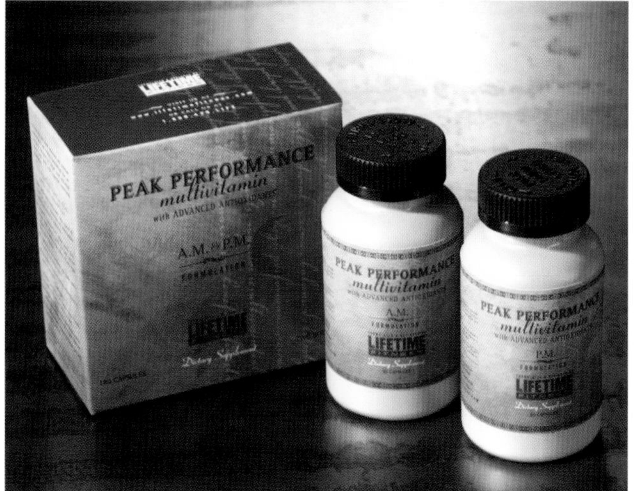

1

2

3

4

5

8

6

7

LIFE TIME FITNESS

1. Nutritional packaging
2. Nutritional product guide
3. Personal care product packaging
4. Identity for personal care products
5. Personal care, nutritional & apparel materials
6. Personal care free sample packaging
7. Ad campaign for Nutritionals
writer: Jeff Mueller
photographer: Rick Peters
8. Event banners announcing the new products

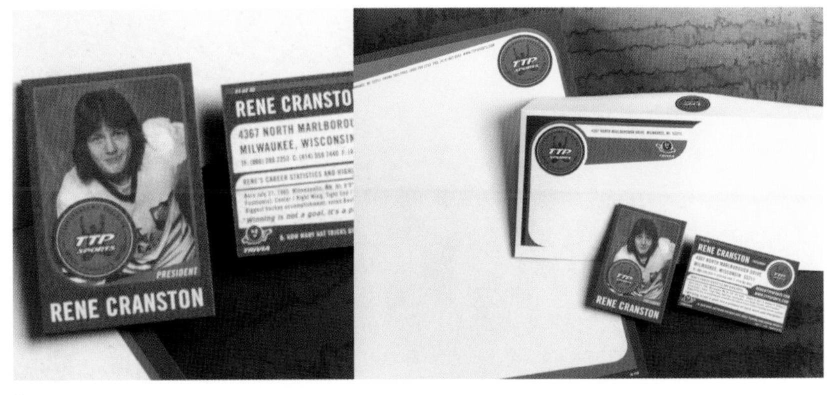

1

2

3

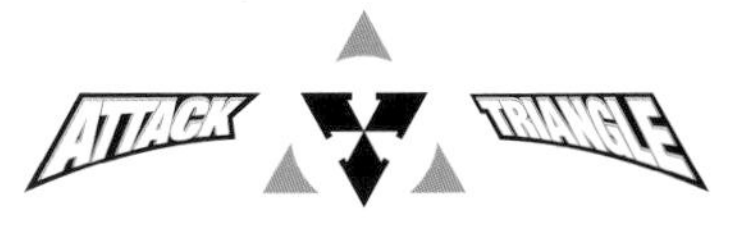

4

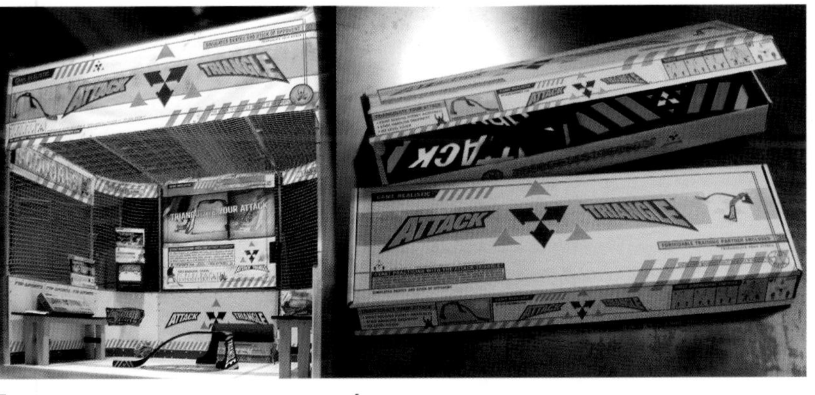

5 6

7

TRANSCENDENT TRAINING PRODUCTS

1. TTP Sports identity system
2. TTP Sports logo
3. Attack Triangle print ad
   writer: Jeff Mueller
   photographer: Joel Sheagren
4. Logo for the Attack Triangle - a hockey training product
5. TTP Sports trade show booth
6. Attack Triangle packaging
7. Attack Triangle product graphics
8. Iron Arms packaging
9. Logo for Iron Arms - a hockey stick weight

8

9

1

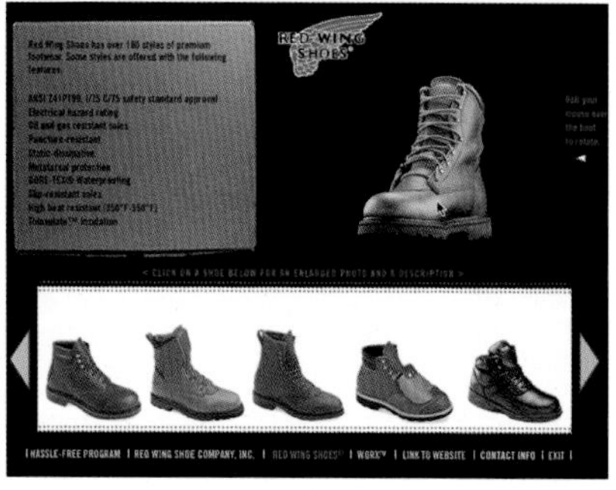

2

RED WING SHOE COMPANY

1. Cd-rom direct mail packaging

2. Industrial Sales Program cd-rom

writer: Jeff Mueller

photographer: Mark LaFavor

interactive development: E-Media Group

1

2

3

DAYTON'S COMMERCIAL INTERIORS

1. Identity system

2. Capabilities brochure
writer: Steve Seidl
photographers: Robert Pearl, Ellie Kingsbury

3. Promotional campaign
writer: Steve Seidl

4. Delivery trucks

5. Capabilities Cube
writer: Steve Seidl
photographers: Robert Pearl, Ellie Kingsbury

6. Icons/signage for a DCI presentation of an office mock-up for Target
writer: Steve Seidl

4

5

6

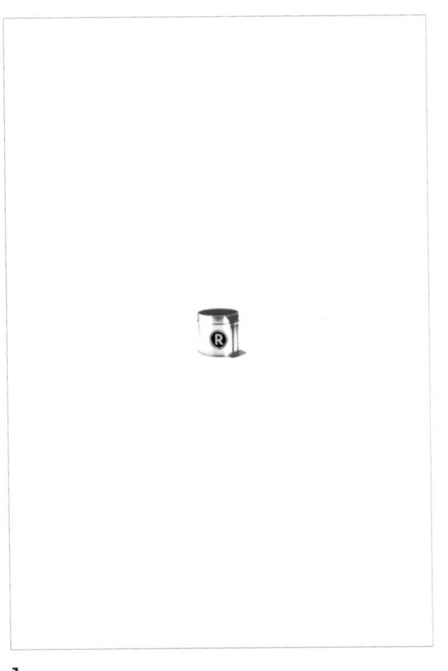

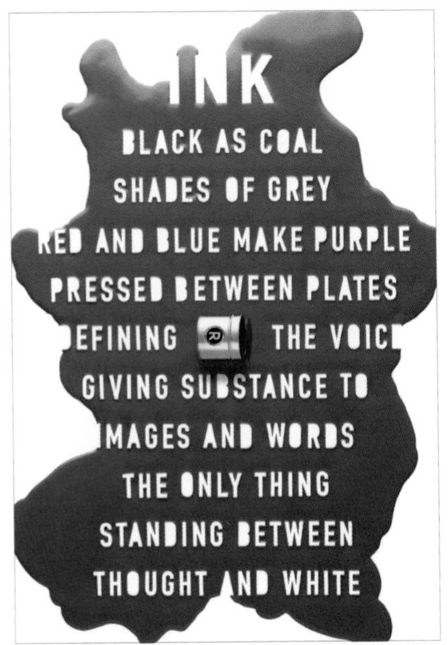

1

2

3

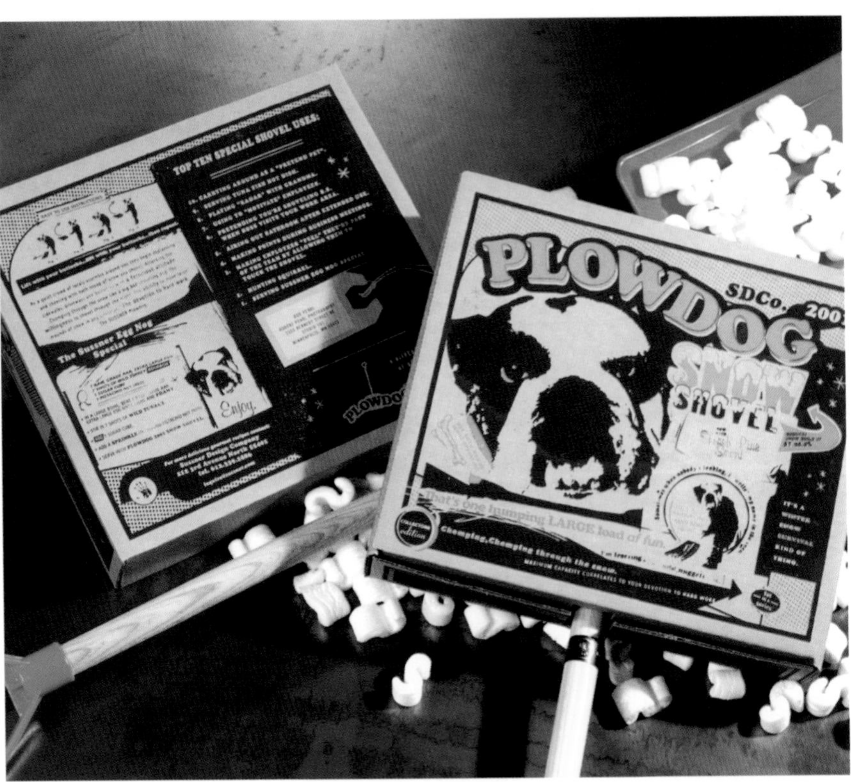

4

5

1. Reflections Printing poster campaign
   writer: Ed Prentiss
   photographer: Michael Hendrickson
2. Reflections Printing delivery truck
3. Learning & Language Specialists identity
4. SDCo. Winter 2001 promotion
5. Best Buy print ad campaign

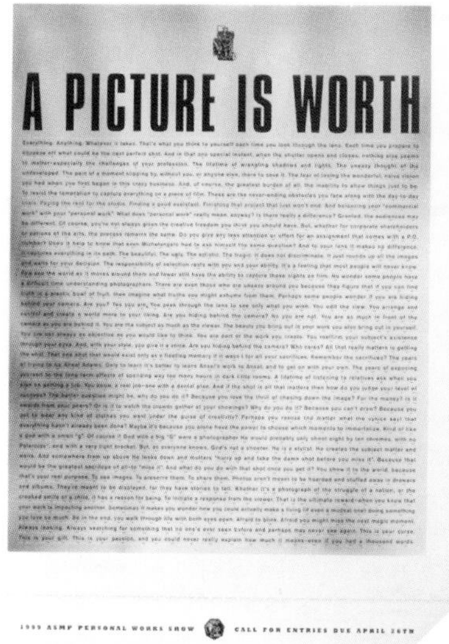

1

2

★★★★ SDCo

AFFECTIONATE
LITTLE
MONKEY

Derek Sussner
October 16, 2000
7:45 p.m.
University of
Wisconsin-STOUT
Micheels Hall
Room 290

Hours of Fun.
Loads of
*Amusement.**

*TINY COAT NOT INCLUDED.

The Sussner makes an adorable pet and an amusing designer. Almost human with his warm eyes, keen wit and effective use of white space. You and your family will love him. The Sussner eats the same food as you (although, digestion can be quite surprisingly different). He'll even lick a lollipop . . . ohmigosh. He's simple to care for with merely a bowl of water and an attentive audience.

The whole gang will love the Sussner. He's a designer. His face resembles that of a very creepy child's face. Just look at his extra cute size 10 1/2 shoes . . . you'll giggle. The Sussner's health is certified and live delivery is 100% guaranteed (God willing).

For ordering info, contact Sussner Design Company at 212 3rd Ave N, Suite 570, MPLS, MN 55401 or call 612-339-2886.

3

4

5

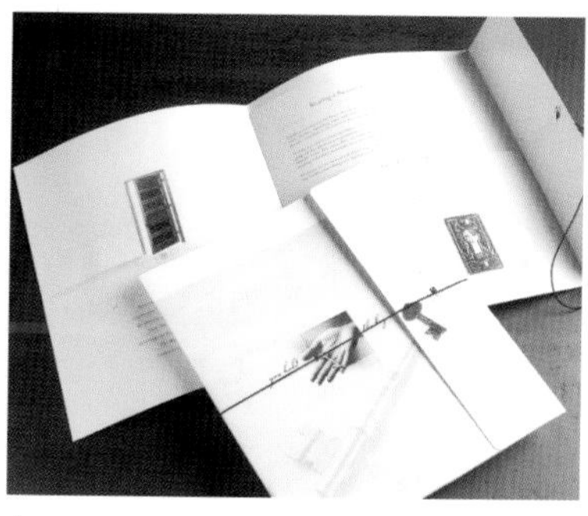

6

7

8

1. American Society of Media Photographers, Personal Works Show call for entries
writer: Ed Prentiss
photographer: Ingrid Werthmann
2. TruckersUnited.com ad
writer: Jeff Mueller
3. UW-Stout presentation poster
writer: Jeff Mueller
4. Bremer Financial annual report
agency: Initio
5. Bremer Financial website
6. BeneChoice - a Bremer product, retirement plan brochure
writer: Steve Kaplan
photographer: Michael Hendrickson
7. Gander Mountain's The Guide, maga-log
agency: Creative Publishing
8. Toro iMow® Direct Mail
writer: Jeff Mueller

1

KKE

2

3

4

BENE C HOICE

5

6

7

8

9

10

PLACES EVERYONE

11

1. eKidtalk.com - a company that creates websites based on children & parent interaction
2. KKE Architects
3. Egis - a developer of industry specific accounting software
4. Porterhouse - a steak & seafood restaurant
5. BeneChoice - a retirement product of Bremer Financial
6. Velte Systems - an enterprise network consulting firm
7. Joe Schaak - director of film & t.v. commercials
8. Twist - a film production company
9. Intelligent Networks - a developer of network and security software
10. Foresight Associates - advisors of workspace and furniture strategy
11. Places Everyone - an urban, teen theater company

Vaughn Wedeen Creative
407 Rio Grande Blvd. NW
Albuquerque, NM 87104
tel 505-234-4000
fax: 505-247-9856
email: vwc@vwc.com
web: www.vwc.com

VAUGHN WEDEEN CREATIVE

Return trips to Vaughn Wedeen's website tell you a lot about us. Each visit may reveal a different splash page. There is -- gasp -- no logo. We are a moving force, not a static one. Our identity is a dynamic, multi-faceted toolbox of targeted images and words that combine to produce an endless series of thoughtful "aha's." Not unlike our work. Strategic. Clever. Original. And smart. Very smart.

Vaughn Wedeen is many things to many clients...one must be resourceful to survive in the high desert since 1982. The altitude and attitude of our blue sky thinking has served us all well.

So the fact that we provide identity systems, collateral, advertising, promotions, posters, packaging, annual reports, environmental graphics, employee communications, videos and new media is not unusual. That we produce dazzling creative solidly based on equally innovative, sound strategies is.

As long as one foot remains strongly embedded in positioning and objectives, we are free to stretch as far and reach as high as our imagination takes us. No one dances the left brain/right brain waltz with more rhythm than we do. And that enables us to keep in step with clients such as *AT&T*, *Levi's*, *Motorola*, *Qwest*, *Citicorp*, *Cox Communications and Time Warner Cable*. Without missing a beat.

Vaughn Wedeen Creative promotional gift crate

I N S I G H T

1.

2.

S T O C K T O N R E

3.

4.

5.

6.

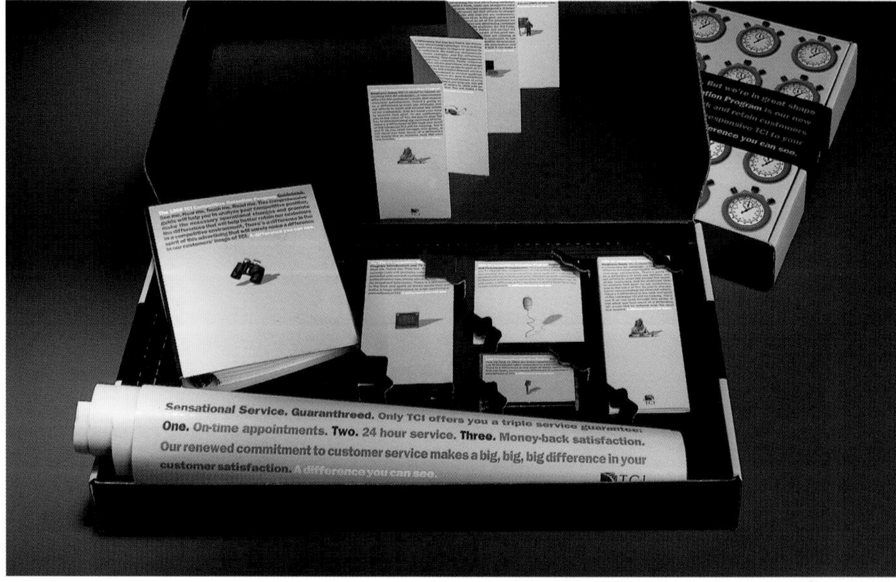

7.

1. Insight Lighting logo
2. Albuquerque: Spirit of the New West logo
3. Stockton RE logo
4. Massage for the Health of It logo
5. U S West internal promotion "Beyond the Call"
6. U S West extended workplace solutions direct mail package
7. TCI competitive advertising kit

1. Biosgroup website & corporate identity
2. U S West recruitment material
3. Qwest.net product package
4. Insight Lighting corporate identity

1.

2.

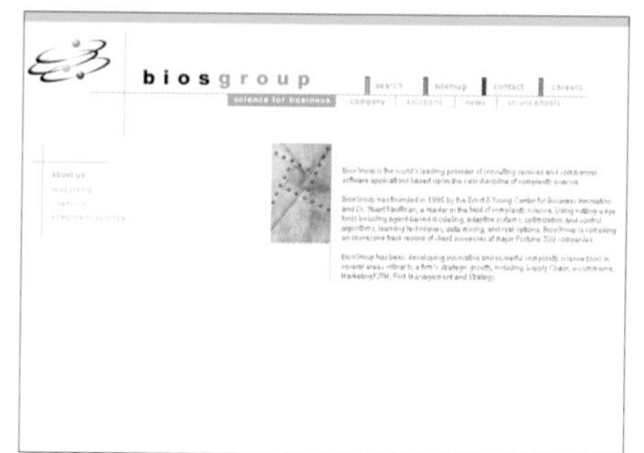

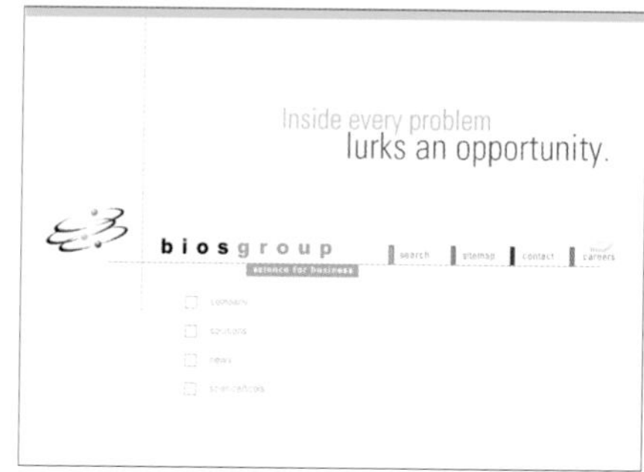

3.

4.

1.

2.

3.

4.

5.

1. U S West Sales Program brochure
2. Aids Walk Poster
3. Solomon Schechter Day School logo
4. Cystic Fibrosis "Hop Scotch" logo
5. Cox Communications internal communication collateral

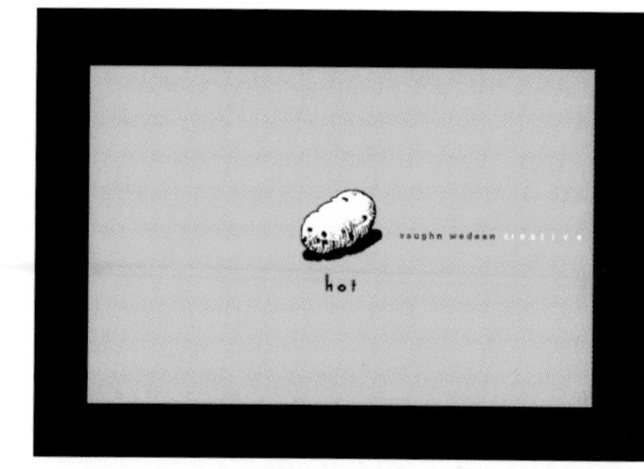

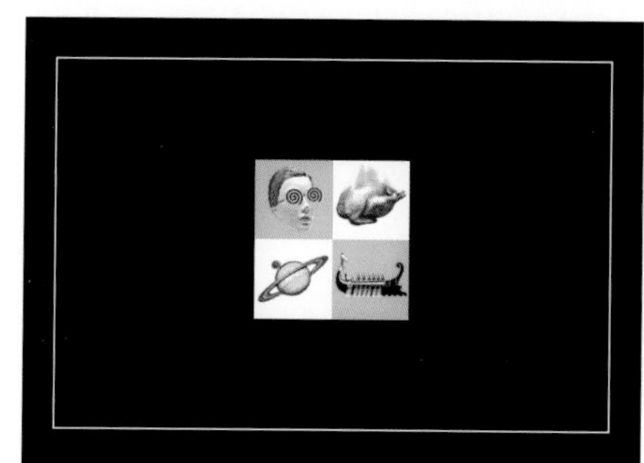

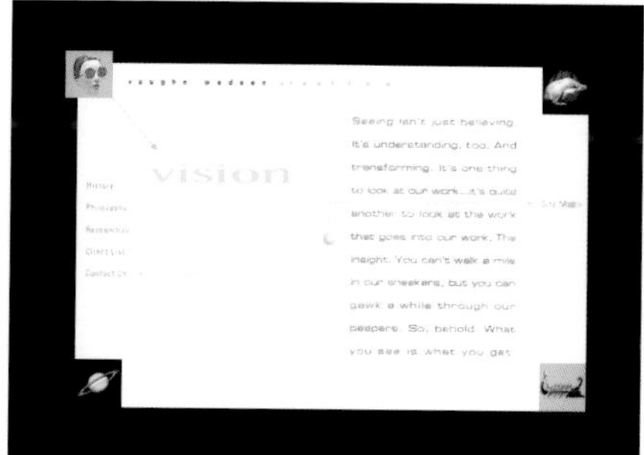

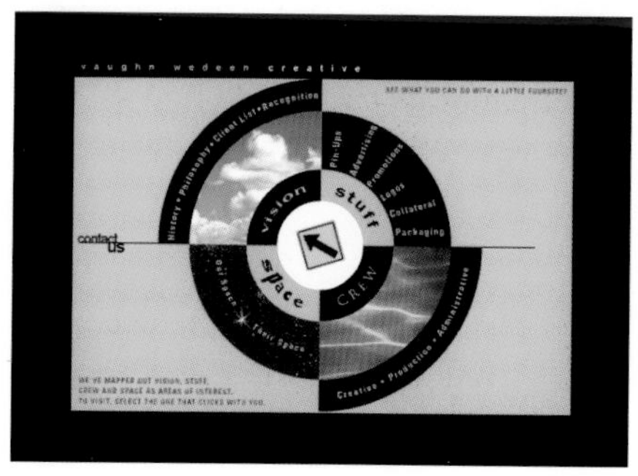

1.

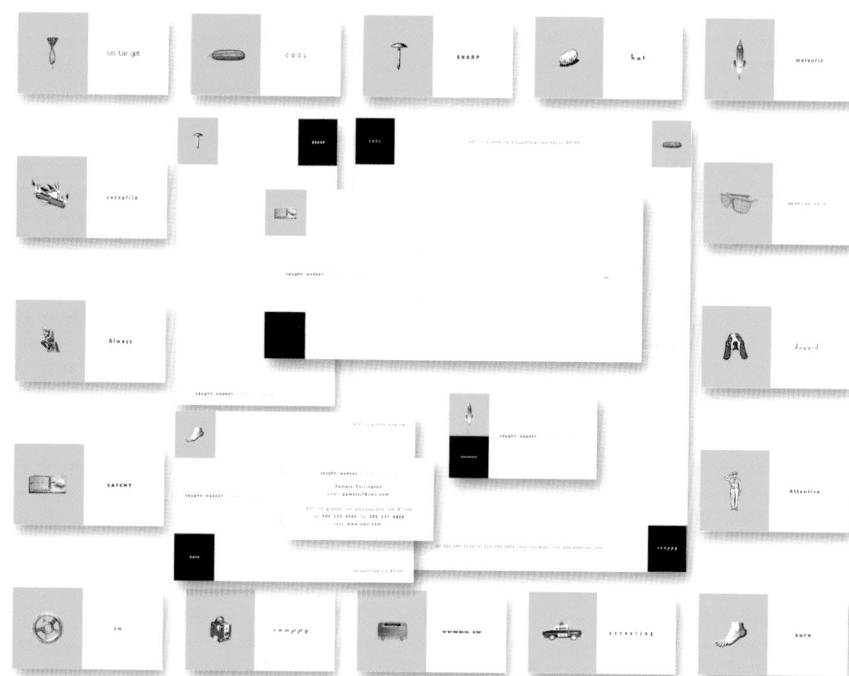

2.

1. Vaughn Wedeen Creative website

2. Vaughn Wedeen Creative corporate identity

3. Gizmo holiday promotion, the build-it yourself toy

3.

1.

2.

3.

4.

1. "25" business theme park identity monument
2. "25" tenant monument sign
3. 4. "25" business theme park sight signage
5. "25" anniversary invitation

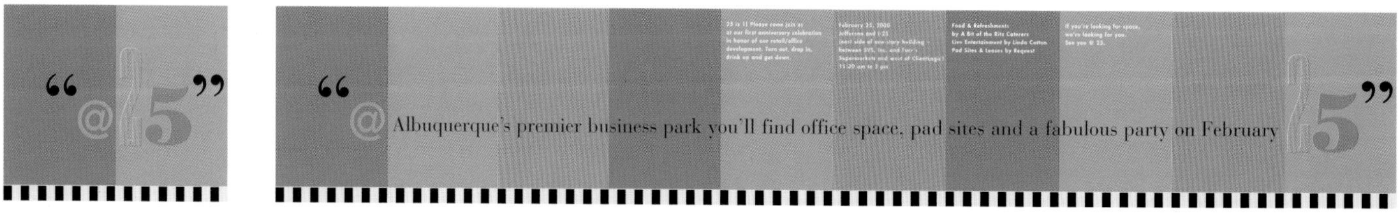

"@ Albuquerque's premier business park you'll find office space, pad sites and a fabulous party on February 25"

5.

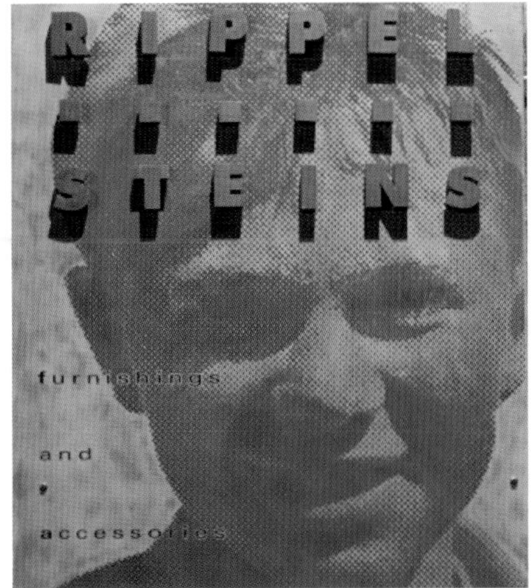

1.

2.

3.

4.

5.

6.

1. 2. Rippelsteins men's accessories store sign

3. Rippelsteins shopping bag

4. University of New Mexico Foundation donor proposal

5. 6. Flying Star Cafe logo and menu boards

1.

Audio:
make me laugh
make me cry
make me smart
make time fly
spread my reach
open the gate
speed my access
end my wait
touch the future
help me prepare
plug me in
take me there

2.

1. Citicorp employee communication kit & collateral
2. Time Warner Cable commercial "Take me there"
3. U S West "Edge Program" recruitment brochure
4. U S West retail video "Opportunity"

3.

4.

1522 San Ignacio Avenue, Suite 4
Coral Gables, Florida 33146
305.667.6667 tel
305.667.9457 fax
www.vortexcomm.com

VORTEX COMMUNICATIONS

What's a Vortex?

Simply put, a Vortex is a constantly changing curve and a perfect metaphor for what we do.

A consumer's interaction with the products and services they use is dynamic and constantly evolving, much like the world we live in. To communicate effectively, while embracing changing needs and audiences, marketing communications have to be responsive, creative and effective. This is the guiding philosophy behind Vortex Communications' design activities.

Whether you need a brochure to solicit new clients, point-of-sale materials to entice visitors to try your product, or a web site that makes hard-to-find information easily available for your buyers, our design process ensures success with the project.

The key is to focus on knowledge and teamwork. Concepting doesn't begin at Vortex until we learn everything we can about you, your business and your audience. We believe the best design solutions come about through teamwork, so our designers work together...analyzing, and improving their ideas while gauging the work against client input as we go. And that process doesn't stop at the approval of a concept. It extends all the way through job completion.

Our team of professionals is as diverse as the clientele we serve. Our designers mix intuitive with analytical, idealistic with realistic, visionary with practical. While we're passionate about beauty, and pride ourselves on creating award-winning work, those goals will always be secondary to the client's objectives and needs.

The selection of work on the following pages is just a sliver of what we've done. It's evidence of where we've been, and a foreshadowing of where we're going. You'll see we've worked in many business and consumer market segments, both in print and online mediums. And while our philosophy of design never changes, the aesthetics of the work does. It's a product of an unrelenting search for what's most appropriate for the audience, the client, the schedule, and budget. It's why we've been successful since we opened our doors in 1984.

1

2

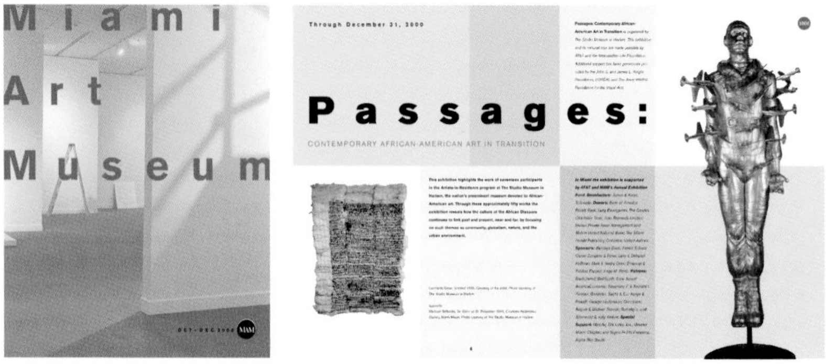

Miami Art Museum

3

MAM

4

5

1-5. Miami Art Museum Identity Program

1

2

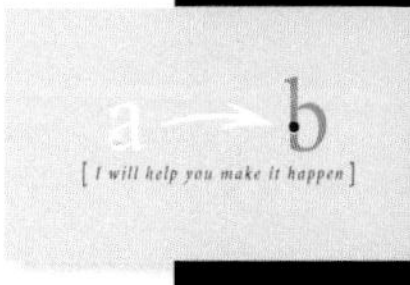

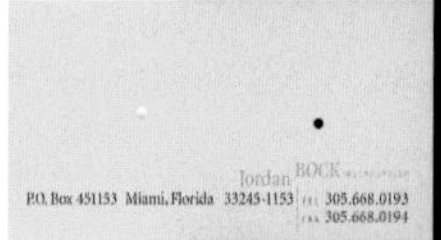

a

b

Jordan BOCK

P.O. Box 451153 Miami, Florida 33245-1153

a

b

Jordan BOCK

P.O. Box 451153 Miami, Florida 33245-1153 305.668.0193 305.668.0194

3

1. Miami-Dade Expressway Authority Annual Report
2. Greater Miami Jewish Federation Annual Report
3. Jordan Bock Logo and Stationery Package

1. American Airlines Employee Newsletter
2. Lash & Goldberg Law Firm Collateral
3. Codina Group's Beacon Cyberport Telecommunications Facility Leasing Collateral
4. Krieger Watch Corporation Product Catalog

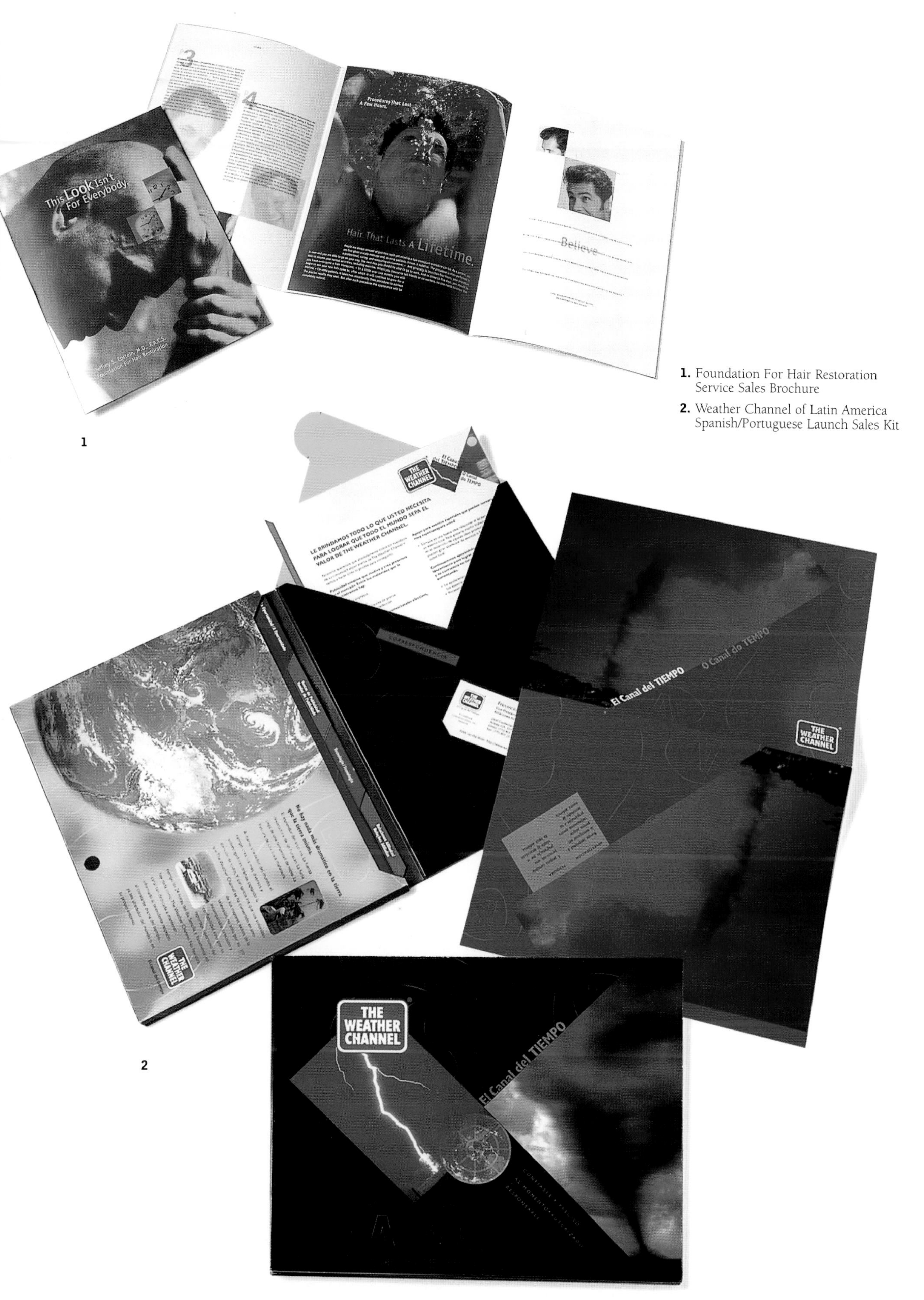

1

2

1. Foundation For Hair Restoration Service Sales Brochure

2. Weather Channel of Latin America Spanish/Portuguese Launch Sales Kit

1

2

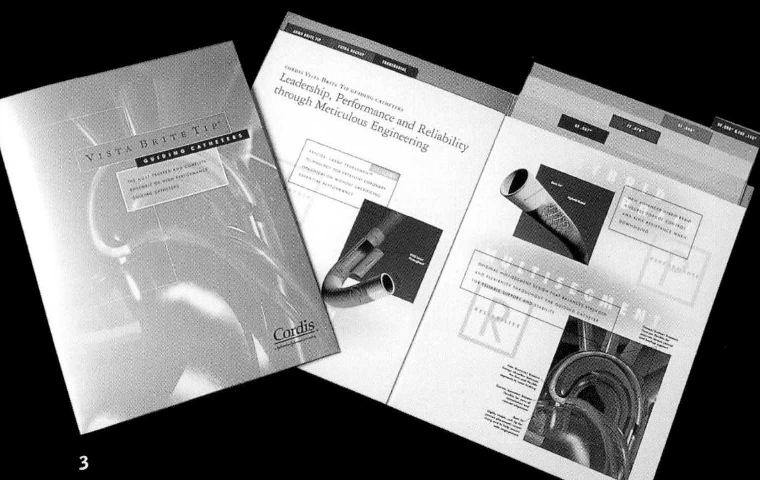

3

1. Radio Unica Network Event Broadcast Promo Poster
2. Johnson & Johnson Cordis Division System 3 Product System Brochure
3. Johnson & Johnson Cordis Division Vista Brite Product System Brochure
4. Minto Communities Madison Green Homebuyer Sales Kit

4

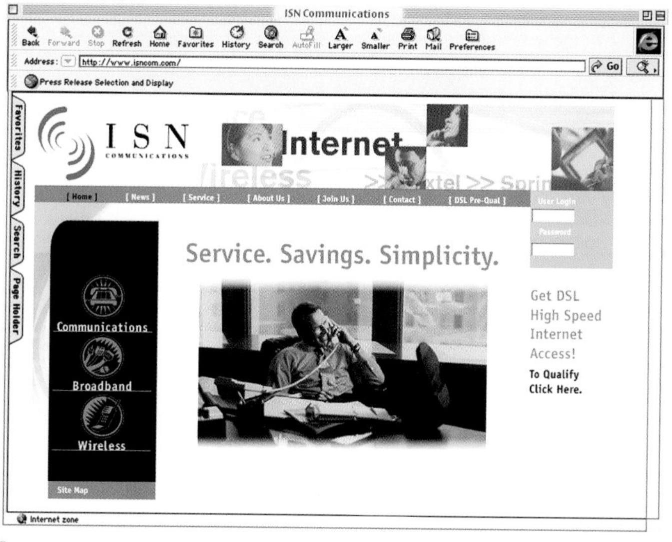

1

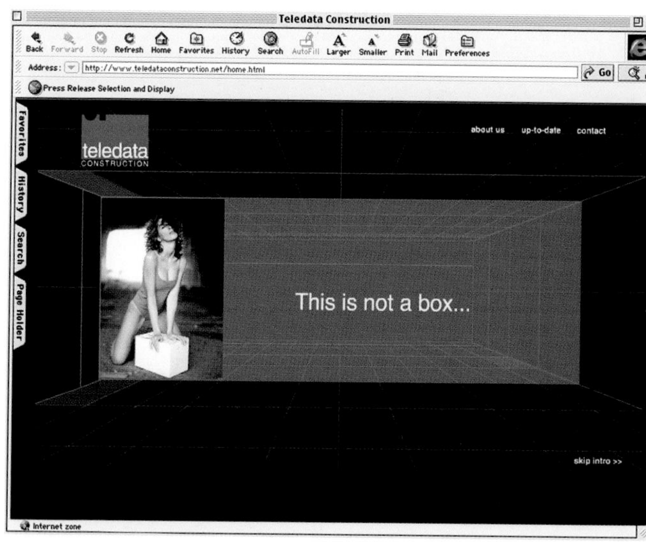

2

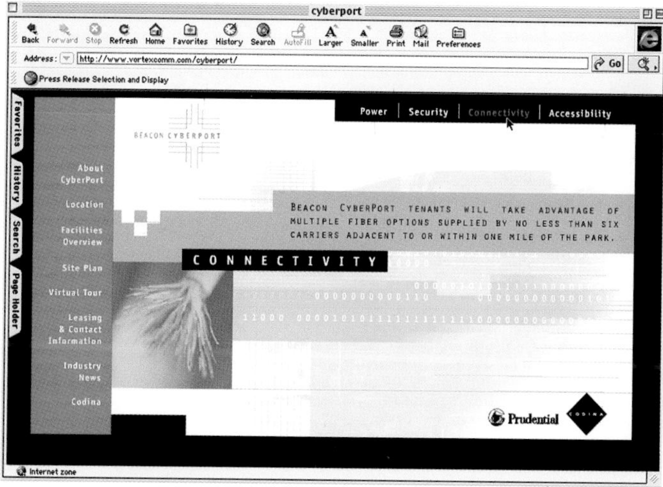

3

Florida Power and Light

FPL

Centro de Información de FPL

Temporada de Tormentas

FPL siempre se interesa por la seguridad y bienestar de usted y su familia, más aún durante la temporada de tormentas. Aquí le ofrecemos algunos consejos importantes para ayudarle a preparase cuando se acerque una tormenta. Queremos que esté preparado. Su preparación comienza aquí.

4

1. ISN Telecommunications Services Web Site
2. Teledata Construction Capabilities Web Site
3. Beacon Cyberport Flash Leasing Presentation
4. Florida Power & Light Spanish-Language Hurricane Preparedness Web Site

1

2

SOUTH FLORIDA
SUPER BOWL
XXXIII
HOST COMMITTEE
JANUARY 31, 1999

3

4

5

Island Dolphin Care

6

msadventure.com

7

8

Madison Green

9

10

11

12

1. Sports-Oriented Caribbean Resort
2. Sleep Clinic Identity
3. Super Bowl Host Committee Identity
4. Fusion-style Restaurant Identity
5. Internet Solutions Web Services Company
6. Dolphin Therapy Center for Children
7. Women-Oriented Web Portal for Travel
8. Art Museum
9. Golf-Oriented Residential Community
10. Music Festival
11. Online Marketing and Development
12. Healthcare-Oriented Transportation Logistics

Wages Design, Inc.
887 West Marietta St.
Studio S-111
Atlanta, GA 30318
www.wagesdesign.com
t. 404.876.0874
f. 404.876.0578

WAGES DESIGN, INC.

THE PLACE: Strategic design consultancy housed in former plow factory turned arts center. It's not heavy farm equipment but 21st century brands we're forging.

THE GOAL: Help clients achieve an integrated presence across all relevant media. From core identity development to full-strength, broad-spectrum branding, we create design that incites positive change. Moving our client-partners and their brands toward accelerated growth.

THE PEOPLE: A staff of highly talented people who speak five languages collectively. Not including their fluency in print, interactive, environmental design and the inspired strategy that drives it. Creative director and founder Bob Wages brings 20 years' experience to the task.

THE PRACTICE: One of the best identity firms in the country continues to embrace print and new media with unbridled virtuosity. Corporate and product naming. Packaging and print promotions. Advertising and annual reports. Exhibit design and dynamic interactive. Including database-driven web sites. We project your voice and vision with power.

THE CLIENTS: Antec, Assurant, Berkeley Process Control, Bowcutter, Canada Life, Cox Communications, Datalex, Delta Air Lines, DuPont, Georgia-Pacific, Georgia State University, Kids II, Rex Corporation, and UPS.

THE RESULT: From broadband networks to child development toys, we build foundation identities and powerful, integrated presence programs for business-to-business and consumer brands, start-ups and multinationals. And we have fun doing it.

1. A brand extension for the UPS Worldship software product lines through packaging and interactive design.

2. ANTEC, a leading manufacturer of cable telephony products. Projects include collateral package, an interactive product catalog, advertising, and promotional materials.

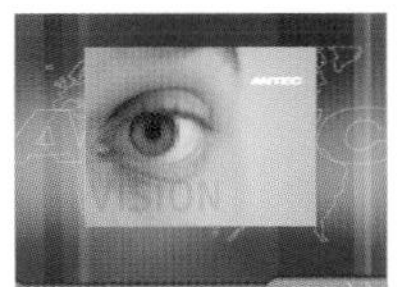

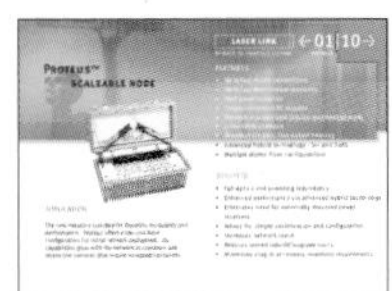

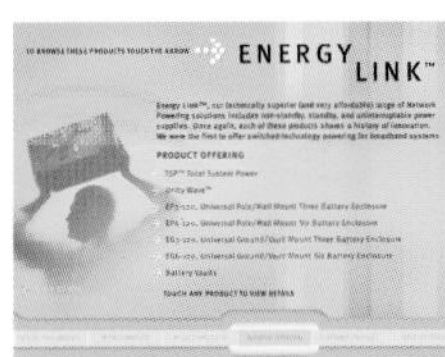
ENERGY
LINK™

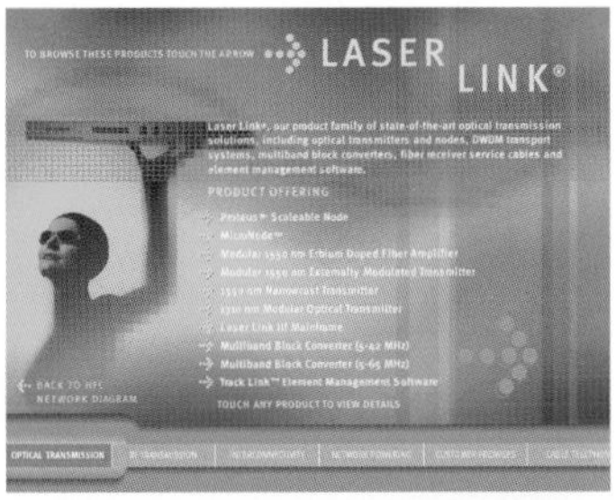

TO BROWSE THESE PRODUCTS TOUCH THE ARROW
CUSTOMER
PREMISES
PRODUCT OFFERING
TOUCH ANY PRODUCT TO VIEW DETAILS

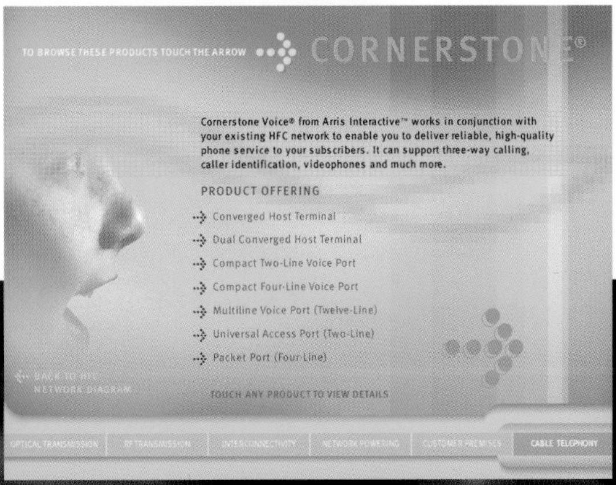

2

TO BROWSE THESE PRODUCTS TOUCH THE ARROW
CORNERSTONE®
Cornerstone Voice® from Arris Interactive™ works in conjunction with your existing HFC network to enable you to deliver reliable, high-quality phone service to your subscribers. It can support three-way calling, caller identification, videophones and much more.
PRODUCT OFFERING
Converged Host Terminal
Dual Converged Host Terminal
Compact Two-Line Voice Port
Compact Four-Line Voice Port
Multiline Voice Port (Twelve-Line)
Universal Access Port (Two-Line)
Packet Port (Four-Line)
BACK TO HFC NETWORK DIAGRAM
TOUCH ANY PRODUCT TO VIEW DETAILS

1

1. Brand identity for Georgia State University to include a clear wayfinding program of campus maps, building and directional signage.
2. Brand identity for Kids II, a manufacturer of developmental toys which included a complete packaging system and web presence.

Kids II
Play to Learn Toys
Musical Mobile
Baby Bugs
Rock 'N Rattle Stacker
Rocks & Rattles!
Teaches stacking skills!
Discovery Pal
It Rattles!
It Crinkles!
It Squeaks!
It Crunches!
It Jingles!
Soothe 'N Smile Rattle
Bath Bean Buddy
Reversible Nesting Blocks
About Us
Play to Learn
Infant Development Graphics
Types of Development
Playing with Baby
Kids II: Play to Learn Toys
Contact Us
Where to Buy
FAQs
What's New
Kids II Products
Educational Resources
Children Learn
and Discover through Play...
At Kids II, this philosophy is incorporated into our products to give babies a healthy foundation to play and to learn. Read about your baby's developmental stages, print a free poster, browse our product line. Don't forget to check back frequently for new information!
WHAT'S NEW
Millie the Millipede
Our newest addition to the Kids II cast of characters! Bright, colorful, and huggable, Millie encourages the development of baby's sensory skills. Crinkle, rattle, and squeak sounds and a variety of fabric textures encourage touching and interaction.

2

1. Datalex, a technology company specializing in the travel industry required brand roll-out to include collateral, web, trade show, and annual report.

2. Identity development for Bowcutter Technologies, a technology company. Roll-out of identity to web site, collateral, and an interactive sales presentation.

1

2

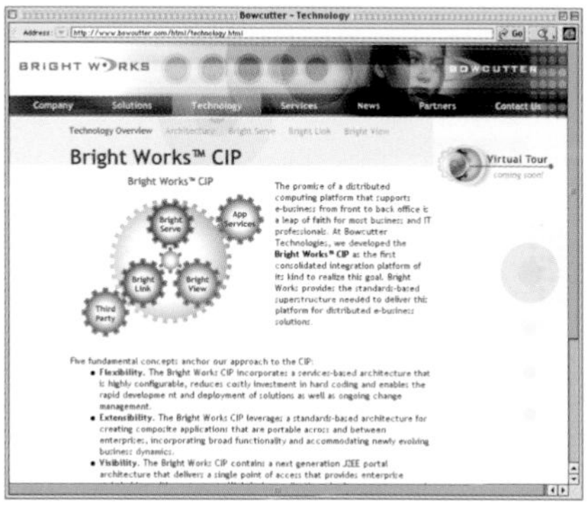

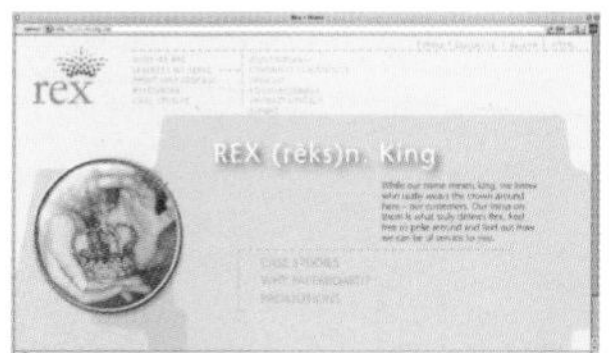

1. Identity development for Rex Corporation, a packaging company. This identity was applied through their corporate web site and promotional sales materials.

1